Yes Dave!

Thanks for
dude! It m...

Hope you enjoy the book.

All the best.

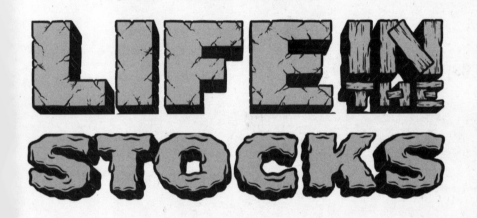

M@A.$

Thanks for the support dude! It means a lot.

LIFE IN THE STOCKS

VERACIOUS CONVERSATIONS WITH MUSICIANS & CREATIVES

VOLUME TWO
MATT STOCKS
FOREWORD BY KEITH BUCKLEY

RARE BIRD
LOS ANGELES, CALIF.

THIS IS A GENUINE RARE BIRD BOOK

Rare Bird Books
6044 North Figueroa Street
Los Angeles, CA 90042
rarebirdbooks.com

FIRST TRADE PAPERBACK ORIGINAL EDITION

Set in Dante
Printed in the United States

10 9 8 7 6 5 4 3 2 1

Library of Congress Control Number: 2021951759

Publisher's Cataloging-in-Publication Data available upon request.

For Marcella Kroll

CONTENTS

FOREWORD

by Keith Buckley

IDON'T REMEMBER HOW I met Matt. Now, usually the phrase "I don't remember how we met" is either mumbled embarrassingly or admitted in a flash and disregarded before anyone has time to process it. With Matt, however, I say that I don't remember how we met with a sense of peace and pride. Considering our friendship currently and the psychic connection it contains, not being able to recall the exact circumstances of our first meeting tells me there was a natural merging of "the seekers spirit" within us both, occurring so naturally as to not even register in my mind. One day he wasn't there and the next day he was. But Matt *knew* me somehow, and I knew him. He was a new friend that not only belonged there but had been there the whole time. It felt surprising but not sudden, and the more I got to know him the less surprising it became. Here was a friend I could be honest with. What was it about Matt Stocks that made me trust him so much?

Matt doesn't just hold up a mirror to anyone he talks to, he kindly gets you to hand that mirror over to him in the first place, and these interviews are as much a testament to his empathic abilities as they are to the honesty of the musicians he allows to reveal themselves through the transformative—the restorative—power of conversation. Matt has a gift for "inquiring further." By listening as closely as he does, he actually begins to *see* you. From there he draws out your truth.

INTRODUCTION

Fɪʀsᴛ ᴏғ ᴀʟʟ, ᴄᴏɴɢʀᴀᴛᴜʟᴀᴛɪᴏɴs! If you're reading this, it means you survived the great global pandemic of 2020–2021, and you lived to fight another day. Furthermore, welcome to *Life In The Stocks Volume Two*. I wrote *Volume One* in the peak of the pandemic during the first worldwide lockdown. I made a conscious effort not to mention COVID-19 at any point, since I figured it would all blow over before long, and I didn't want to date the book by referencing an ephemeral virus. The more you know, right?

I'm writing this introduction in September 2021, and we're still not entirely out of the woods. But things have been slowly reopening, and I just DJed my first post-pandemic full-scale festival, which was nothing short of incredible. So we all remain hopeful. However, if the last couple of years have taught us anything, it's that anything can happen. "Pray for the best, prepare for the worst, and expect the unexpected," to quote the great Gary Busey.

As soon as the world did shut down, I, like many people, lost a lot of work. I make most of my money from DJing, and as we all know, live music was the first thing to go and the last to return. It's been a lean, mean eighteen months, my friends; I'm sure many of you can sympathize. But we're still here because we found a way to get by. For me, it was the support of my podcast listeners. The financial aid that I received via Patreon was invaluable, and because of that income, I was able to scrape by. If you supported me in that way, even if it was just with a dollar a month, thank you so much. You guys saved my ass. The book project also saved my soul. During those dark and depressing early days of COVID, it really did feel like a gift from "whoever"—insert preferred word here.

Here's how it all came about. On March 10, 2020, I got an email out of the blue from a gentleman named Tyson Cornell, founder and owner of Rare Bird Lit, an LA-based independent publishing company responsible for releasing both *Life In The Stocks* books. Tyson was in London for a book conference that had just been canceled due to you know what (*cough, cough*), and he was trying to make productive use of his time in the UK after all his initial consultations fell through. So, he reached out to a few of his friends to ask if they could suggest any British people for him meet up with. And Keith Buckley from Every Time I Die threw my name in the mix.

Apparently, Tyson was already a fan of my podcast. He'd discovered it a year or so prior via the Keith Buckley episode, and I'd soon learn that Rare Bird were the publishing company behind Keith's novels, *Scale* and *Watch*. Can you see the pieces falling into place? After hearing Keith's podcast, Tyson jumped full force into my back catalogue, which at that point contained almost 150 (now over 250) episodes, and he instantly fell in love with the show. This is all what he's told me by the way; I'm not exaggerating any of it for dramatic effect.

It turns out Tyson and I had several friends, acquaintances, and business associates in common. And that was the premise of his email: "Hi, Matt. I love your podcast. We know a lot of the same people. You've interviewed several of the writers that I've worked with. I'm in London right now. Would you like to meet up tomorrow?" The next day was in fact my birthday. And I already had plans to go see Bryan Ferry at the Royal Albert Hall. It turns out Tyson also had tickets to the show, and he was staying at a hotel in that area, so he suggested we meet up for a drink and a chat ahead of the gig. I love it when a plan comes together.

Now, some people might think it's strange to take a business meeting on your birthday. But here's the thing: I always do. First of all, if you take a business meeting on your birthday, it shows the other party how committed you are. But that's not my move. I don't take business meetings on my birthday because I'm after any sort of job opportunity. My needs are much simpler. I do it because I know there'll be a slap-up meal in it for me or at the very least a free drink. And what better way to start celebrating? So I happily agreed to meet Tyson and his colleague Hailie at the pub that day. And I planned on making my drink a double.

Here's where the plot thickens. And again, this is all verbatim to what actually went down. It was a little after lunch on Wednesday March 11, 2020. I was in a group chat with some of my best friends as we were all off to Brighton that weekend, and I'd already had a few texts come through to wish me happy birthday. So I sent a message to the group saying, "Thanks lads. Stoked for the weekend. Bukowski's on his way to get a book deal." Then I put my phone on flight mode, and I walked into The Courtfield pub on Earls Court Road to meet Tyson and Hailie from Rare Bird.

Half of me said that as a joke. At this point, there was no reason to believe there was anything on the table except for a large gin and tonic, thank you very much. But the other half of me—and this is the part that materializes all of my professional opportunities—figured, "Fuck it!" If you don't will that kind of thing into being, it's never going to happen. By saying it out loud and writing it down in a group chat with my mates, I was putting it out there into the universe. And boy did the universe have my back, especially considering what was just around the corner.

I walked into the pub that day expecting a free birthday drink, and within fifteen minutes of me sitting down, Tyson looked me in the eye and asked if I'd ever thought about writing a book. I had, but I hadn't ever really developed any ideas, so I just started pitching stuff off the top of my head—that was how unprepared I was to be offered a book deal that day, despite what I'd said to my friends in the group message. After babbling some impromptu bullshit on the spot,

Tyson politely interrupted me to say, "Those are all wonderful ideas. But I was thinking more along the lines of something based on your podcast." And that's when the penny dropped, ladies and gentlemen. In that moment, the idea for what eventually became *Life In The Stocks Volume One* fell into place. I was good to go. And I had a legitimate publishing house who wanted to work with me. Best. Birthday. Ever.

Later that day, I met up with my friends Ben and Derek, who took me out for champagne and oysters to celebrate my birthday and my newly secured book deal. We went to see Bryan Ferry at the Royal Albert Hall that night, and on Friday we went to Brighton with the rest of the gang for a full weekend of birthday and book deal festivities. Then the following Monday, the UK went into nationwide lockdown, and I spent the next three months trapped indoors writing my first book. It was one of the most insane experiences of my life, as I'm sure that time was for you. And if it wasn't for my book deal, I definitely would've lost my mind. So thank you, Tyson Cornell. And thank you, Keith Buckley. You guys will never truly know how grateful I am to the pair of you. And your timing was absolutely impeccable.

Incidentally, Keith was my first choice of author for the foreword to the first book since he's solely responsible for getting this project off the ground. But when I wrote down the list of guests for the first two *Life In The Stocks* books—did I forget to mention that I signed a deal for TWO books that day? *Best. Birthday. Ever.*—I realized he wouldn't be appearing until the second one, since I planned to work through the episodes in chronological order. And I wanted Keith to write the foreword for the book that he'd be in. Hence why I enlisted the services of Jesse Malin for *Volume One*, who I'm sure you'll agree did an amazing job.

Speaking of Jesse Malin, he's one of only two guests to appear in both books. The other is Jesse Leach. Both Jesses are repeat offenders. And the reason for that is simple: they were the first two guests to return for a second podcast appearance. And both episodes were so good, I had to include them in separate books—I couldn't just condense them into one. Very few people understand my podcast or presenting style better than the two Jesses. That's why I asked Jesse Malin to write the foreword to the first book. And that's why I started a second podcast with Jesse Leach. But more on that later.

This book is very much a continuation of *Life In The Stocks Volume One*. It follows exactly the same structure and format: thirty-five guests share their personal stories and thoughts on a wide range of subjects. And the extracts are again highlights from the original podcasts, sewn together in a way that hopefully tells a story, with a setup to each chapter from yours truly. I've also chosen to focus primarily on American guests once again, save for two Germans (Richard Kruspe from Rammstein and Nadja Peulen from Coal Chamber) and a Swede (Dennis Lyxzén from Refused). Coincidentally, I'm saving all my conversations with UK guests for a British book, which will likely be my next release.

The main difference between this book and the last one is that there are fewer chapters, and the contents and titles of the chapters have been tweaked to reflect the restructuring of certain topics. That's purely down to what was discussed in the original conversations. I obviously didn't plan on turning these podcasts into books when I first recorded them, so what gets covered here is just what came up along the way—I can't very well have a chapter called "Booze & Drugs" if there aren't enough observations and anecdotes to fill it.

That being said, the chapters are longer and more comprehensive this time around. The book itself is also a good size bigger, which means you get more bang for your buck. And speaking of bucks, this book will once again be presented in American English as opposed to the Queen's proper English. That's because most of the guests are American, so I've adopted their mother tongue for clarity and consistency. I'm sorry, England. Please forgive me—again.

I should also point out that you don't have to read *Life In The Stocks Volume One* to fully understand or appreciate this book, just as you don't have to read either book from start to finish in linear fashion. But it certainly helps. I wrote both books with a chronological overview and narrative arc in mind, so the best place to start is indeed book one, page one, then go from there. But you do whatever you like. It's your life, my friend. I'm not here to tell you how to live it.

If I was going to tell you what to do, however, I'd say listen to the playlist at the end of each chapter before moving on to the next. You'll find them all on Spotify—just search for Matthew Stocks. That's what I had in mind when compiling these audio conversations into books. Any other method of consumption is really just a bastardization of my original vision. But like I said, feel free to go rogue and explore both books at your leisure. Be sure to check out the original podcasts in their entirety, too. These compendiums are like Greatest Hits compilations, but there's still plenty of gold to be mined from the full conversations.

With that in mind, all that's left for me to say is thank you for buying this book. I hope you enjoy reading it as much as I enjoyed writing it. Thank you to all the guests who agreed to be in it as well. And thank you to Keith Buckley, for not only writing me such a fantastic foreword, but for getting me a book deal in the first place. It's all down to you, brother. Now let's get this show on the road.

—**Matt Stocks**, Birmingham, September 2021

ALL THE YOUNG PUNKS

"That's when we did a lot of bonding and being creative together."

I F YOU HAVE READ *Life In The Stocks Volume One*—I'll try not to keep doing this throughout the book, but I can't promise anything— you'll recall the first two chapters were titled "Adolescence" and "Punk Rock." Here, I've combined those two topics into one mega chapter: "All The Young Punks."

Our adolescent years are when 99.9 percent of us discover punk music, after all. I'm yet to meet a middle-aged person who's just uncovered the joys of anarchy and rebellion or an old-age pensioner who's had their whole world turned upside down by the power of punk. That's not to say that those people aren't out there, of course. And if you know of any, please send them my way. I'd love to interview them. But it's safe to say that you and I, and everyone that we know, got into punk music young—specifically during our teenage years.

What also happened with my podcast over time is I found myself asking less questions about people's childhood experiences and familial environments, and more about the musical and cultural movements that were going on around them while they were growing up. It's always a delicate blend; I try to walk the line between the personal and the cultural when interviewing anyone for my show. But as *Life In The Stocks* evolved, the budding musicologist in me overtook the wannabe psychologist and discussions evolved from what was happening in people's homes to broader sociological and historical accounts of certain cities at specific points in time.

As I transcribed the next round of interviews for this book, it became apparent that many of my guests' stories were intrinsically linked to the burgeoning music scenes in their respective areas. And as someone who missed out on those artistic uprisings, I selfishly wanted to hear all about them. It is my podcast after all. And there's nothing to stop *you* starting your own podcast where *you* interview interesting people about the things that *you* like. That's the most important lesson you should take away from punk: do it yourself.

Coming up in this chapter, Casey Chaos remembers the time pro-skater and renowned hell-raiser Duane Peters switched him onto Black Flag as a kid; Perry Farrell recalls his misspent youth living at the infamous Wilton House in Hollywood, which became the birthplace of Jane's Addiction; Charlie Paulson from Goldfinger provides one of the most detailed accounts of LA punk history that you're likely to read outside of a book dedicated to that subject; Walter Schreifels, Lou Koller, and Vinnie Stigma regale us with tales from New York City back in the day; Richard from Rammstein describes his escape from East Berlin before the fall of the Berlin Wall; and Nadja from Coal Chamber explains what it was like to move from Holland to Los Angeles as a teenager at the tail end of the hair metal movement. What a time to be alive!

I enjoy all the stories from every chapter for a variety of reasons, and this one is all about pure nostalgia. I identify with the following fables because they remind me of my own musical upbringing—those carefree juvenile years discovering punk rock for the first time. And whenever I find myself jaded by the state of modern music or the entertainment industry today, I dive into these anecdotes to remind myself that rock 'n' roll was fresh and exciting once upon a time and that it can be again.

The future of music is in the hands of the youth, of course—same as it ever was. And it's up to them to make rock 'n' roll great again. I'm just happy that I caught the tail end of the nineties alternative era because it was an incredible time to be young. Through my podcast,

I get to hear all the stories from the seventies and eighties as well. And that shit keeps me forever young. It really is a blessing to host these discussions, and it's my absolute pleasure to share them with you here.

But first of all, I'd like to hand over to Tom Morello to talk about his amazing mother, Mary Morello. Because there's always time for insights into the family lives of your favorite musicians. It just so happened that my interests shifted, and the conversations became more about music and what was going on socially and culturally than what was happening in people's homes, but it always comes back to the biographical. If a story's not personal, then I'm personally not interested. And I have a sneaking suspicion you feel the same way.

TOM MORELLO—*RAGE AGAINST THE MACHINE, AUDIOSLAVE, PROPHETS OF RAGE, THE NIGHTWATCHMAN*

MATT: Tell me about your mother, Mary Morello. I gather she's one hell of a lady.

TOM: Yes, that's an understatement.

MATT: And she's ninety-four years old?

TOM: She'll be ninety-five on October 1, God willing. Mary Morello is a force of nature. She grew up in a small coal mining town in central Illinois—the kind of town where no one leaves—and she left as a single woman and traveled the world for twenty years.

MATT: What was her drive to do that?

TOM: She can't explain it. I've asked her that many times, and I don't know why. She says she doesn't know why. She said she had a history teacher who was inspirational, but everyone had that same history teacher in that class, and only one of them became Mary Morello. She taught in Spain and Japan and post-war Germany, and after taking tramp steamers around the globe multiple times—having many adventures—she eventually found herself in Kenya, where she met my dad—in the midst of the Mau Mau Uprising. She was teaching at a school in the Aberdare Range where the Mau Mau lived, on a residence where you couldn't go out at night for fear of leopards.

MATT: We're talking real outback business?

TOM: You're in the bush, yeah. And while she was there, she met some of the people who were involved in Kenya's independent struggle, and one of them was my dad.

MATT: Am I right in thinking your dad was Kenya's first ambassador for the UN?

TOM: He wasn't Kenya's first ambassador for the UN, but he was Kenya's ambassador to England for eight years, and he was part of the first UN delegation. That's why I was born in New York City.

MATT: Is it safe to say he wasn't present during your childhood?

TOM: That would be very accurate, yes. I didn't meet him properly until I was thirty years old. He was always a visage and a presence without ever really knowing who he was. But the good news is Mary Morello is no joke.

MATT: Did you grow up in Illinois?

TOM: Yeah, in a town called Libertyville, Illinois. And she was obviously an overqualified world history teacher given her travels and her intellect, but she wasn't allowed to teach at a lot of the local high schools because we were an interracial family. They said, "You can teach here, but because you guys are Black you have to live elsewhere." And she wasn't having that. But someone finally vouched for us in Libertyville, and that's why I grew up in that town.

MATT: I'm assuming politics and academia were both there for you from an early age?

TOM: Yes, without even really thinking they were part of life. Even though I grew up in a staunchly conservative suburb, the politics of my home were very radical, and I didn't realize the sharp juxtaposition of that until I was in high school. That was when I realized I had a very different worldview to my teachers—and most of the student body.

MATT: Did your mom teach you?

TOM: She did. But I was in my senior year, and I was already on my way out; it was the last quarter of my high school career, and I'd already been accepted into university. She taught African Studies, which is a very interesting topic, but I'd be like, "Mom, I'm going to skip class today to go and practice with my punk band—I'm just letting you know."

MATT: And she was cool with that?

TOM: Yeah, she was actually the only parent who would allow us to rehearse in the house, which was very sweet of her because we were a cacophonic group, and we probably weren't very pleasant for her to listen to.

MATT: Didn't you go to school with Adam Jones from Tool?

TOM: Yeah, he was in that band with me; we were called the Electric Sheep.

MATT: Isn't it crazy how life works out? There seems to be points in time when you can trace key artists of their generation back to previous lives together as kids. It's mad.

TOM: It is mad. It's crazy.

JESSE LEACH—*KILLSWITCH ENGAGE, TIMES OF GRACE, THE WEAPON, STOKE THE FIRE PODCAST*

JESSE: I was born in a trailer park in Florida. I'm not even joking. My parents were the managers of a fucking trailer park in Florida. We also moved to Missouri for a while and survived a tornado, apparently. But I don't remember that. Then from there we moved to Rhode Island, which is the Luxembourg of the United States. It's a teeny, little place filled with a ton of very interesting characters and a very dangerous organized crime syndicate that nobody talks about.

My first real memories are living in Philadelphia, Pennsylvania, in the 1980s. My very first memory is actually saying, "I hate Philadelphia." We had a moving truck and a Volkswagen Bug, and I remember screaming at the top of my lungs, "I hate Philadelphia!" That's my first memory. Music caught me soon after that. I got really into break dancing and Whodini, and Run-DMC and the Beastie Boys were in the charts—that shit was popping. My first love was break dancing, b-boying, and hip-hop. I still love hip-hop to this day. It's my first love over anything rock, punk, or metal. That's something most people don't know about me; I'm a huge hip-hop fan. I love the old school shit.

MATT: Could you break dance?

JESSE: Kind of. Keep in mind, at this stage in my life I'm five years old. I managed to cut the sleeves off the denim jacket that my parents got me, and I wore my mom's bandana, which was one of those aerobic exercise ones—look them up on the internet, they're not masculine at all. I'd go down to the corner store where the kids would have ghetto blasters, and I'd go in to buy my bubblegum, then stand there and do my b-boy stance and watch the older guys break dance. They used to call me little man. That's where my whole love affair with music began.

MATT: I imagine Philadelphia was a predominantly African American community at that point. So were you in the minority as a young white kid?

JESSE: Yeah. During that time—and rightly so, for many reasons—there was a radical movement going on in Philadelphia, and they were trying to keep the neighborhood safe and clean. There were some radicals who didn't think we were very safe because we were white people. My dad was in bible college at this point, studying to be a minister, and we had a next-door neighbor named Moses, who was a pimp. He used to carry around a sawn-off shotgun underneath his trench coat. And he had love for my father. He used to call him "The Minister."

We were the only white family living there, and Moses was like, "I'm going to protect The Minister." I didn't know this at the time, obviously because I was only five years old. But I found out later on that Moses protected my family. He would escort us to and from the train station, and once word got out that he had my family's back, we were totally left alone. My father would also do repair work for the community—fixing people's houses up and doing odd jobs, just to show God's love—and we started to become an acceptable presence in the neighborhood.

I went back to that old neighborhood recently and the mother of Moses, who's called Mary—it's so funny, Mary and Moses—is still alive. Moses got shot down in the street unfortunately, but Mary is still around, and she gave me a big hug and showed me around the neighborhood. They have community gardens there now, and there's a house that my dad fixed up that's still there. So that's where I come from: Germantown, Philadelphia. That's where I first found out who I was, and it's firmly rooted in African American culture. That's why I'll always stand in solidarity with anyone of color, especially in our country right now with everything that's going on. It breaks my fucking heart. Fuck that racist shit.

RICHARD KRUSPE—*RAMMSTEIN, EMIGRATE*

MATT: The *Rammstein in Amerika* documentary was a real education for me as to the roots of the band. You guys have really stuck to your guns since day one.

RICHARD: Well, we're German, you know?

MATT: It's the only way you know?

RICHARD: Yeah, especially coming from the East. We had to fight a lot.

MATT: At what age did you get out of East Berlin?

RICHARD: I escaped when I was twenty-three. But it wasn't planned; there was a situation where I was captured by the police at a demonstration, and I just felt like I couldn't breathe anymore.

MATT: Were you actively a part of that demonstration, or were you just in the wrong place at the wrong time?

RICHARD: It was just bad timing. Normally, that's my strong suit—to be on time. But on that day, I was in the wrong place at the wrong time. I was investigated for five days, and when I got out, I was like, "I need to leave."

MATT: That was enough for you to realize it was time to move on?

RICHARD: Yeah.

NADJA PEULEN—*COAL CHAMBER*

MATT: Was it a culture shock for you moving from Holland to LA?

NADJA: No, not at all. I've been wanting to come here since I was around fourteen years old. When I was a teenager, I was a big Guns N' Roses fan after *Appetite for Destruction* came out. So I always wanted to go to The Rainbow and do that whole Sunset Strip thing.

MATT: So you were a rock 'n' roller from an early age?

NADJA: Oh, yeah. My parents are rock 'n' roll, so it's always been like that, you know? And I always wanted to come here, so for me it was a dream come true.

MATT: What year did you move out to the States?

NADJA: I think it was '93 or '94—something like that. I just missed the height of the Sunset Strip days, which was fine because Guns N' Roses were really the only hair metal band that I liked.

MATT: What else were you listening to around that time?

NADJA: Back then it was Faith No More, Soundgarden, Alice in Chains, and all the alternative Seattle bands. And I was into older rock and punk stuff, like The Stooges and The Stones.

MATT: The good shit.

NADJA: Yeah. You've met my mom; she's a proper rock 'n' roll lady.

MATT: She's amazing. Was her first gig out here managing Jumbo's Clown Room?

NADJA: No, she's been working there for a long time, but that wasn't her first gig. When we first came here she did all kinds of stuff just to survive.

MATT: Was money tight?

NADJA: Oh, yeah. We came over here with one suitcase each—that was it. But it was fun. LA was way more rock 'n' roll then than it is now. I still love it, but back then there was so many bars and clubs and bands. And it was all new to me.

MATT: Were you able to get into all the bars and clubs despite only being eighteen?

NADJA: I grew up in Europe, so I started going out when I was fourteen. My mom would take me out to pubs and clubs and stuff like that. Then when I was fifteen or sixteen, I started going out by myself without any adult supervision. So when I came out here when I was almost eighteen, there was no way I was waiting until I was twenty-one to go out because I'd already been going out for years. So I found creative ways to get into the clubs.

MATT: Would you get drunk?

NADJA: No, I just wanted to go out and meet people. I like alcohol a lot more now than I did in those days, even though I'm still not much of a drinker.

MATT: Was LA touristy back then?

NADJA: It was. But Hollywood Boulevard used to be a lot more shady and scary. Now, it's cleaned up and become a lot more gentrified.

MATT: I think it's the same all over the world: everywhere has been gentrified.

NADJA: Yeah, it's boring. I don't like it at all. There's obviously good and bad that comes with everything, and there's, of course, good that comes with this too, but the traffic is worse, the people are less exciting, and there's definitely less shows.

MATT: It does still have a certain magic about it, though. I feel magic here. Is that what's kept you here all this time?

NADJA: Yeah, I feel the same way. When I first landed here I fell in love with the smell of the city, and it's not necessarily a great smell, but it did something to me. I love the whole energy of the city. But it's not for everybody; a lot of people come to LA, and they absolutely hate it. It all just depends on who you are and what you're looking for. But whatever you are looking for, you can find it here. That's the beauty of it.

DEAN KARR—*DIRECTOR, PHOTOGRAPHER*

DEAN: My parents weren't really into music, other than hating my music, but I was into it very young. It was a way to reach out and rebel against my parents. I had locks on the inside of my bedroom to keep them out—and the music *up!* I used to listen to a lot of classic metal back then: Sabbath, Maiden, and Priest.

MATT: So you've always been a heavy metal dude?

DEAN: Hell yeah. Those guitars are angels, man.

MATT: Were you artistic from an early age?

DEAN: Yeah. I loved cooking, music, and photography. I used to sneak cameras into concerts. I have albums and albums of all those right-on-the-wall shots of K.K. Downing [Judas Priest], Tony Iommi [Black Sabbath], and Eddie Van Halen [Van Halen]. We were little kids starting early, and the big kids would let us come right up in front of them. And if we weren't on the wood barricade then we didn't make it. We didn't do our job.

MATT: What were you shooting with back then?

DEAN: Shitty little 110 cameras to begin with, then my grandpa gave me a Canon A-1. The shots came out really cool, man. But it was bigger and bulkier, so we had to take the camera apart. We'd put the body and the lens in sandwich bags and put them in our underwear. Then we'd run into the bathroom, get in two stalls, and my friend would hand me the lens under the bathroom stall. I'd build the camera in there, then I'd put the camera under my T-shirt with the strap around my neck, and we'd run as fast as we could to get out in the crowd.

MATT: I love it. A lot of people were probably sneaking into the bathroom to do blow, but you guys were going in there to get your camera set up to shoot the gig.

DEAN: Yeah, that's all we were doing back then.

MATT: After you finished school did you go to college?

DEAN: I did.

MATT: In Seattle?

DEAN: Six hours away, at Washington State University, which is a huge university.

MATT: What was your degree in?

DEAN: Probably partying. I was six hours away from my parents for the first time—you learn a lot about life is what that is. I basically didn't learn shit about photography the whole time I was there, but I had a great time. Then I got accepted at the ArtsCenter [College of Design] in Pasadena, which is definitely one of the top five elite schools in the country for photography and filmmaking.

MATT: Was that because you were doing a lot of photography in your spare time? Because it obviously wasn't on the strength of your academic achievements.

DEAN: Actually, they didn't accept me twice. Then I got accepted the third time with a half scholarship, which didn't make any sense to me, but that's how it went down. And I'm still one of their most successful alumni.

LINUS OF HOLLYWOOD—*NERF HERDER, SOLO ARTIST, PRODUCER*

LINUS: My dad was a very strict military guy, and I immediately got into music when I was a teenager. I was teasing my hair and wearing eyeliner because I was really into hair metal, and my parents tried to be supportive at first, but after coming to see some shows where their son was basically dressed as a woman, I think they became very confused as to what I was doing with my life. And I was in gifted classes growing up; I skipped a grade when I was a kid, so I think they thought I was going to be a doctor or something like that. But as soon as I heard *Van Halen II*, I was like, "That's what I want to do!"

MATT: At what age did you start playing an instrument? And what was the first one you learned to play?

LINUS: I started playing guitar when I was five.

MATT: *Five?*

LINUS: Yeah. I taught myself, too.

MATT: How do you teach yourself guitar when you're five?

LINUS: I really don't remember. I have friends who are really great teachers because they remember how they learned, so they can tell other people how to do it. But I don't remember how I learned; I just took an early interest in it, and it feels like I've always known how to play. I don't remember learning at all.

MATT: That's wild. I guess some people just pick up an instrument and immediately there's a bond.

LINUS: Yeah, and it's weird because no one in my family is musical at all, but I have pictures of me when I was two years old with these giant headphones on my head, listening to *Rock and Roll Over* by Kiss. I just loved music, and I didn't get that from anyone in my family.

SCOTT SHIFLETT—*FACE TO FACE, ME FIRST & THE GIMME GIMMES, VIVA DEATH*

SCOTT: I came in on rock, mostly sixties and seventies hard rock. So I'd already been messing around, and I had a bit of an established approach to playing before the shred movement came along in the eighties. And that was exciting to a degree, but for the most part all the attention was paid to blistering licks, and that seemed to be to the detriment of everything else: bass, drums, and the songs. Bands just became a boring backdrop for the inevitable histrionic guitar solo that would rip your head off, and though that had a certain novelty, and some of the guys had some character to their playing, by and large it just felt exhausting and unfulfilling. I missed the days of Deep Purple, Black Sabbath, Queen, early Van Halen, and Led Zeppelin.

MATT: Were you a bassist first or a guitarist first? Or both?

SCOTT: It's hard to say. I have an older brother who is a guitar teacher, and he's only two-and-a-half years older than me, but he was a huge influence on me growing up. So the reason I started playing bass was because of my older brother, Mike. Now, a lot of people know my younger brother, Chris.

MATT: Is there three of you in total?

SCOTT: There's three of us in total, not counting our stepbrother, Steve. But we never actually lived with Steve. He is family, but we're the core three Shiflett brothers. So Mike started on guitar, and I unofficially started messing around on his guitars; I watched and studied his moves and picked up his licks and stuff like that. Then when it came time for proper lessons, my mom said, "What's it going to be?" In my mind, I always figured I would be a lead guitarist or a drummer. But when the day came and she hit me with the question, "We're going to sign you up for lessons, so what's it going to be?" I just said bass in a panic. It wasn't that I had some drive for bass or even an affinity for bass. I just knew that guitar looked scary and daunting, and my older brother was already on it. And I figured if I picked another instrument that would get us one step closer to a band, so I picked the bass.

MATT: When did punk music come into play? At the same time as the sixties and seventies hard rock?

SCOTT: Yes and no. I've got a picture of my record collection from 1974, and you see The Beatles, David Bowie, Grand Funk Railroad, and The Rolling Stones. There was no real beginning for me. I've always been listening to music. Periodically, I'll come across somebody who will say, "I was studying to be an architect, and then I discovered rock music out of college." But not the Shiflett boys. This was an obsession from as far back as we can remember.

MATT: Did that come for your parents? Were they big music fans?

SCOTT: They had their musical tastes. My dad was mostly into blues and jazz, and my mom was into the California sound. And I loved their tastes; I still listen to their tastes to this day. But my older brother Mike was really the forerunner of what was our music, which tended to be late sixties and early seventies hard rock. Then I kind of ran with a little bit more of the heavy metal, and my little brother [Chris] got into some of the glam rock. But we all loved each other's stuff, too. We all covered part of the spectrum, and we all dug each other's music, even if we were all focusing on different things specifically. And that medicine ball of music gets lobbed back and forth generationally. The early sixties Stones and Beatles—and the garage rock bands of the sixties—definitely influenced the American protopunk bands, like the MC5 and The Stooges, and even early Ramones, which then came back over here and helped inspire all the British bands, like the Sex Pistols, The Clash, and The Jam.

MATT: It's always been this transatlantic love affair between the US and the UK hasn't it?

SCOTT: Yeah, and each iteration spawns a new haircut or pair of trousers that seem appropriate to wear with it, and that sort of pushes the thing forward. It's interesting because people are always looking for ground zero for things like the terminology, but most things have to percolate for a while before they get their chrysalis and the moment where the name meets the sound meets the look, which for punk was probably London in 1976, when all the bands spawned out of there.

I still remember in 1977, my older brother, Mike, and I were sat watching the news with my dad, and this was back when this burgeoning new movement was enough of a threat and a cultural scare that it merited its own news coverage. It was like, "What are these people doing sticking safety pins through their clothes and faces?" In the little inbox they had a picture of Johnny Rotten, and they'd airbrushed flames all around him so he just looked dangerous and menacing. I remember when that came on the screen, I looked over at my brother Mike and he looked back at me, and we were both, like, *"What is this?"*

JIM ADKINS—*JIMMY EAT WORLD*

JIM: When I was growing up and starting to play in bands, and starting to go and see other bands play, that was all pre-internet as we know it, so you found out about things from friends and flyers at record shops. Record store clerks were like the gatekeepers to what was cool and happening back then. And the Phoenix area where I grew up was pretty spread out—it's a large metropolitan area—so something could be happening on one side of town and you would never know about it.

MATT: Did any other well-known bands come out of that area?

JIM: When I was growing up, probably the biggest Arizona band was the Gin Blossoms. To call it bar rock wouldn't be exactly accurate, but there was this whole scene of bands influenced by The Replacements, and it was rock 'n' roll music with a respect for songwriting. If you've heard Gin Blossoms—*that*. So there was that whole thing going on.

MATT: What was the local live music scene like?

JIM: When we were kids, there was a law that got put into effect where if you were an establishment that served alcohol, you had to be above a certain capacity or sell a certain amount of food to have people under the age of twenty-one in your space. Otherwise, you had to have a partitioned area separate from any bar that was monitored. And no bar owner wanted to eat up their capacity with kids who weren't going to buy booze, so a lot of places became straight up twenty-one and over, and a lot of people who were putting on punk shows had to find their own place. And in a weird way that energized things because we realized we had to do things ourselves, and that spawned a whole host of different places that were super sketchy and only open for about eight or nine months at a time before they got shut down—all-ages art space-type venues with vocal PAs only.

MATT: Did you get out and do any desert generator parties?

JIM: We played some desert generator stuff, yeah. That definitely happened. If you were under twenty-one and you wanted to play, you figured it out. And we just sort of fell in line with like-minded people who were doing that. Our scene in Arizona was comprised of people who were doing it on their own because no real promoters wanted to take a chance on acts who were at our level, which was zero back then. Some friends of mine decided they would start a record label, and they didn't know what they were doing. They just decided, "We're a record label now." And our record was one of the first ones they released. Then some other friends of mine said they wanted to be promoters. And so on. Another way that people found out about music back then was in zine reviews. Zines were like the podcasts for the pre-internet era; you found out about music through magazines like *Maximumrocknroll* and *HeartattaCk*.

MATT: I genuinely think pre-internet was the last good era to be young.

JIM: Yeah, we got to experience a crazy point in history that'll never appear again: the crossover of pre-internet and then the internet. And there were no smart phones. It was really, *really* expensive to have a cellular phone back then. That was a rich person thing—no one else had them.

MATT: And when mobile phones first came along, people didn't used to spend all their time on them because all you could do was call and text to begin with. You wouldn't just sit there looking at your phone the way everybody does now.

JIM: Yeah. When we'd tour, we'd use our road atlas to find directions to the edge of town. And when we got to the edge of town, we'd find a payphone to call the promoter and try to get directions to the venue where we were playing that night. Can you imagine trying to navigate anywhere now without any GPS help? I do it automatically because I want to find the best traffic route, even if I know where I'm going. And you had to memorize all your friend's phone numbers. How many phone numbers do you have memorized now?

MATT: My own—that's it. But what were you saying about zines?

JIM: *HeartattaCk* and *Maximumrocknroll* were two zines that were kind of big, and there was a dozen or so smaller ones that you would look at to find out what was going on. And *Maximumrocknroll* would put out a yearly periodical called *Book Your Own Fuckin' Life*.

MATT: Of course. That was the bible of touring back then.

JIM: Yeah, and we utilized that thing on all our early tours. You could call up promoters in different towns, and if none of them called you back you could just start calling bands in other towns to see if you could get hooked up with a show somewhere else. In turn, when they came to your town, you would help them out with something. That was how everybody toured back then.

CHRIS DEMAKES—*LESS THAN JAKE, CHRIS DEMAKES A PODCAST*

MATT: What was the Gainesville music scene like when you were growing up?

CHRIS: Gainesville is this little microcosm in Florida—it's its own little thing. It's a very liberal college town of about 100,000 people, then you go five miles either way, and you're in the sticks.

MATT: Alligator country?

CHRIS: Alligator country. The middle of nowhere. I actually came from a place three hours south of Gainesville, called Port Charlotte. That's where Vinnie [Fiorello] and I grew up.

MATT: Did you two start the band?

CHRIS: Yeah. And we grew up three hours south of Gainesville in a place that couldn't have been any different—it would be like going from Scotland to Pittsburgh. We didn't have any good record stores, let alone punk record stores. So we'd have to drive half an hour to get to a good record store, and probably an hour and a half to get to a show.

MATT: Do you know what though? I believe there's magic in the quest. And now that all music is accessible at the touch of a button, that element of discovery has gone. When we were kids, you'd save up a certain amount of money, and you'd buy the one record you really wanted because that was all you could afford. And you'd play it out, and you'd know all the words inside and out. I feel like that culture has disappeared with streaming.

CHRIS: It's gone. And I don't know if it can ever be replicated because that's all young people know nowadays. My son and daughter are never going to know what a CD is—it's going to look like some relic that your grandparents used. Technology is what it is, I guess. It just isn't the same nowadays. We started in what I like to call the analogue era, where it was all recorded to tape and all your mistakes were there. I've always said that I'd love to make a reality show where you send a band of nineteen-year-old kids out on tour with no smart phones, just maps and payphones, and see if they can make it. They wouldn't find any payphones, though, so they'd be screwed.

MATT: How old were you when things started taking off for Less Than Jake?

CHRIS: I was four months shy of my eighteenth birthday when I moved to Gainesville in the summer of '91. I'd been corresponding with Vinnie back home and writing these songs, but we didn't have a name yet, and Vinnie sent me a demo with "Less Than Jake" written on it. I was like, "What the hell does that mean?" And he said, "Well, you know how my mom always comes to bother us when we're practicing at the house and tell us that the music is bothering our family bulldog, Jake? He'd always start howling, and we'd have to stop playing. So, we're Less Than Jake." I thought it sounded so stupid, but we needed a name and that's what we went with.

MATT: I think it's a great name, and it really suits your sound. There are certain band names that make no sense, but they just work, and I think yours is one of them. It's the same with Reel Big Fish. That name makes absolutely no sense, but it's perfect for them and what they do.

CHRIS: Yeah, Less Than Jake was definitely meant to be. So we had this demo that I was handing out at shows for free in early 1992. And in June of that year we got a new bass player. So I always count July 14, 1992, as the inception of the band, because that's when we played our first show. You're only a legit band when you play your first show. That was with this guy Chris, who was with us until about October or November of '92. But things weren't working out with him, and Vinnie and I wanted to go on since we had another batch of songs written. And that's around the time I met Roger [Lima].

MATT: Was Roger in a band at that time? What was he up to?

CHRIS: He wasn't. I actually met him through my roommate. She met him at a dorm party one night, and she was like, "I heard this guy playing guitar. Aren't you looking for someone to play guitar?" I said, "No, we're looking for a bassist." But she suggested we still meet up, so she had him come over one night. I had my guitar in my room, which I handed to him, and he started playing. I was like, "This guy's great!" So I asked him if he played bass, to which he replied, "I've never tried." He went out and bought a fifty dollar bass the next day. Then he wired a car speaker to make a bass cabinet for his amp. And he became the bass player in Less Than Jake in January of 1993.

BEN OSMUNDSON—*ZEBRAHEAD*

MATT: Where did you grow up?

BEN: In Orange County, Southern California. And when I was in high school, you'd go to a backyard party, and Sublime, No Doubt, and The Offspring would be playing. Lagwagon were always around, too. They all played the local parties. Every weekend there was something cool to do, and all those bands were from near my hometown, so it was always easy to see them play. I didn't even know how spoiled I was, I just thought going to shows was fun. It was only later on that I realized how lucky I was.

MATT: When you say house parties, do you literally mean parties at people's houses, with bands in the back garden?

BEN: Keggers, yeah.

MATT: And they just happened to be the bands that went on to define a generation?

BEN: Crazy, right? Even today watching Guttermouth play, I was like, "Those guys went to my high school as well."

MATT: Who was the first band from that area to take off? Social Distortion?

BEN: Yeah, in Southern California, Social Distortion are like gods. They're so big.

MATT: They're like The Clash of that region, aren't they?

BEN: Yeah, it's insane. But he deserves it. He's freakin' Mike Ness, you know? Then after them, it was The Offspring and No Doubt—kind of at the same time. Then Reel Big Fish and Lit took off. All those bands were a stone's throw from my house, and I'd go see them all the time. It was kind of incredible.

MATT: Talk to me about Sublime.

BEN: Going to see Sublime back in the day, there was a fifty-fifty chance that Bradley [Nowell] would be sober enough to play. It was a weird experience. You'd go to the show thinking, "They might play tonight. They might not." Some nights it would just be him on an acoustic guitar trying to play songs. Then other nights it would be the best thing you've ever seen in your life. There was something about him, though.

MATT: What do you think it was?

BEN: His voice was so soulful and amazing.

MATT: He was connected to that reggae spirit, wasn't he?

BEN: Yeah. And they played every night of the week in Southern California, so if you wanted to see them then you could. They would literally sell CDs out the back of their car, and everywhere they played people showed up. It's obviously depressing that he died before they hit big, but you could tell there was something about them that was going to be huge.

MATT: Did you know Bradley personally?

BEN: I didn't know him at all. I went to about fifty freakin' Sublime shows, but I never met him. I was always the timid kid at the back of the venue, just quietly watching the show.

MATT: What about No Doubt? Was it obvious even early on that Gwen Stefani was a star in the making?

BEN: The weird thing about No Doubt is they were humongous in Orange County for about ten years before the rest of the world caught on; she was a superstar in Southern California way before *Tragic Kingdom* hit. And it was bizarre because you'd see them play in Southern California, and there'd be thousands of people watching them. Then when you went outside of Orange County, there'd be like a hundred people watching them. So we had ten years of No Doubt in Orange County before they got big. And everyone looked up to them already because we didn't realize the rest of the world didn't know who they were. We just thought they were big everywhere.

GREG ATTONITO—*THE BOUNCING SOULS*

MATT: Where did you see most of your live shows as a kid growing up in New Jersey?

GREG: There was a place called City Gardens in Trenton. It was in a terrible neighborhood, and it was a scary place to go. But when you look at all the old bills, there was so many great shows there. I saw

Toots and the Maytals there. I saw Debbie Harry—solo, not even as Blondie—there. I saw lots of hardcore shows, and bands like The Meatmen there. And I saw the Red Hot Chili Peppers there.

MATT: How good were they back in the day? Chili Peppers, Fishbone, Jane's Addiction, Thelonious Monster—that whole eighties LA alternative rock scene.

GREG: Did you see Fishbone back then?

MATT: No, dude. I wish. I've only watched them on the internet. But I had Perry Farrell on the podcast a few weeks back, and he was telling me all about that scene and time and place.

GREG: It was great seeing the Chili Peppers at City Gardens. There was probably only about three hundred people there, and it was cool as a teenager to see what they were doing.

MATT: Were they in the whole "Socks on Cocks" phase at that point?

GREG: Yeah. I saw them at Halloween one year in New York City, and they played fully naked with glow-in-the-dark body paint—socks and everything. It was such a freaky scene, The Ritz in the city in the late eighties. I was like, "Are people even wearing costumes? Or are these just their regular clothes?" Because they might've dressed like that in August, too. It was out there.

MATT: Was New Jersey dangerous back then?

GREG: In some areas, but where we grew up it was pretty suburban. And I feel very fortunate now to have grown up there. We lived among trees and nature, and we rode our bikes around, and we were so close to Philly and New York. We could take the train right into the city to go skate and watch shows. But going back to Fishbone, they were one of the greatest live bands I've ever seen.

MATT: I've heard so many people say that; Fishbone and Bad Brains seem to be the two bands who inspired almost everybody to start a band and take that live show to the next level.

GREG: Yes. Sadly I didn't see Bad Brains back in the day with HR on vocals, but a little bit later when CBGB was doing their string of closing shows, we opened up for Bad Brains and HR sang. That was really cool.

MATT: How important was skateboarding to you growing up? Was it right there alongside punk rock?

GREG: Yeah, Bryan [Kienlen] and I would skate on his driveway after school. That's when we did a lot of bonding and being creative together. And when we lived in New Brunswick later on, we'd go out on late night skate missions. So it's all part of the same soup, you know?

MATT: Definitely. My introduction to so many bands came from skateboard and BMX videos. It was a golden age of discovery.

JOBY FORD—*THE BRONX, MARIACHI EL BRONX, ARTIST, PRODUCER*

JOBY: *Thrasher* used to put out these compilations called *Skate Rock*, which they'd put out once a year. A lot of them featured bands who were skaters, like Steve Caballero's band, The Faction. I got turned onto that band by the *Skate Rock* comps, and bands like D.I., JFA, and all that stuff. There's something about skateboarding that identifies with faster music; I don't know what it is, but it makes total sense. All the *Bones Brigade* videos that we'd watch as kids featured music by all these punk bands, too.

MATT: Back when skateboarding and punk rock were both very much outsider subcultures.

JOBY: One hundred percent.

MATT: They weren't mainstream or popular in the slightest. And the likelihood was, if you were rolling round on a skateboard or wearing a mohawk back then, you would probably get arrested or beaten up.

JOBY: Exactly. They weren't cool at all. But they captured the youth of America—at least a certain type of kid who didn't want to play football or be a jock or whatever. And the two things went hand in hand. There was a lot of bands who would play at these skate demos, and all of us skaters would go to the shows and donate cans of food, which they would then give to the homeless. No one ever made any money.

MATT: Before Nirvana, the idea of making a career out of punk rock was totally inconceivable, wasn't it?

JOBY: One hundred percent.

MATT: Then Nirvana changed the whole game, followed by Green Day and The Offspring.

JOBY: That's right. Before those bands, a career in punk rock was inconceivable. We had no aspirations of ever making a record or anything like that. We would just get together and play music and go skating, and that was just what we did.

MATT: It was a great time to be young—without sounding like two old geezers.

JOBY: I think so. I look back on those times, and like you said earlier, there was a lot of discovery. It was tough to find those records because most record stores didn't carry punk. You had to order records out of magazines or from the labels themselves. I remember every record that I bought would come with a catalogue of all the rest of the records that label had put out, so I'd read about bands and save up my money, then send off a check to SST records for the new Minutemen album.

MATT: I spoke to Casey Chaos about that. He said he became pen pals with Glenn Danzig, Ian MacKaye, Henry Rollins—all those guys.

JOBY: That was a big part of the punk scene back then. I remember when I first started playing shows, we'd go up to San Francisco and play like a matinee show with all these different bands, and we'd exchange addresses and write each other letters. That's the way the punk community worked back then. No one else wrote letters, but we did because it was cheap and easy, and that's how you knew what was going on. People collect email addresses now, but we used to have postal mailing lists; you'd play a show and people would sign up and leave you their address, then you'd send them out flyers of whatever you were doing that month in the mail. That's how people did it back then.

CASEY CHAOS—*AMEN, CHRISTIAN DEATH, SCUM*

MATT: Tell me about your history with punk music. What does it mean to you?

CASEY: I grew up in New York, then my mother decided to move to the backwoods of Florida. It was like *Deliverance* town, you know? Swamp land. And I didn't get along with people at all. Everybody kind of took the piss out of me with my New York accent. So music, to me, was kind of like the enemy's tool. I really hated music. "Freebird" and all that seventies rock stuff was shit that I didn't identify with at all. Then I went to a skateboard competition around that time, which was a really big competition where they had pros from all around the world. It was an amazing event. And it was a week-long, so they roomed people with other skateboarders.

Ironically, they roomed me with Duane Peters, who was a skateboarder that I really admired. He was full of life in his pictures, and he had a punk rock image, even though I didn't understand what punk rock was yet. When we got into the room together, he said, "Hey, man. You like punk rock?" I was like, "What's that? What's *punk rock?*" He goes, "Music, man. You like music?" And I go, "No, I fucking hate music." And he said, "*What?* How can you hate music?" So I explained how all the people back home that I hated loved music, and he was like, "Oh, well, you'll love this!"

He put a cassette tape into this big boom box that he had, and I'll never forget it. It was a song by Black Flag called "Police Story." The lyrics went, "This fucking city / Is run by pigs / They take the rights away / From all the kids." It was as if I saw God's asshole open up. It was like the fucking universe revealed itself to me. It was beautiful. I was like, "How can they say that? How can you do that?" It was so noisy and full of life and energy. I was blown away. And I was completely addicted from that point on.

MATT: Tell me about that photo on your wall of you as a kid in the crowd at a Black Flag show. It's classic.

CASEY: I was twelve years old in that photo, and that was the first punk rock show I'd ever seen: Black Flag. I arrived at the show early because I was corresponding with Chuck Dukowski at the time, and I got to meet the band. I'd never seen anything like it—to this day. It was one of the most powerful things I've ever witnessed in my life.

MATT: Were you a big Misfits fan from the start as well?

CASEY: Yeah. I remember Henry [Rollins] had a tattoo of the Misfits skull, so I was always interested in them. When I got turned onto them, I loved them. But in Florida you couldn't buy these records. You couldn't get them anywhere. You'd have to correspond with the bands or the label. So I used to write to all those guys: Ian MacKaye, Glenn Danzig, the SST Records office. I still have a lot of those letters. It's interesting now, in retrospect, because the Misfits just headlined The Forum, and no one would've ever thought they'd do that back then.

JOEY CASTILLO—*QUEENS OF THE STONE AGE, DANZIG, THE BRONX, CIRCLE JERKS, ZAKK SABBATH*

MATT: Who's the first band you ever saw live?

JOEY: The first punk rock gig that I went to was X, The Blasters, and The Gears at The Whisky [a Go Go]. That was in late 1979, early 1980— right around that time. And that's when I knew that's what I wanted to do. My girlfriend's older sister took me to the show. She was like, "You like punk rock? You want to come with me to Hollywood?" I remember I snuck out of my parent's house that night, and I went to the show and my mind was blown. That's how it all happened.

MATT: What was the first proper band that you were in?

JOEY: The first proper band that I played in was LA's Wasted Youth. I'd been going to shows with a bunch of punk rock friends, and I got to know these other kids, and it kind of led to that. I came in after Allen [Stiritz] the original drummer left. That was probably late '84.

MATT: How old were you then?

JOEY: Well, I went on their first US tour with them when I was underage, so I had to sit outside a lot of those twenty-one-and-over clubs until we played.

MATT: And your parents let you go on tour?

JOEY: Yeah, they kind of knew what I was going after at that point. And I think I must've been about eighteen.

MATT: Did you have your head screwed on in the sense that you wanted to try and make a career out of playing music?

JOEY: No, and that's what I tell everybody: I was just living in the moment. My parents were great—they were totally supportive. And I went out on the road for a month and a half, which was a long time for a first tour. We were in a van, we got robbed, and we did this, and we did that. But we did it, and we finished it, and it was awesome.

MATT: It was a real rite of passage?

JOEY: That was it. And that's when I knew coming home, "This is what I want to do."

MATT: There was no going back?

JOEY: No. And there really wasn't.

MATT: What's that old punk documentary with Social Distortion?

JOEY: *Another State of Mind.*

MATT: That film documents exactly what you're talking about so well.

JOEY: Absolutely.

MATT: The van will break down; you will get into fights.

JOEY: You'll make friends; you'll lose friends.

MATT: But if you finish it—

JOEY: And you make it home, and you have a clear memory of what just happened—because a lot of the time you do something and it's a total blur. But I can almost remember every second of that tour.

MATT: Meal by meal, mile by mile, moment by moment. Because you were aware of the importance of it as it was unfolding?

JOEY: Yeah, and it was happening for the first time—to me at least. So I wanted to live it to the fullest, I suppose. That's how it felt at the time.

MATT: Presumably, you were the youngest person in Wasted Youth at that point?

JOEY: Yeah. I was eighteen and the rest of the guys were a little bit older.

MATT: Were the rest of them drinking and partying the whole time?

JOEY: Yeah, but I was too. We all were. And it wasn't outrageous, but we were having fun, you know what I mean? We were doing the typical young band on the road thing. That's when I met all my buddies in the New York scene, too. We did a CBGB matinee show, which was awesome, and that's how I know John Joseph, Todd Youth, Jimmy Gestapo, and all those guys.

MATT: Isn't that the beautiful thing about touring? You get to travel the world and make friendships all over the place, and you can be so far from home, yet still enjoy these connections that feel so familiar.

JOEY: Exactly. And back then there was no cell phones or internet or any of that stuff. It was all payphones and letters.

MATT: And you built genuine friendships that way because it wasn't as flippant and noncommittal as the social media age.

JOEY: That's right. And over the years, through all the different changes in bands and times, and deaths and sad stuff like that, you remain somehow connected to these people because of those early formative experiences. I say this to a lot of people: growing up in Southern California in the 1980s, coming up on punk rock and going to shows and meeting all these kids, it schooled me in a lot of ways and opened me up to a lot of different things, whether it was bands or authors or places or ideas. And there's nothing wrong with anybody taking the other path and staying at home, but I knew for me, I had to get out and see the world. And when it comes to music, if it's in your mind that it's what you love and what you want to do, then it's attainable—you can do it. That's how it was for me. All these different doors open and you keep growing and learning. That's how I try to live my life to this day.

JOHN FELDMANN—*GOLDFINGER, PRODUCER, SONGWRITER, A&R EXECUTIVE*

MATT: Would it be safe to say that punk rock has afforded you a career, and by extension a life?

JOHN: Punk rock has definitely changed, altered, and given me a life beyond anything I could've ever imagined. When I was going to punk shows as a little kid, I would never have imagined that I'd be here in Manchester speaking with you about punk rock all these years later, because those shows were so small: the Adolescents, T.S.O.L., Social Distortion, GBH, and all those bands that I saw when I was growing up. They were always in some Veterans Hall with thirty to forty people—there was really no one there back in those days. And it didn't feel like there was ever going to be a future.

MATT: It wasn't built to last?

JOHN: No, it wasn't. If you think about it, Bad Religion and Social Distortion are the only bands that really persevered, and neither of those bands went on to become as big as The Offspring, Green Day, or Blink-182. It must've been 1982–1985 when most of those Southern California bands were really affecting my life when I was in high school. Then that whole movement kind of went away.

MATT: Until Bad Religion released *Suffer* in 1988?

JOHN: I guess so. Fat Mike claims that NOFX wouldn't have made *White Trash, Two Heebs and a Bean*, or *Punk in Drublic* without *Suffer*. I know he's said that. And without NOFX, would there be a Blink-182? I really think NOFX was the gateway band for a lot of the pop punk bands of the nineties.

MATT: Am I right in thinking that UK punk was a scene and a style that impacted you?

JOHN: For sure. I was a huge fan of The Police; they were a massive band back then, and they were sort of my guilty pleasure to a certain extent. They always had the greatest songs. And he [Sting] had the greatest voice. And he was just an amazing bass player. I was a bass player as a kid, so I would learn his bass lines and study how he wrote music, starting with the bass. And when I found out he was in *Quadrophenia*, I would go over to my friend's house and watch that movie all the time. My parents would never let me watch it because of that scene in the alleyway.

MATT: That alleyway is still there in Brighton.

JOHN: I've been there and done the whole fucking thing. I listened to *Quadrophenia* while walking the [Brighton Palace] Pier when I was making a King Blues record. It was a seminal moment in my life—a full circle kind of thing. And *Quadrophenia* gave me the fashion sense of bands like The Jam and the Buzzcocks, with the skinny ties and the three-button sharkskin suits—all that stuff.

MATT: That's still a big part of the Goldfinger look to this day.

JOHN: Yeah, it's definitely still part of what we do. But as much as The Specials influenced our style, I'm equally influenced by Bad Religion. And they look nothing like how I dress on stage, but their sound is definitely part of it.

MATT: Your first band was called Family Crisis, correct?

JOHN: That was my first band, yeah.

MATT: How old were you then? About fifteen?

JOHN: I was twelve.

MATT: Twelve?

JOHN: Yeah, I started that band at twelve, and it lasted until I was fifteen. We were influenced by the Southern California skate punk bands. There was a band called The Faction that we grew up with down the street in San Jose, and Steve Caballero was part of that band. He was a legendary skateboarder. So we were sort of thrash punk, but I was also really influenced by the Buzzcocks. It doesn't sound that different to Goldfinger to be totally honest, it's just more bass driven because I was writing songs on the bass back then.

MATT: Did you tour in that band?

JOHN: The farthest we ever went was Lake Tahoe. We did a Northern California run up to the Bay Area, and we played shows with 7 Seconds and Bad Religion. It was great to play those shows and experience that style of punk rock back in 1983. I had liberty spikes in my hair, and I literally took the dog collar off my dog to put the Sid [Vicious] chain on. I ripped up my pants and all that shit. Back then there was no Hot Topic or anything like that; you had to make your own clothes. A friend of mine actually came to London back in the early eighties and bought a pair of creepers from Malcolm McLaren's store [SEX], which he then brought back, and I bought them off him for thirty dollars. That was a lot of money for a pair of shoes back then, but they were blue suede creepers, and I felt like such a stud in them.

MATT: Were your parents supportive of you going out on tour as a kid?

JOHN: No, they called the cops on me, and they tried to put me in rehab. I ran away a lot. So they were the opposite of supportive—they were scared. I remember going to see the Dead Kennedys when I was a kid, who I saw a bunch of times, and my parents were going to drop me off in San Francisco while they went to see an opera. But when my mom saw all the people waiting in line for the concert, she was like, "There's no chance." Everyone was doing speed and all the other shit that people did back then.

MATT: It sounds like a crazy time.

JOHN: There was a lot of drugs. And people would tape razor blades to their combat boots and swing chains around in the circle pit. It was a very different era. There was *so* many fights back then. And look, now that I'm a parent I understand how they must've felt. But they thought punk rock was some form of mental illness—that's really what they believed.

MATT: Did you get into drugs and alcohol at a young age?

JOHN: Yeah, and that's exactly what my parents were scared of; they didn't want to see me overdose and die or become some homeless kid on the streets. Everyone was scared back then because they didn't know what the fuck punk rock was. I remember being at the Democratic Convention when they were protesting Ronald Reagan, and Jello Biafra from the Dead Kennedys had a Reagan mask on. I was in the middle of it all, and they had cops on horsebacks with their fucking batons out beating people up. It was wild, man. I don't think I've ever felt as alive as I did back then when I was in the movement. I was really deep into it for about three or four years, then I started exploring other music as I got older. T.S.O.L. made a record called *Beneath the Shadows*, which was a new wave record with keyboards, and I felt like that was the turning point. Bad Religion made a full synth record [*Into the Unknown*] around the same time too, and everyone started exploring things outside of hardcore punk. I grew my hair long like Henry Rollins, and I was like, "Punk rock is dead."

GREG HETSON—*REDD KROSS, CIRCLE JERKS, BAD RELIGION*

MATT: What was the eighties LA punk scene like?

GREG: It was an adventure because you had no idea what was going to happen. There was only a couple of mainstream clubs that would book punk bands, so most shows happened in halls without permits. And even if they were permitted, if the cops wanted to come in and bust it, they would come in with their billy clubs, or truncheons as you would call them—

MATT: And you'd get a beating?

GREG: You'd get a beating, yeah. I went to this one gig before I was in a band or anything, and my friend and I still had long hair—we hadn't cut our hair off yet. We were at a punk show standing on the staircase that led up to the hall, when all of a sudden a riot squad came in out of nowhere. It was a totally mellow gig, and they just started beating all the punk kids up. They looked at us, and because we didn't look like punks—because we had long hair—they didn't hit us. Before that night, I always thought the cops were our friends; I never bought into that whole "fuck the police" mentality. But when I saw that, I was like, "What the hell?" It really opened my eyes. And the LAPD at that time was ran by this police chief named Daryl Gates, who was notorious. He was really bad.

MATT: And that obviously peaked with the Rodney King incident.

GREG: Yes. It was a very racist and homophobic organization back then. They were against anything that was different. They overreacted a lot, too. They'd go in with tanks and bulldoze people's houses down—people who they thought were drugs dealers, and a lot of times they weren't. It was crazy.

MATT: As someone who missed out on both eras but has read up on and watched a lot of documentaries about both time periods, it reminds me of reaction to rock 'n' roll music in America during the 1950s, when the powers that be thought, "This is a threat to society as we know it."

GREG: Yeah, and the hippies in the sixties as well.

MATT: Absolutely.

GREG: They eradicated the hippies and then they got the punks. And the punks weren't singing about peace and love, they were singing about how everything was fucked up, and saying, "Let's destroy the establishment!"

MATT: Were you affected by hippieism at all or was punk very much your youth movement?

GREG: It was punk. But I was born in 1961, so I lived through the sixties.

MATT: Were your parents political?

GREG: Yeah. My dad would take me to political rallies and stuff like that. He was always watching the news and reading the paper. He was really into folk music in the fifties as well, which was obviously the protest music of its day. But I hated folk music. I still don't like it.

MATT: I love Bob Dylan. But when it comes to people like Joan Baez singing "Kum Ba Yah, my Lord," that's when it gets too schmaltzy for me.

GREG: Yeah, my dad was into a lot of the schmaltzy crap.

MATT: Which band got you into punk music?

GREG: The Ramones. I was already learning guitar at that point, and I'd never heard anything quite like them. I was like, "I can play like that!" Then I heard The Dickies on the radio, and I went to go see them live. That was the first punk rock show that I saw. Immediately, I was like, "This is what I have to do."

PERRY FARRELL—*JANE'S ADDICTION, PORNO FOR PYROS, LOLLAPALOOZA*

MATT: When you were a kid and you rode out on that Greyhound coach to California like so many young dreamers do, did you know you were going out there to try and pursue a career in music? Or were you just going out there to figure out life?

PERRY: No, I just wanted to surf.

MATT: That was the sole goal?

PERRY: Yeah.

MATT: And you lived on the beach for years before any form of success or notoriety found you?

PERRY: Yeah. I was an artist, and I did freelance graphic art for magazines. I could also design jewelry, so I designed jewelry for custom jewelry houses along the coast. That's how I made my living. I was a framer and a carpenter, too. I built track homes and banks and all sorts. I waited tables, and I washed dishes. And I did some other things that I'm not too crazy about admitting.

MATT: You did what you had to do to get by?

PERRY: Yeah.

MATT: Am I right in thinking that you started out performing as a Frank Sinatra impersonator?

PERRY: Yeah. I used to be a liquor distributor, so I would drive around in a van and deliver liquor to liquor stores and nightclubs. I was doing a delivery in Newport Beach, and I was waiting to sign off the delivery of the liquor when this woman came up and asked me if I was a model. I said, "Oh, yeah. I'm a model, I'm an actor, I can sing, I can dance—I can do it all." She said, "Well, why don't you come back when we're doing our next modelling show?" And I said, "That's pretty cool. But I can actually do something for your show: I can impersonate Frank Sinatra, David Bowie, and Mick Jagger." She said, "All right, cool." So that's what I did: I modeled for her, but I also pumped up her show and did some Bowie, Mick Jagger, and Frank Sinatra impressions. From there, this guy Tony Rizzo was looking for models. He was a photographer, but he also had a stable of young guys, and he got me onto some soap operas doing bit parts and stuff like that. So he managed me for a while. That relationship didn't last very long, but it got me up into LA, and that's where I got in with the punk rock kids.

MATT: That's when you found the whole Black Flag, X, Go-Go's scene that was exploding at that time?

PERRY: Yeah, and I started auditioning to be in bands. I'd look through the *LA Weekly* or the *Music Connection*, which at the time was how it went. There would be ads that would say stuff like, "Singer wanted! Must like The Psychedelic Furs, The Cure, Siouxsie and the Banshees, and Joy Division." So I would go off on those auditions. And that's how I ran into my first group, Psi Com. We were a post-punk goth band that formed in 1982.

In 1983, we all got five hundred dollars together and made a record in one day. We went to Ethan James's studio in Venice Beach. He was recording all the punk rock guys at that time. We had to track everything in one day. Then we'd go to all the punk rock and indie record stores and give them records to sell. Then we'd come back a couple of weeks later and see how many we sold. That was my first introduction to the record business. But that band broke up when everybody started going the way of Hare Krishna, and I was going the way of black magic.

MATT: And when they said, "You can't have sex," you were like, "I'm out!"

PERRY: Yeah, "Count me out." They were great guys, though. And it was a great record. Plus, when you're young you're trying to find yourself. I gave everything a try at that time; I studied comparative religion because I wanted to know where they were all coming from. And I was young so I had the time to figure out where I wanted to go. I studied religion, I read science-fiction, I read J. G. Ballard, Phillip K. Dick, William S. Burroughs, Aldous Huxley, Charles Bukowski. I loved to read. And the downtown punk scene was really all about the gay community, and the art community, and that's where we felt most comfortable.

MATT: It was all based on the philosophy of being an individual and an outsider, then all those outsiders grouped together and an alternative community started to form—back when the word "alternative" truly meant something.

PERRY: Yeah, and they took me in. I felt very fortunate to be a part of that scene. There wasn't any money in it back then. But there was a lot of fun and experience, and we were all enriched with art and culture. That's where we were really rich. I really felt that was where we had the edge on everybody.

MATT: What was the name of the house that you used to live in?

PERRY: The Wilton House. There were six rooms to fill, and I kind of oversaw the whole thing because I found the location, so it was up to me to come up with rent every month.

MATT: I bet that was a fun task.

PERRY: It was tough. A lot of people would come and go. And I was trying to fill the house with artists and musicians and the intelligentsia.

MATT: Who aren't always the most reliable people.

PERRY: They're not the most reliable people, no. They usually cause a lot of headaches and chaos. We all did. We built a rehearsal unit in the back and the neighbors were always angry at us about the noise. They would constantly call the cops and shut us down. But we had to rehearse, so we'd just wait a day or two and then start again. We did try to fortify the sound with egg cartons and carpet that we'd find in dumpsters, but it didn't work. We also had this one guy, who was a musician, bring in his girlfriend from Phoenix. They were trying to make it, as was Jane's Addiction, and she raised animals—dogs. So the place became a puppy mill. The guy didn't want to open his door, so he kept it locked. But eventually he moved out, and I was able to see what had been going on in his room.

The house was built in the 1920s, so it was a very old building with wooden floors. And this guy had put newspaper down to soak up the puppys' pee, but there was six dogs and their pee had saturated through onto the wood floor, and the wood floor was buckling up from all the urine. The landlord got so mad at me. He would show up to the house with a pistol on his holster and pat it, as if to say, "I want to shoot you." But we had laws in LA back then, which meant you couldn't kick people out of houses or apartments if they were coming up with the rent. Our landlord knew this, and he knew that I knew this, so he hated me.

MATT: Was that house the birthplace of Jane's Addiction?

PERRY: That's where we started, yeah. Jane [Bainter] was living there as well. In another room was Stuart Swezey, who was the guy behind Desolation Center, and he taught me how to put on shows out in the desert. Eric Avery moved in for a while. And D. H. Peligro from Dead Kennedys lived with us.

CASEY CHAOS—*AMEN, CHRISTIAN DEATH, SCUM*

MATT: Charles Bukowski is one of my all-time favorite writers. He had such a unique style and voice. Was he someone that you spent time with?

CASEY: Yeah. I met him when I was sixteen, right after I moved out to LA. I got to hang out with him at a bar that he used to be a local at, right across the street from a restaurant called Miceli's in Hollywood, on Las Palmas Avenue. They used to let me go inside this bar and hang out and drink cokes with him, and he bought me some real drinks sometimes. I have some books that he signed for me and everything. He was an amazing guy. What a character, right?

MATT: What a character.

CASEY: And a brilliant writer. He was a fucking genius.

MATT: Would he surround himself with a lot of people, or was he more of a lone wolf kind of dude?

CASEY: No, he'd show up to the bar by himself most of the time, or maybe with a friend, or some chick that maybe wasn't quite a street girl, but close.

MATT: The type of girl you wouldn't necessarily take home to meet your mother?

CASEY: Yeah. But he was amazing, man.

MATT: How do you become aware of someone like that at such a young age? I didn't discover Bukowski until much later on.

CASEY: Punk rock.

MATT: Were a lot of early punk bands referencing his work?

CASEY: Totally. And punk rock magazines back then exposed you to all kinds of art—not just music. That's what makes punk rock so important: it was all about exposing real shit that was punk rock in other cultures and facets of art. You just don't see that in metal magazines—and I love metal. Punk rock magazines used to turn you on to all kinds of writers outside of music, like Charles Bukowski and J.G. Ballard. I learned all about writers like that through *Slash* magazine, which was based out of LA and used to have amazing articles. It was a record label, too. They signed the Germs and worked with a lot of great artists. It was an incredible magazine. I learned about artists like [Jean-Michel] Basquiat at a really early age, just from reading their articles.

CHARLIE PAULSON—*GOLDFINGER, BLACK PRESIDENT*

CHARLIE: If there wasn't a drag scene and there weren't any gay people, there would be no punk rock—period. The gay community was welcoming to the kids on the LA punk scene back in the day. They were fucking outcast kids. Punk rock later developed this sort of testosterone, macho-type thing, but that's not what it was about in the beginning. In London, New York, and LA, it was about misfits. It was about kids that didn't fucking belong anywhere, and they got fucking picked on because they were fucking weirdos. So there's a spiritual connection with the gay community. Punk rock and drag have a long history together.

MATT: What was your first exposure to drag, do you remember? And do you remember being enthralled and excited and enticed by it?

CHARLIE: Yeah, and a little bit scared. I was living in West Hollywood, and I was sort of a street kid; I was about seventeen or eighteen, and I was kind of just living wherever. I used to go into gay bars in Boys Town because I used to get hit on and men would buy me drinks. So I'd go and hang out in a gay bar for an hour, get fucked up for free, then walk up to the Sunset Strip and go hang out at the clubs. And I know that's sort of duplicitous and taking advantage of people, but I'm an alcoholic, and it was free alcohol.

MATT: How did you get involved in playing drag shows?

CHARLIE: There was a club in LA from 1999–2001 called Club Makeup. It was built out of the ashes of the old New York club, SqueezeBox. Are you familiar with *Hedwig and the Angry Inch*?

MATT: Yes.

CHARLIE: Okay, Hedwig was born at SqueezeBox. The guy who wrote that film and those songs [John Cameron Mitchell] used to be a drag performer at SqueezeBox. Originally, they used to get up and do covers. But over time he started bringing his own songs in, and those songs would later become the soundtrack to *Hedwig and the Angry Inch*. He developed them over time with the house band at SqueezeBox, and then some promoters in LA, including Joseph Brooks, who used to be the DJ—I don't know if you're familiar with the Cathouse?

MATT: Riki Rachtman's old club?

CHARLIE: Yeah, the club where Guns N' Roses, Faster Pussycat, and that whole scene came out of. But what a lot of people don't know is that it wasn't just this whole glam metal thing. I mean, it was to an extent, but it was also about Siouxsie and the Banshees, Gene Loves Jezebel, and Christian Death. I don't know if you want a full punk rock history lesson by the way.

MATT: Lay it on me, dude. LA history is fascinating to me.

CHARLIE: Right, and I was born and raised there so I fucking love my city; it's my identity. That's why I have you bring us [Goldfinger] on to "California Love" every night. We touched on Death Row Records and the Crips and Bloods earlier, and I'm just as connected to that as I am the drag scene. To me, LA is the greatest city in the world. But I digress. There used to be a punk rock record store on Melrose called Vinyl Fetish, started by this guy Joseph Brooks. Izzy [Stradlin] from Guns N' Roses used to hang out in front of it all the time and smoke cigarettes. Joseph eventually gave him a job, and when Izzy got himself a band, he was like, "You have to check out my band." And that was Guns N' Roses. Joseph was an early adopter of that band,

and when Riki started the Cathouse with Taime [Downe] from Faster Pussycat, they tapped Joseph to be their DJ.

MATT: Was this the whole scene that Jane's Addiction came out of, before it split into the two divided sections of alternative rock and glam metal?

CHARLIE: Yes. And I always try to explain to people what Hollywood in the eighties was like, because occasionally the Red Hot Chili Peppers will come up in a conversation, and people will shit on them. And to an extent I agree: I'm not a fan of anything they've done in the last twenty years. However, when I was fifteen, sixteen, seventeen, Hollywood was Guns N' Roses, Jane's Addiction, Fishbone, the Chili Peppers, Thelonious Monster, and Faster Pusscat—all of these bands that now seem so different on paper. Guns N' Roses would open for the Circle Jerks back in the day, you know what I'm saying? At the core of everything was punk rock. Man, I could go on for hours about that shit.

MATT: It's all good. I love it.

CHARLIE: So anyway, Joseph was the DJ at the Cathouse, and later on he teamed up with this other guy [Pat Briggs], and they started this club night at the El Rey called Club Makeup. It was essentially a drag queen, glam rock, punk rock, disco club. If all of those things made sense to you together, then you fit in at Club Makeup. It was LA's answer to Studio 54 for a while; people would come in these crazy fucking costumes, or they would be decked out in formal attire like they were going to the Oscars, and street punks would come in there half naked, and everybody belonged. You'd walk into the bathroom and people would literally be fucking on the floor—anything went.

MATT: It sounds decadent as hell.

CHARLIE: It was. And every night at midnight, a group of musicians would take the stage and we'd back-up these famous drag queens from all over the world. We played with Wayne/Jayne County and The Voluptuous Horror of Karen Black—

MATT: Did you ever encounter Divine?

CHARLIE: No. I think she was in poor health by that point, so she wasn't travelling a lot. But it was an amazing time. It lasted for three years, then E!—this cable network in America—came and did a special on Club Makeup one night, and that was the end of it. All of a sudden, all these people from Orange County and looky-loos from all over town started coming to check out the freaks in Hollywood, and that was the beginning of the end of the club. It sucked after that.

MATT: What happened to the band?

CHARLIE: Queens have volatile personalities, and the people that I was playing with would cut off their nose to spite their face. So it fell apart.

MATT: Any choice anecdotes of top-drawer insane behavior?

CHARLIE: Okay, I'll tell you this: the last time Tranz Kuntinental played together, we had been tapped to headline the West Hollowood Halloween Carnival. Now, if you know anything about this event, it's fucking massive. 200,000 people gather all over Boys Town, which is a strip of Santa Monica Boulevard where all the gay clubs are. The whole area shuts down, and it becomes just like a carnival—literally. We'd been tapped to headline the main stage, which was huge. They'd paid us a ridiculous amount of money, it was put on by the city, and it was a big fucking deal. The band was tight, and we were ready to go.

We were halfway through the set, and our queens—again, being punk as fuck—were up there saying whatever they wanted to say. And I love it: they're Darby Crash, they're Stiv Bators, they're fucking GG Allin. They're doing their thing, and I think it's awesome. But at one point, the lady who had essentially hired us pulled me over to the side, and said, "Look over there!" So I looked over to the side of the stage. And she said, "That's the Mayor and his children. This is supposed to be a family event put on by the city."

I pulled a couple of the main queens aside, I showed them the mayor, and I said, "Could you please cool it with all the cocksucker,

AIDS, faggot shit that you're saying?" And they were like, "Yeah, no problem." We play the next song, and I'm thinking, "All right, cool. This is going to be good." Then at the end of that song, this one particular drag queen—who I'm sure you've heard of but will remain nameless—says, "Oh, my God! That fucking sucked my cock, you fucking faggot! It was so bad, I think I just got AIDS." I was like, "*Fuck.*" And that was effectively the end of Tranz Kuntinental.

GREG HETSON—*REDD KROSS, CIRCLE JERKS, BAD RELIGION*

MATT: Was Redd Kross was your first band?

GREG: That was the first band that I was in, yes.

MATT: How did that group assemble?

GREG: I was a senior in high school, and back then there weren't a lot of kids in my high school that were into punk rock.

MATT: Where did you go to school?

GREG: In Hawthorne, California. Hometown of The Beach Boys. But I don't really get that band. So I was in class one day, and there was a younger kid who had a folder, and he had a punk flyer on it for this band, The Bags. I was like, "Are you into punk rock?" And he kind of looked at me as if to say, "Are you going to give me shit?" He said, "Yeah." And I was like, "So am I." So we started talking. He said, "I play guitar, and my brother plays bass, and we're looking to put a band together." That kid was Jeff McDonald, and that's how Redd Kross was formed. But I was really only in that band for less than a year. I left in December 1979.

MATT: What was happening musically in LA in 1979?

GREG: The punk scene has just started to change from a small artistic older crowd where everybody knew each other to the suburban kids picking up on it, and that's when the whole scene just exploded.

MATT: In a good way or a bad way?

GREG: Good and bad because a lot of good bands came out of that time. And it was less cliquey, which was cool. But it also brought an element of jock mentality.

MATT: And gang violence?

GREG: That was a little bit later on. But in 1980 things exploded in LA, and bands went from playing 200-seater shows to a thousand people showing up. So they had to move the shows to bigger venues, and it took a while to get proper promoters to start doing the shows because I think people were still afraid of punk.

MATT: I guess the agents were still figuring it out, too. Like, "What the fuck is this new punk rock phenomenon?"

GREG: Agents? There were no agents, there were no managers, and there were no major record labels putting anything out. It was all very DIY. It wasn't like the English punk movement, where everybody was signed to a major label. We didn't have that luxury over here.

MATT: That's why I love the Buzzcocks; everyone always talks about the Sex Pistols and The Clash, but the Buzzcocks were the first band in the UK to self-release music. They basically invented DIY culture in our country with the *Spiral Scratch* EP. That record was the absolute embodiment of that idea: do it yourself.

GREG: For sure.

MATT: Who were the early LA punk bands that stood out for you as a fan of the music who was there at that time?

GREG: Black Flag, X, Adolescents, and The Germs. I was definitely in the right place at the right time. There was a lot of good stuff coming out. What was also cool about that time, which is finally getting some recognition, was the contribution of women in punk rock.

MATT: And not just women's rights and gender equality, but also vegetarianism and veganism, and ecological awareness, and all these ideologies that are now mainstream concerns. A lot of that stuff initially came out of punk—doing away with homophobia, sexism, racism, and all the other "isms."

GREG: Yeah. The hippies stood for a lot of that stuff too, but I guess it was more in your face with punk rock. Nobody cared if you were gay or black or this or that. Everybody was accepting and accepted. That's what was so cool about it. I didn't fit into any set crowd until I met some punk rockers, and they were totally accepting of me, even though I still had long hair or whatever.

MATT: It was about celebrating individuality.

GREG: Exactly. There was no uniform, and the bands didn't want to sound the same, which I think happened in the punk rock revival of the nineties when you started hearing a formula.

MATT: Why do you think the LA punk scene died out in the mid-eighties?

GREG: What killed the LA punk scene was the gang mentality and all the fights and violence at the shows. People were getting really fucked up, and there were all kinds of riots caused by the fans—not by the police. So the promoters just stopped booking shows because of the insurance liability. And that's when you saw the rise of thrash metal.

WALTER SCHREIFELS—*GORLLIA BISCUITS, YOUTH OF TODAY, QUICKSAND, RIVAL SCHOOLS*

MATT: I guess you were right there on the frontline when New York hardcore morphed from that first wave of bands—Murphy's Law, Cro-Mags, and Agnostic Front—who perhaps came from quite broken backgrounds, to the next wave started by Youth of Today and other bands like that, where it was more about positivity, education, and the message in the music. Would that be safe to say?

WALTER: Yeah, I think so. I would credit Ray Cappo with that shift—both stylistically and philosophically. The bones of that New York scene were already there, but it was really in a state of limbo when I first started going to shows. With that initial blast of bands there was only a very small group of people who were there for those early shows. I was too young, and I didn't make it to any of them. When I finally did get in there, that wave was dying out and those bands were looking for a new audience, so they started leaning more into metal music and bands like Corrosion of Conformity and DRI.

When I first heard Youth of Today with Ray Cappo, they sounded like the hardcore that I wanted to be there for; they sounded like Negative Approach. But Ray had this added charisma and ability to organize, and he got people from the New York scene—like Raybeez [Raymond Barbieri, Warzone vocalist] and Roger [Miret, Agnostic Front vocalist]—to work with him and build a real community. And like with any sort of scene, once there's enough people doing the same thing from different angles, then they get healthily competitive with each other.

MATT: Strength in numbers.

WALTER: Yeah. You go see a band one week, and maybe you don't rate them too highly. Then you go see them like a month or so later, and they've got some new songs.

MATT: Because they've been taking note of what the other guys are doing, and that's inspired them to up their game.

WALTER: Exactly. I'd hear certain mosh parts and be like, "Damn! I have to do something to get up to that stage because I'm out there feeling it." You know what I mean? And in hardcore, the ultimate form of expression is to dive into the void—the stage dive. And you're counting on people to catch you with the very real possibility that they won't.

MATT: It's a leap of faith.

WALTER: Yeah, it's a leap of faith. And you feel it. I can remember being in the pit for Agnostic Front and being like, "Holy shit! I might die in here. I need to figure out how to get out of this storm of bodies."

MATT: Big, older, burly bodies, too.

WALTER: Yeah, and I was just a skinny kid. If you've ever been knocked over in a mosh pit, you know what I'm talking about.

MATT: I took a hit to the face last night taking photos down the front. But I loved it. I felt like I was right there among the action.

WALTER: Yeah, it's a real physical thing, and you feel it in your body. Anyway, that's a very longwinded answer.

MATT: There are no longwinded answers in podcasts, Walter. It's all good.

WALTER: But getting back to my original point, I would credit Ray Cappo with that change of color within that local scene. And for people that know about it and who were there, it was pretty amazing. It was such a cool location, too. I knew what CBGB was before I even knew what hardcore was. The first time I tried to go there, I was too scared to walk in; I thought I was going to get stabbed or killed.

MATT: How did the parents feel about a venue like that? Was it on their radar as this den of iniquity?

WALTER: My mom wasn't worried about it, as long as I got home a reasonable hour. And that was the beauty of the afternoon matinee shows: you'd be there all day and you'd get home by nine o'clock. There was obviously plenty of people who stayed out all night getting fucked up, but I always kept it low-key.

MATT: Did you ever get into alcohol or drugs? Or did you look at the older kids and what those substances did to them, and that put you off?

WALTER: Yeah, there was probably a few times where I realized I was hanging out with the wrong kids. Some of them were down to do stuff that I knew wasn't going to take them to a good place, so I'd slide away from those people. And I became straight edge after being inspired by Youth of Today. I wanted to be straight edge because Minor Threat were my favorite band, but then Youth of Today created a way that we could be straight edge and still be a part of this thing that was happening right there and then. That was very appealing to me.

MATT: Did veganism come into your life at the same time, or was that a little bit later on?

WALTER: Vegetarianism came a little bit later—about six months or so. Ray added vegetarianism to straight edge, and you had to be vegetarian as well to really be legit.

MATT: What happened if you weren't? Were you ostracized?

WALTER: No, but it was like, "That's cool, dude. Kill the animals."

MATT: "I'm not pissed off, I'm just disappointed."

WALTER: Yeah, sort of like that. It was like, "I guess killing animals is all right for you. I'm just a better person than that." That was kind of the attitude. There was definitely a zealotry to it, but I think it was headed in a positive direction.

MATT: There's so much information around plant-based diets these days, it's very easy to live that lifestyle. But back then it must've been a challenge?

WALTER: Yeah, it's definitely become a lot more mainstream and that's incredible to see. When we got into it, it was only really the hippies who were vegetarian. But we all worked at health food stores in Manhattan.

MATT: Were they like gathering places for musicians and artists back then?

WALTER: In hardcore, yes. Health food stores were filled with hardcore people, and at that time they were all independently owned. The one that I worked at the most was owned by Swami Satchidananda [Saraswati], and a lot of them were owned by hippies or gurus. It was the opposite of capitalism.

MATT: It sounds like an innocent time in many ways.

WALTER: It was. When you're a teenager or you're going into your early twenties, some people say, "You don't know anything at that age, and you haven't lived." But you're also really smart in a way because you can look at something and say, "Here's what I think is right, and I'm going toward that in a clear direction." Whereas when you get older, you see so much more nuance, and I think a lot of people lose sight of those initial feelings, which are so pure.

MATT: They get convoluted in your head because life has ground you down.

WALTER: Right. And things aren't always black and white, but it's good to have that compass set early in life. Vegetarianism was a great one for me. And straight edge was a great one, too. They both branch into so many different things to do with consciousness and an awareness of what's happening in the world. I was made hyperaware of the straight line that I was trying to walk and that's where the zealotry came from: I believed in our cause one hundred percent. I wanted to convert everybody to vegetarianism and the straight edge lifestyle, and hardcore that was played in the spirit of the original '81–'83 vibe.

LOU KOLLER—*SICK OF IT ALL*

MATT: Were you old enough to catch the first wave of New York punk bands?

LOU: That was just before my time, but growing up in Queens I used to see Dee Dee Ramone all the time in my neighborhood. We were snotty little punks, though. We'd see Dee Dee heading to the subway, and we'd be across the street, and we'd yell, "Dee Dee! You suck!" Then we'd all hide behind cars. But we were just little punks, you know? That's what you did: you loved the Ramones, but you also fucking hated them. I never got to see them at CBGB, but they did play for free in the park in Queens a couple of times, which we all went to, and it was amazing. My era was a couple of years later with Reagan Youth. They were the first band we'd go and see in Queens. Then we'd venture to CBGB a little later on. Our big bands were Agnostic Front, Murphy's Law, and the Cro-Mags.

MATT: I've still never been to New York, which is a crime. But I'm obsessed with the city. I'm fascinated by how gritty and sketchy and dangerous it used to be, but also what an artistically led community it was back in the day, before all the money came in and the rent prices went up.

LOU: I can't remember his last name, but this guy Jesse who used to play in D Generation—

MATT: Jesse Malin. I love Jesse. He's like the Major of the Lower East Side.

LOU: He is. And it's cool because you hear his story, and I read in an interview somewhere that he was living in Queens where I grew up, and he just looked up an apartment in the Village Voice and found one for about three hundred bucks, because nobody wanted to live on the Lower East Side back then. So he moved from Astoria, Queens to the Lower East Side. And when you ventured into Alphabet City back then, where the avenues went from numbers to letters—Avenue A, B, C, and D—then the farther you went in, the worse it got.

MATT: All I think about when I hear people say that is that movie *The Warriors*.

LOU: Here's a story that will give you an idea of what it was like back then. One day, me, my brother Pete, and my best friend Tom went down to this store on St. Marks Place called The Pit, where they sold skull rings and all this biker shit. We were about thirteen years old. I was wearing a denim vest with Black Sabbath *Vol. 4* painted on the back, and my brother had the Motörhead logo painted on the back of his jacket. We were walking down the street, and we walked past this café with three Hells Angels inside. We were just these little kids excited to be down on St. Marks Place, and when we got into the store these Hells Angels said, "Give us your colors!" We were like, "Colors? What colors?" And they were like, "Your fucking jackets." I tried telling them it was just a Black Sabbath jacket, but they said, "You don't walk through our neighborhood with your colors on." I was like, "It's not gang shit. It's fucking music." And we were just little kids, but they didn't give a shit. They even told the store owner, "Fuck you, too. We don't like a lot of the shit you got in here. You better take this, this, and this out of your window." And he was like, "Yes sir."

VINNIE STIGMA—*AGNOSTIC FRONT*

MATT: How important was New York to the sound of Agnostic Front when the band was starting out?

VINNIE: It was everything. Even back in the early days of CBGB or Max's Kansas City, I'd go see a band and think to myself, "I could do that. And I could do it better, louder, faster, and harder." You know what I mean?

MATT: Were you watching bands like the Ramones, Television, Suicide, and the New York Dolls?

VINNIE: Yeah, I saw them all.

MATT: Were you inspired by any of them?

VINNIE: It was a funny inspiration: an inspiration to say, "Fuck you! I can do it better!" Those bands weren't hard enough for me. I like straight up hardcore punk, like Discharge and GBH.

MATT: So you were coming from the UK side of things?

VINNIE: Yeah, I would say I was coming from the UK side. But I put my own twist on it because I wanted to play faster. That was the hook.

MATT: Why do you think those original CBGB and Max's Kansas City bands were a lot more art school, and when hardcore came along, it was a lot more street?

VINNIE: Well, they came from the glam era. And I'm from that era, too. But I also made the jump. And a lot of those guys didn't make the jump. You know what I mean? And when the hardcore kids started coming around, the older punk rockers had an attitude toward them. I was like, "What the fuck is your problem? They're with us. Take care of them. Bring them in." That's just how I am. And all those fucking cock suckers aren't around today.

MATT: Did they have an elitism about them?

VINNIE: Yeah, they were elitists. It's like, "Who the fuck are you? You're a punk rocker, you jerk!" Let me tell you something, I act like a moron on stage, but my act stays on the stage. I never take my act off the stage; I'm not any better than anybody else. And if I can help a young band out, I love it. I get a kick out of that. And I should do that; I'm an older guy.

MATT: You want to help pave the way for the next generation?

VINNIE: Yeah.

LOU KOLLER—*SICK OF IT ALL*

MATT: Who were the first punk bands that you got into?

LOU: I'd gotten into UK bands like The Exploited and Discharge when I started going to high school. We'd met our drummer Armand [Majidi] by this point, who was like, "You know there's a whole scene here in New York, right?" And he played us Agnostic Front. We were like, "What the hell is this?" Their album *Victim in Pain* came out in 1984, and that was it. I got that record and I was like, "Holy shit." It's a full album that only lasts fifteen minutes, and it was so powerful. It had the punkness of GBH, but it had its own New York sound—it sounded like where we would go to hang out. That album put New York on the map. And it gave them nationwide exposure, which was both good and bad.

MATT: How was it bad?

LOU: *Maximumrocknroll*—the big punk fanzine back then out of California—would say that Agnostic Front were Nazis. And *Victim in Pain* caught a lot of shit from *Maximumrocknroll* because of the cover, which is a picture from World War II of a Nazi shooting some Jewish guy in the head as he's about to fall into a mass grave. They started referring to the band as Nazi skinheads from New York after that. But what they didn't realize was that the skinhead scene was eighty percent black and Hispanic back then.

MATT: Do you remember the first time you saw them live?

LOU: I first saw Agnostic Front on their Back from US Tour at CBGB in 1986. Me and my friend were the only guys with hair in the whole place; I think everybody had shaved their heads in honor of them coming back home to New York. Tommy Victor from Prong was the only other guy in the building who didn't have a shaven head—he was the soundman there, and he still had his long hair.

MATT: I know Tommy. He's got some great stories from that time.

LOU: I fucking love Tommy, man. I remember I was standing in the crowd that night with my denim jacket with Motörhead on the back, and this guy came up to me and asked, "Do you like Agnostic Front?" I was like, "Yeah, I love Agnostic Front. *Victim in Pain* is my favorite album." It was Vinnie Stigma. He just walked up on stage and that's when it hit me. I was like, "I love Black Sabbath. I've been to see them at the [Madison Square] Garden. But I'd never meet Tony Iommi in the crowd right before he walked up on stage. *This* is where I want to be." And that was it.

ALAN ROBERT—*LIFE OF AGONY, COMIC BOOK CREATOR*

MATT: What year were you born? 1971?

ALAN: 1971, yeah. You nailed it.

MATT: So, you were slightly too young for the original wave of CBGB punk bands, but you would've been right there as a teenager when New York hardcore came along?

ALAN: The second round of it, yeah. It was the tail end of Agnostic Front, Cro-Mags, Leeway, Sheer Terror, and Carnivore, who'd already broken up and then reunited. LOA [Life of Agony] started in the summer of '89. We were more involved in the Brooklyn scene, so L'Amour was our home. We'd be at L'Amour every week. It didn't even matter which bands were coming through, that would be the place to hang out.

MATT: Who did you see play there?

ALAN: Slayer, Faith No More, Quicksand, and White Zombie. Biohazard was rising in the scene at that time, too. When they got signed it was like our friends got made in the mob. We were like, "They're a national act now? Holy shit!" That was inspiring for us to see; those guys were a couple of years older than us, and we really looked up to them; Joey [Zampella] and I would draw T-shirts for them back in the day. I actually grew up right across the street from Evan [Seinfeld] as a kid, before music was even in our lives. We literally lived right across the street from each other.

MATT: Was he always a larger-than-life character?

ALAN: Yeah, he was. There was one time when it was snowing, and he was shoveling snow wearing these fuzzy knee-high mammoth boots, ripped jeans, no shirt, and Bon Jovi-style hair. And his mother was screaming at him: "Evan, get your ass inside! What are you doing? You're crazy!" I was looking at him across the street through the window, and I said, "Mom, what's up with Evan? Why is he shoveling snow with no shirt on?" She just shook her head.

We ended up moving house when I was in my early teens, and I had some kind of accident where I needed stitches. So there I was in the hospital, and Evan was delivering pizzas to the emergency room. He was working at Lenny & John's, which was the local pizza hangout spot, and he recognized my father—he didn't recognize me because I had long hair down to my ass by this point. He came over, and he was like, "Alan?" And I was like, "Yeah." I was probably about sixteen at that point, and he gave me a pass to come see Biohazard at L'Amour. That was my first time seeing a heavy metal concert in the flesh.

MATT: That was your first gig?

ALAN: Yeah, Biohazard at L'Amour. I think they played with White Zombie, who also came up in that scene.

MATT: What I really like about the nineties, maybe more so than any decade before—or since—is every band was so unique, even within specific scenes.

ALAN: Yeah, especially the bands who would come through L'Amour— that was the spot. You'd get bands from the West Coast, like Excel and Suicidal [Tendencies], come through. Then you had different flavors of punk and hardcore influencing the East Coast bands, and it was always cool to see that. You could discover bands without even having to search for them, because they came right to our spot. Then you'd go to the record store and find their cassette tape or vinyl; there was no internet back then, so if you were into music you'd find out about bands through trading tapes and going to see live shows. It was a fun time.

LOU KOLLER—*SICK OF IT ALL*

MATT: Are you friends with Life of Agony? Do you go back a long way with them?

LOU: Yeah, I remember Joey Z handing me their demo. When I went home and I listened to it, and I first heard Mina's voice—Keith back then—I was like, "Woah! This guy can sing opera. What the hell is he doing here?" I knew then and there they were going to change shit. And they did. I think if they stuck more toward the style of their first album, they would've been way bigger. I mean, people talk about Pantera all the time, and Pantera are fucking amazing, but they didn't have that style until Life of Agony came out.

MATT: What about Pete Steele? Were you friends with him?

LOU: I knew him, but we weren't buddies or anything like that. I remember his first band Carnivore played CBGB, and the band came out in their Road Warrior outfits with meat hanging off them and shit. We were like, "What the fuck is this?" But the music was so good. Then he cut off his hair and wrote songs with Agnostic Front for the *Cause for Alarm* album. He was a cool guy.

MATT: Were Type O Negative another one of those inimitable bands on the scene at that time?

LOU: Yeah, and it's funny because I never went to Brooklyn to see them, but I remember catching one of their early shows at some basement bar in Manhattan. Pete was standing there with a stand-up bass strapped across him like a regular electric bass, just hanging on chains. Then he started playing *The Munsters* theme. I was like, "What the fuck?" But that's what he was into. I like a lot of Type O Negative.

MATT: What an amazing voice, too.

LOU: Oh, yeah. There was a place that we rehearsed at one point in Soho, New York—on Greene Street—in the basement of this snooty apartment building. And in one room there was Prong, the next room was Helmet, the next room was Cro-Mags, and the next room was the Bad Brains. When the Bad Brains were in practicing, us and one of the guys from Prong would be out in the hallway listening. And when we got done rehearsing, we'd open the door and the drummer and bass player from Helmet would be there, like, "Do you guys mind if we listen?" And it was cool because all of those bands went on to do pretty amazing things.

ALL THE YOUNG PUNKS PLAYLIST

RAGE AGAINST THE MACHINE—"KNOW YOUR ENEMY"

WHODINI—"FREAKS COME OUT AT NIGHT"

RAMMSTEIN—"DEUTSCHLAND"

GUNS N' ROSES—"NIGHTRAIN"

VAN HALEN—"DANCE THE NIGHT AWAY"

SEX PISTOLS—"ANARCHY IN THE UK"

GIN BLOSSOMS—"FOLLOW YOU DOWN"

LESS THAN JAKE—"ALL MY BEST FRIENDS ARE METALHEADS"

SUBLIME—"SANTERIA"

RED HOT CHILI PEPPERS—"OUT IN L.A."

THE FACTION—"SKATE & DESTROY"

BLACK FLAG—"POLICE STORY"

WASTED YOUTH—"FUCK AUTHORITY"

BAD RELIGION—"SUFFER"

T.S.O.L.—"WASH AWAY"

THE DICKIES—"GIVE IT BACK"

PSI COM—"HO KA HEY"

HEDWIG AND THE ANGRY INCH—"THE ORIGIN OF LOVE"

RED KROSS—"COVER BAND"

YOUTH OF TODAY—"BREAK DOWN THE WALLS"

AGNOSTIC FRONT—"VICTIM IN PAIN"

BIOHAZARD—"PUNISHMENT"

TYPE O NEGATIVE—"I DON'T WANNA BE ME"

SICK OF IT ALL—"BUILT TO LAST"

THE PURSUIT OF HAPPINESS

"This is the luckiest job there is."

L AST TIME AROUND, THIS chapter was presented under the banner of "Success." This time, I've gone with something a little more earnest: "The Pursuit of Happiness." And no, I'm not talking about the Will Smith movie. I'm referring to the actual pursuit of joy and living your life in such a way that makes you happy. You Americans should know all about this, as it's in your Declaration of Independence. Cheers to you, Thomas Jefferson!

I've been thinking a lot about "success" over the last couple of years. And when you're thirty-five, broke, and living at home with your parents, it's very hard to call yourself successful. But then I'd never refer to myself as successful anyway, even if I was absolutely killing it. And I get that message from friends and random strangers on the internet all the time: "Dude, you're absolutely killing it!" But I'm not. COVID completely stripped me of my livelihood, and I wasn't exactly in the most financially stable place to begin with.

This isn't a pity party though. I'm just outlining my stance on the subject. And there's definitely a silver lining to the entire pandemic experience: I, like many people, used the downtime during lockdown to reevaluate my priorities. I took a long hard look in the mirror, and for the first time in my life I asked myself, "Who am I? Who do I want to be? And what do I want out of life?" I can safely say success no longer factors near the top. It never really did, to be honest. But now that I've seen how trivial all that stuff is, and how quickly it all can all go away even once you've attained it, I really couldn't care less if anyone else thinks I'm successful or not. And that's all success really is: someone else's evaluation of your life.

Happiness, on the other hand, is something only *you* define. And it's about so much more than material gain. Happiness has always been the holy grail for me, probably because I've only ever experienced it in fleeting doses. And don't get me wrong, I'm not so naïve as to think that there are people out there who are blissed out every single second of every single day. We all have our ups and downs, obviously. My highs and lows just seem a little more intense than your average Joe's. I think I'm borderline bipolar. It runs in my family so it'd make sense if I was. But that's another story for another book. I'm not quite ready to open that can of worms just yet.

I spoke in my first book about how difficult life as an independent freelancer in the music industry can be, so I don't need to go into that again here. But let's just say if you want to enjoy a good quality of life, then the music business probably isn't for you. It will chew you up, spit you out, and piss in your face you just as soon as look at you. It's done that to this penniless podcaster countless times, and I'm not a unique case; I know dozens of people who've had their lives turned upside down by the music business. She's a cruel mistress.

Right about now you're probably thinking, "Well, why don't you do something else if it's really that bad?" And I did think about packing up and moving on a couple of times over the last two years, just as I have done many times during the last decade. But the truth is, I'm too stubborn to quit. I've given my entire adult life to this industry, and I've made far too many personal sacrifices to walk away now. Plus, I'm still excited by what's around the corner. I love the thrill of the unknown. And things do seem to be constantly moving in a positive direction for me, even if the speed of travel is a little slower than I'd like. So I think I'll stick around for the time being.

I recently read a quote by Winston Churchill that rather aptly applies to the story of my "career." The late British Prime Minister once famously said, "Success is not final, failure is not fatal; it is the courage to continue that counts." Old Churchill may be somewhat of a problematic figure in today's woke society, and people may want to tear down his statues and brand him as a racist nowadays, but there's no denying what an inspirational statesman he was once upon a time. And the geezer knew a thing or two about never giving up. He helped us defeat the Nazis after all.

Churchill's laconic and iconic quote can be also applied to the pursuit of happiness. Throughout my own personal journey, I've been to some very dark places. But there's always hope of a better tomorrow. So if you are going through hell, as we've all collectively been through over the last two years, and will all individually go through to varying degrees in the future, all you have to do is keep going. No matter what happens to us in our personal lives or our professional careers, we just have to keep searching for the courage to continue. Never give up. Never surrender. I think Churchill said that, too.

During this chapter, you'll hear from Dennis Lyxzén on the breakup and reformation of Refused, you'll read about how John Feldmann beat the odds and became one of the biggest producers of his generation, why Greg Hetson was fired from Bad Religion, why Jesse Leach left and then rejoined Killswitch Engage, how Scott Shiflett's brother got his gig in the Foo Fighters, how Vinnie Stigma beat cancer, why Jesse Hughes loves drugs, and a wide range of other guests discuss being grateful, staying humble, and living life to fullest. We also discuss the validation of your peers, spirituality, mindfulness, and mysticism, and there's even some words of wisdom from the illustrious Gene Simmons.

Coincidentally, these are all people who've made a living out of doing what they love. And the most valuable lesson that I've taken from talking to them is that happiness is the key to success—not the other way around. Personally, I'm not quite there yet. And maybe none of us are. Maybe we're all just constant works in progress because happiness will always come and go. But the trick is to enjoy it in the moment and try not to mourn it too much when it passes; for as long as we keep pursuing it, it will always come back around.

It's also worth pointing out that happiness isn't about feeling intense joy all the time. It's more about a general state of well-being, satisfaction, and contentment with your overall life and current situation. And that's enough right there. I'd happily go without the manic highs and crippling lows, and trade it all in for a quiet and contemplative peaceful existence. Once you've cracked that, you've cracked life. You lucky bastard! Speaking of lucky bastards, let's see what Tommy Lee has to say.

TOMMY LEE—MÖTLEY CRÜE, METHODS OF MAYHEM, SOLO ARTIST

MATT: How old were you when you did your first arena tour?

TOMMY: Let's see, Mötley Crüe's first arena tour was opening up for Ozzy Osbourne on the *Bark at the Moon* tour in 1984, so I think I would've been about twenty-one.

MATT: Were you old enough to legally drink? Can you remember that?

TOMMY: When Mötley Crüe first started playing I was seventeen, and for a couple of years it was really difficult to get me into a lot of the shows. I remember the band lying about my age, and people would follow me around to make sure that I wasn't drinking. But of course I was.

MATT: Of course you were. What's it like being thrown into that arena world at such a young age?

TOMMY: Dude, I will tell you the most endearing and amazing story— and I'll try to condense it a bit. But just so that everybody gets the context of the story, let's rewind to my final year of high school, where I had three months left until graduation. I was faced with the choice between finishing high school and getting my diploma or touring around the world and going to fucking rock shit balls out. I was like, "I'm out!" And my parents were like, "Dude, are you serious? Fuck! You've only got three more months. What if this music thing doesn't work out?" And I was like, "Oh, it's going to fucking work out. Just you wait." They told me that I had to have something to fall back on in case it didn't, but I assured them it was going to work out.

Now, fast-track to the LA Forum in 1984. It's sold out, and we're opening up for Ozzy Osbourne. There's about 15,000 people at the show, the fucking big blinder house lights come on, and I can see my mom and dad standing at the soundboard. I saw them look around at the sold-out show with everybody going fucking crazy—it gives me goosebumps just talking about this—and I'll never forget that moment. They looked at each other after looking around the whole venue and seeing all that, and they were both like, "Fuck! He really did it."

MATT: What an amazing proud parent moment.

TOMMY: I really do have really supportive parents—especially my father, dude. He was on a whole other level. He gave up half of his garage so I could practice, and he was a mechanic. For a man to give up half of his mechanic workspace so his son could play the drums was amazing. He built me a soundproof room in there so I wouldn't make everyone fucking crazy. He even built a pyrotechnic show for my band in high school, and we played out in my backyard blowing stuff up. My neighbors must've been like, "What the fuck is going on over there?" So I had a really supportive family growing up, and I think I was a fun project for my dad to see what kind of mischief he could get up to.

MATT: I guess he got to live vicariously though you, his rock star son.

TOMMY: There you go.

TOM MORELLO—*RAGE AGAINST THE MACHINE, AUDIOSLAVE, PROPHETS OF RAGE, THE NIGHTWATCHMAN*

MATT: You went to Harvard to study social studies, correct?

TOM: Political science, yeah.

MATT: Did you ever think about pursuing a career in politics?

TOM: Not politics with a capital P. I was a fired up, committed anarchist when I went to Harvard. I was going there to intellectually arm myself for the coming struggle, not to seek elected office. But while I was there an unexpected thing happened: I was a freshman; I was nineteen years old, and I had a religious calling to play guitar. I started playing when I was seventeen, but I was nineteen when the skies opened, and I realized that was my fate.

MATT: Do you remember having a specific epiphany to pick up the guitar?

TOM: I don't know if there was an actual moment, but that was when my ability started to catch fire. At first I was practicing for an hour a day, then it was two hours a day, then it was four hours every day, while also pursuing an honors degree in political science. In a world of chaos, this was something I had control over. The only deciding factor of whether I would sink or swim was my own will, and I had that in abundance.

MATT: I think there's certain musicians who appear throughout history, and you can't imagine them ever doing anything else. Obviously, Jimi Hendrix is one that comes to mind.

TOM: Sure.

MATT: Slash is another one.

TOM: Sure.

MATT: It's almost like a physical connection to the instrument.

TOM: Yeah, I really had no choice. It didn't feel like a choice that I was making; it felt like a choice that was made from the outside.

MATT: So, you pack your bags, and you move out to LA?

TOM: Yes, I went seeking my fortune.

MATT: What year did you arrive?

TOM: I arrived in Hollywood in 1986. I left home on September 2, 1986, and I arrived thirty-six hours later.

MATT: Talk me through that first month in LA. What was going on?

TOM: It was not an awesome month. I went out there with all these lofty ambitions, and I thought I had it all figured out; I thought it was going to be a city of shredding guitarists like Steve Vai, and I was going to fit right in because I'd been doing my eight hours of practice a day, so I was going to get myself a band of virtuosos and rocket to the top. But that was not what happened. This was the period of Faster Pussycat and bands like that.

MATT: Ratt, Poison—all that stuff.

TOM: Yeah. It was all very image heavy, and it was a very particular image that I did not fit. Musicianship wasn't high on the scale of priorities either. When I saw those bands playing out at the local clubs, I was like, "I'm in trouble here. You have to be *that* in order to be a rock star, make records, and be successful. And there's nothing in me that can do any of that: I don't look like that; I don't play like that; I don't pose like that. I can't do any of it." And even though I had a Harvard degree, I didn't have any work experience. My only work experience was at the Renaissance fair.

MATT: What's that famous restaurant in LA? Medieval Times?

TOM: Yeah, I could've probably worked there. I missed a trick there. I ended up doing a lot telemarketing in the end. And I had a stint as an exotic dancer.

MATT: Did you really?

TOM: Yeah.

MATT: Wow! What was your jam?

TOM: "Brick House," are you kidding me?

MATT: The Commodores?

TOM: Yeah. That's the moneymaker right there.

MATT: I bet you had some crazy experiences doing that. Was it all bachelorette parties and stuff like that?

TOM: It was exclusively bachelorette parties, yeah. That's where the money is. So I did that while trying to figure out how to be in a band. And it wasn't evident, at that point, how I could be in a band. Finally, I joined the one band in Hollywood that would have me, which was not a particularly good band. It was a semi-talented singer-songwriter who rehearsed us mercilessly over the course of eight months to play these not-so-great songs. While I was doing that, my buddy Adam Jones convinced me to go out and be his wingman at some club one night, which is where I first saw a band called Lock Up, who became my favorite local band. They were a different kind of band, and one that I had never seen before. They were from the Eastside of Los Angeles. I soon became friends with people in their circle, and they needed a guitar player, so I joined the band. It had nothing whatsoever to do with the Sunset Strip. And they didn't care how long my hair was. We just had fun making music together—as opposed to being driven to get a record deal.

HYRO THE HERO—*RAPPER, SOLO ARTIST*

MATT: Were you a talented basketball player as a kid? Am I right in thinking that?

HYRO: Yeah.

MATT: And I guess it could've gone either way, so what took you in the musical direction?

HYRO: I'm good at basketball—no ego!

MATT: You're just stating the facts.

HYRO: Yeah. But the music just caught me. And I had a bad attitude. I wasn't going to listen to no coaches. I was more about the streetball game, and I had a problem with authority all the way through high school. I got kicked out of Milby High School for talking too much shit. So I moved to Chavez High School and graduated from there. And the music just got me, you know what I'm saying? I was making music during that whole time, and somewhere along the line it really became my passion, when I realized I wasn't ever going to the NBA. I could make beats, and I could rap, and people were feeling what I was doing. I performed at a talent show in school where I sampled "La Bamba" by Ritchie Valens, and I made it a rap song and people loved it. I even got it played on a radio station in Houston: Mega 101. And I got some attention for that, so that's when I started making my little mix tapes.

MATT: Did you make three of them?

HYRO: Yeah.

MATT: I've got all three. You gave them to me when we first met back in 2011. You sample Pantera and Rancid and all these other bands—

HYRO: Yeah, what I would do is sample the parts of the songs that I thought were cool, like the breakdowns, because I thought, "Oh, shit. I could rap to this." So I took them, sampled them, put my beats behind them, and then they got hot on Myspace. I feel like I'm ahead of my time sometimes, and I was doing something that was so different back then—people almost weren't ready for it.

MATT: There was a gap, I think, after bands like Rage Against the Machine and Cypress Hill started winding down, and there was a void for that kind of mix of rock and hip-hop to be filled.

HYRO: Yeah, and I was just sampling at the start, so it was still kind of hip-hop influenced with the way that I was sampling it. But the more I got into rock, I started building it up with the live instruments and all that stuff. Then I came out to LA and started developing more of a heavier sound with all the live instrumentation, which eventually led to where I am now. And I thought I was going to be a star overnight, but it's not like that. I had to learn the groundwork, man. And it ain't easy. If it does come easy then it probably won't last long.

MATT: That's it. I think if you're an overnight runaway success, the only way to go from there is down. I feel like it's better—and it's obviously harder that way, too—to play the long game and build things gradually.

HYRO: Yeah, man. You build it up from a grass roots level, and it might take longer that way, but you get more respect in the end. And you have a career.

MATT: Let's talk about your debut album, *Birth, School, Work, Death*.

HYRO: That album was crazy. Ross Robinson produced it. And I had Paul [Hinojos] from At the Drive-In, Mark [Gajadhar] and Cody [Votolato] from The Blood Brothers, and my boy Daniel [Anderson] from Idiot Pilot—who lives across the street from me right now—play on it. It was crazy, bro. We got in the studio, and within two weeks we'd made the record. It was just fire. It was insane. People talk a lot about what Ross does, because he likes to do crazy stuff with artists, but he heard me on the mic and he was just, like, "Go!" I love the raw, rugged feeling of that album. It got a lot of respect from people, too.

MATT: Jonathan Davis from Korn called it his favorite album of 2011.

HYRO: I know. Shout out Jonathan Davis. That was insane.

DEAN KARR—*DIRECTOR, PHOTOGRAPHER*

MATT: Where did your career in photography begin?

DEAN: NWA is really where I started—shooting NWA at Priority Records.

MATT: That must've been such an exciting time. NWA were so dangerous and fresh back then.

DEAN: They just seemed like cool cats to me. They were always nice as could be. I only did maybe three shoots in the studio with them, but that's definitely where I started. I was doing a lot of hip-hop stuff before I was doing any rock. Then I did the Tool thing [*Undertow*], and Pantera [*Far Beyond Driven*], and Alice Cooper [*The Last Temptation*].

MATT: Those were all the album covers?

DEAN: Album covers, yeah. Then an artist from Canada—somebody named Sass Jordan—was at one of my photography exhibitions, and she said, "Man, I'd love you to do my music video." I was like, "I've never had a film class, but that'd be kind of neat to try." So I did. I didn't really learn how to move a camera properly for a few videos, but it was really cool to see moving pictures instead of just a still photograph. And I loved the collaboration with all the different departments on a film set, as opposed to just me and my assistant on a photo shoot.

MATT: Does it all kind of spiral from there? Do you get one gig, then get a bit of a rep off the back of that, then the next one comes through, and so on? Is that basically how it happens?

DEAN: Yeah. When that stuff gets a certain level of attention then the phone doesn't stop ringing. But it could ring a little more. RING!

MATT: Have you noticed the industry change? Obviously records don't sell like they used to, and there's no longer the budgets that there once was. Have you noticed a drastic change in your lifetime?

DEAN: Absolutely. It all changed about fifteen years ago, I'd say. It started with downloadable music and all that stuff. It affected everybody's job protection at record labels; everybody got fired and had to move back home with mommy and daddy and figure out what the hell they were going to do next. I think a lot of them got their real estate license. Nobody expected it. That's called having the rug pulled from underneath your feet.

MATT: Did it all happen quickly, seemingly overnight?

DEAN: It probably went through kind of a six-year transition, and then it was like, "Oh, yeah, it's over." And budgets started fizzling down fast. We used to work with budgets of $150–200,000 per video. Then it went down to about $50–60,000, and that would've been a generous budget. Now it's $5–20,000 max. They don't give a fuck what it looks like anymore.

MATT: Have you noticed the artistry suffer as a result?

DEAN: Yeah, because it takes money to make something cool. My art department, my stylist, my camera department, all those people have a level of expertise and respect that they deserve. And they deserve to be paid what they're worth. I had an interesting experiment in Portland last month, though. I actually pulled off a pretty cool production for $5,600. I really liked the song, and it was by a friend of mine, Joseph Arthur, who's a singer-songwriter from New York, and he plays with Peter Buck, the guitarist from R.E.M.

I only had an hour to plan the thing, as I was flying to Portland to do the photoshoot for the album cover. Joseph and I were going back and forth, and we both really wanted to make it happen because the song was so good. And I had some really cool locations sorted out. I hit the ground in Portland and the film gear place was open for another hour, so I just went straight there. I got the "okay" from the manager that we could spend $5,600, and I went in and bought every slider and piece of motion film thing they had within an hour of them closing. We extended the shoot to two days, and I did it, dude. I produced it, art directed it, and shot it myself. I'd never even used my Nikon D810 as a movie camera before. But it does a really nice job.

MATT: What was the first big music video that you shot? Was it "Sweet Dreams" by Marilyn Manson?

DEAN: Yeah, that was the over the moon one, for sure. And I did "Crash into Me" by Dave Matthews in the same month, which was an equally huge video. I know a lot of people overseas don't know who Dave Matthews is, but he's a massive artist. So within one month, I had made my two signature pieces.

NADJA PEULEN—*COAL CHAMBER*

MATT: When did you first join Coal Chamber? After the third album [*Dark Days*]?

NADJA: No, I joined after the second album *Chamber Music* came out in 1999. The first record [*Coal Chamber*] came out, they did the touring for that, then I came in early '99, right before *Chamber Music* dropped.

MATT: How did you get the gig? How did that call come about?

NADJA: Well, it's funny. I'd seen Meegs [Miguel Rascón] around town at after-hour parties, Bar Delux, and other places that we used to hang out. He was a friend of the then-guitar player of this girl band that I was playing in. So I'd see him around, and I didn't really know him, but there was this girl Heather, who I used to party with, and she ended up being Meegs's girlfriend. Heather called me up one day, and said, "Hey, my boyfriend is in this band, and they need a girl bass player. I've seen you play, so I know you can do it. You should try out." And I was like, "All right, I'll check it out." Meegs then showed up at Jumbo's [Clown Room] one day and dropped off a CD. I checked it out, and it was different from the music that I was playing back then; I was just starting out with my girl band at the time, and we were playing more indie rock 'n' roll music. This was way more metal than what I was playing.

MATT: So you hadn't heard of Coal Chamber at this point?

NADJA: I hadn't heard their music because I wasn't into that kind of music, and I wasn't in that kind of world. I had heard the name, and I'd seen pictures of them in magazines here and there, but I wasn't familiar with their music at all—or their live performances, or anything like that. So Meegs dropped off the CD and said, "Call my manager and come in for an audition." And their manager at the time was Sharon Osbourne.

MATT: Was it really?

NADJA: Yeah. And I did know who she was, obviously. So I went to see her at the office that she had across from The Troubadour back then on Santa Monica Boulevard. I was like, "Oh, shit. That's Sharon Osbourne." And it was funny because she was very cool to me, but I think she sized me up in five minutes. She was slightly intimidating back then, and I was only twenty-four years old. I went in for the audition and Dez [Fafara] and Meegs were there. Mikey [Cox] wasn't there because he was living in Albany, New York, at the time. So his brother Travis came in and played drums instead, and he was really cool. The audition went well. Then I went in a second time, and I didn't hear anything from them after that.

I had actually made plans to go to Europe at this point. I had already bought my ticket to go and see my grandmother in Germany, and when I didn't hear back from them for a few days, I was like, "Well, I guess I didn't get it. So I'm going to go to Europe instead." I thought I'd better call Sharon just to make sure because I was leaving in three days. So I called her up, and I was like, "Hey, so I guess I didn't get the gig. And it's cool. I just wanted to make sure because I'm leaving for Europe in three days." And she goes, "What are you talking about? You got it!" Nobody fucking told me.

MATT: That's so typical of this business.

NADJA: Yes, it's super typical. But I didn't know that at the time. I was just like, "Oh, fuck." Then I had a month to prepare, so I canceled my trip to Europe because I had to learn those two records for the tour. And I locked myself in a room for a month to learn all the material.

MATT: How was your first show with them? Do you remember it?

NADJA: Of course.

MATT: Did you ace it?

NADJA: Yeah. I mean, I was a little bit intimidated and shy at the time. But the show went really well. It was in Philadelphia at the Electric Factory. That place has always been special to me.

MATT: You know when a new member joins a band and the fans get up in arms? Did you experience any of that?

NADJA: People would sometimes ask, "Where's Rayna [Foss]?" But that was about it. Nobody booed me out or anything like that. I was a different type to Rayna, though. I dress different, I move different, and we're both very individual in what we do.

MATT: Have you two ever connected with each other?

NADJA: No, which is kind of a shame, you know? I replaced her when she was pregnant, and I knew it was only a temporary deal; I knew once she'd had the kid that she would come back. And during her pregnancy I never met her, which is when I was doing all the touring. Then she came back after she'd had the kid, and I went to their show at The Palladium, which I believe was on that same touring cycle, and I only met her briefly for about five minutes. That was pretty much it. She asked me how I liked the show, we had a friendly five-minute conversation, and that was it.

I remember years later when the internet happened, there was someone who created a Nadja fan page and some of my fans were talking shit about her on my forum. I never paid any attention to that stuff. But I got an email from her one day that said, "Hey, there's some people talking shit about me on your website. Can you take care of that?" And I was like, "Yeah, sure." So I did. And then she sent me an amp. She said, "You played this amp way more than I did, so I think you should have it," which was very nice of her. And that's all the communication I've ever had with her.

MATT: So what happened? She came back and rejoined the band, then she left again?

NADJA: After she had her kid, she came back and did a month or so of touring for *Chamber Music*, then she recorded *Dark Days* with them. But the minute she was done recording the album, she quit the band. Then I came back in and did that entire album cycle.

MATT: Was that weird for you, dipping your toe in the water, then going away, then coming back again? Did you sort of feel, like, "Am I in? Am I not in?"

NADJA: Yeah, it was a little weird. I toured for pretty much the whole *Chamber Music* album cycle and that lasted almost a year, so I got pretty used to that lifestyle. But I knew after that first tour cycle that Rayna was coming back, and I never had any false illusions of her not coming back. So I accepted it for what it was and that wasn't too hard on me.

It was harder when I came back for *Dark Days*, because at that point Rayna had left the band and I was back in. And I figured, "Cool. Now we're going to continue." So when we broke after the *Dark Days* album cycle, that was really hard for me. I was like, "Now I'm in the band, and we're breaking up. This really sucks." Whereas before I knew I was just filling in.

MATT: It's like you were presented with an opportunity, and then it was snatched away.

NADJA: Exactly.

JOEY CASTILLO—*QUEENS OF THE STONE AGE, DANZIG, THE BRONX, CIRCLE JERKS, ZAKK SABBATH*

MATT: You and I do different jobs, but there's a similarity in the sense that we're not a fixed full-time employee of any one company. And when we get to the end of one experience, I think there's a certain mindset where some people would just go, "That was amazing," and they're content with that.

JOEY: One hundred percent.

MATT: Whereas, I think people like you and me—without assuming too much—do one fun gig, and that sets alight in us this hustle and drive, and at the end of it all that we're thinking is, "How do I make the next thing happen?"

JOEY: That's right.

MATT: And it just keeps on rolling.

JOEY: A hundred percent.

MATT: And you're not worrying about tomorrow or yesterday, because you're living in the moment and trying to make the most of it.

JOEY: And that's the thing: it can get a little bit cloudy at times. You get comfortable, and you start thinking, "These people are my life." And some are and some aren't, as you find out. But with age, and if things keep growing, like you say it becomes easier to take that next step into the unknown. And it becomes easier to figure out a room when you walk into it.

MATT: It's about being confident without being a jackass.

JOEY: And it's about not being held back by fear, because moving forward and stepping into the unknown, for some people, is very scary.

MATT: I don't feel like it is. And I imagine you're probably the same way.

JOEY: I'm absolutely the same way, I just keep going.

MATT: Fake it 'til you make it, right?

JOEY: That's right. I've been doing that my whole life.

SCOTT SHIFLETT—*FACE TO FACE, ME FIRST & THE GIMME GIMMES, VIVA DEATH*

MATT: When your brother Chris moved to San Francisco to work at Fat Wreck Chords, is that how he ended up in No Use for a Name? And were you already in Face to Face by that point?

SCOTT: No, he actually joined No Use for a Name before I was in Face to Face. I had a little bit of time off after Chris and my last band dissolved in a sea of drug addictions and fist fights. So he went up there because he had that job, and he was only there a month or two before he got tapped. My brother is well-known now as a wealth of talent on the guitar, and I know he didn't take but three seconds to be discovered. No Use for a Name needed a guy, and he got the gig.

It's funny, the first time I actually saw the band perform, they were playing a place formerly called The Palace—I don't know what it's called anymore—and I just came in off the street. My brother was up on stage, and they were setting up their stuff, and he looked out and saw me and motioned for me to come over. I came around the side, and he got me up on stage, and he said, "I don't have a tech. Will you tech for me?" So I watched my first No Use for a Name gig with my own brother in it, sitting on the side of the stage tuning his guitars and handing him fresh ones every couple of songs.

MATT: Amazing.

SCOTT: Yeah, it was a cool vantage point. So he was in that band, and he made a couple of records with them.

MATT: Then he joined the Foo Fighters?

SCOTT: Yeah, and whatever people want to say about it being a chump move or a sellout move, I couldn't disagree more. I think my brother's talents have been put more to use in the Foo Fighters than No Use for a Name. There was a lot of that toeing the line in the nineties, where people were almost afraid to stretch out for fear that they were going too far. But I've always been well aware of what he's capable of. No Use were a cool band, and Tony [Sly] wrote cool songs, but I always felt like my brother could do more. And I'm glad to see, for a number of reasons, that he landed another gig and continues to stretch his wings and do other music.

MATT: The punk police make me laugh. They somehow believe that success is the enemy.

SCOTT: Right. When Chris first joined the Foo Fighters, I was playing a Face to Face gig, and as we were walking out on stage a voice in the crowd yelled, "Your brother's a sellout!" And I knew damn well they were talking to me. But I didn't get into a confrontation about it because you can't win with that kind of person. I just remember in my mind thinking, "You have no idea how much I disagree with you, sir. And I'm not going to get into now because I've got a gig to play. But you're wrong. End of story."

MATT: Do you remember the day you heard the news that he was joining the Foo Fighters?

SCOTT: Yes. The original Face to Face guitarist Chad Yaro was always a bit difficult to rely on to make tours. It seemed like he was quitting the band every other Thursday back then. And we were constantly faced with the threat of him pulling out a day or two before tour. I remember we had a desperate situation going where we had a tour coming up, and Chad was pulling his usual, "Fuck this, I'm out." And I'm not saying this to slag him off. There's so many differences between us, but I love him so much. I consider him a lifelong family friend, and he will always be my dear brother Chad. But he was a difficult little fucker back in those days. So Chad pulled out of a tour again, and I was just looking to temporarily fix a flat. I wasn't asking Chris to join our band or anything like that—unless he wanted to. I'd always be open to that.

So, I called him up, and I was like, "Hey, we have this thing. If you're free and you feel like doing it, I'd love to have you come out." And he goes, "Actually, I'm about to drive down to LA to audition for the Foo Fighters. Please don't tell anyone." And I was like, "No way! That's unbelievable." Maybe a day or so later, Chris called me up with the good/bad news: "The good news is, I got the gig. The bad news is, you've got to figure out your own problems." And I was nothing but happy for him.

Not to spill too much of his personal life, but things weren't great at that time with No Use for a Name's career. My brother was delivering pizzas between tours and worrying about where his life was headed. He was confiding in me that he was interested in going to business school and moving back in with our dad to facilitate that. So for me, him landing that gig was a godsend, and I've only ever been for it. And the rest of the dudes in that band are great. I would never profess to know them well, but they've only ever been kind and gracious to me, and I'm very thankful for that.

MATT: I think people sometimes forget that the Foo Fighters come from a punk rock background, and although they're a massive arena rock band nowadays, they're still very much in touch with those roots.

SCOTT: Right. And I didn't see any of these tours, but one of my best friends saw one of the early Foo Fighters tours when they were opening for Mike Watt. They were driving around in a van setting up their own gear, and Dave was barely saying two words to the crowds back then. So they had to fight their way to the top. Granted, they had the vapor trail of public sympathy on their side after the death of Kurt Cobain. But it takes more than that to continue; it takes talent, perseverance, charisma, and mother fucking charm. And Dave Grohl has all of that in spades. He was just able to parlay that into a huge career, and I see nothing wrong with that at all.

JOBY FORD—*THE BRONX, MARIACHI EL BRONX, ARTIST, PRODUCER*

MATT: You put out the first Bronx album [*The Bronx*] on your own label, correct?

JOBY: Yes.

MATT: Was that a conscious choice?

JOBY: Yes. But you have to realize, we'd only played about ten shows at that point, and we had about twelve labels trying to sign us. It was a joke. So we used the internet to our advantage. Record labels would contact us, and we would write back in Morse code because I found some website that would change whatever you said into Morse code. And we developed a moniker for this person called The Governor who would write these cryptic messages to all the record labels.

A friend of ours worked for Jive Records at the time, and he said he could spin this PR campaign to the whole industry, and it would be hilarious, so we agreed to do it and see what happened. We'd tell record labels if they wanted to meet with us they had to send us all these albums, and we'd get fucking records up the ass from all these labels because they didn't care. I remember one time, this steroided-out A&R guy was like, "Send me the rock!" So we wrote back as The Governor: "Give me your FedEx number." And we filled a FedEx box full of rocks and sent it to him. It cost about $150 to post.

I used to work at a record label myself back then, so I kind of understood the pecking order and the ladder that you had to climb. The way I saw it, we had two choices: we could either sit there and take a ton of money, and our careers would have ended just as fast as they started—

MATT: I guess that's the mistake most bands make: as soon as that carrot is dangled in front of them, nine out of every ten bands just grab it without the long-term game in mind.

JOBY: Absolutely. And that's the thing, I wanted to play music for a living. That's why I took a job at a record label, so I could be closer to bands and maybe meet somebody and get in a band, or something like that, you know? Our manager at the time was baffled that we turned down all the offers, but I was like, "This is what I want to do." And because we'd recorded our record, we owned it, and that stacked all the cards in our favor. So we licensed the record to a smaller label, and as soon as we did that, we signed for another record with Island Def Jam. That meant we were able to retain the rights to the first album, and we licensed it all over the world. We were able to tour on that for about two-and-a-half years before we went and did the money pit record.

MATT: What was that experience like? Was it a total leap from the first record?

JOBY: Yeah. I've never experienced anything like it—before or since.

MATT: Who produced the second album?

JOBY: A guy named Michael Beinhorn, who did Soundgarden's *Superunknown*, Marilyn Manson's *Mechanical Animals*, and Korn's *Untouchables*. But actually the really cool thing about Michael Beinhorn is that he wrote the Herbie Hancock song "Rockit." I was like, "Man, that's cool." When we were meeting with all the big money producers and deciding who to go with to make the record, that's what sealed the deal for me. It was great, man. It was an exercise in extravagance. We were in the studio for about six months, right down on the beach in Venice. We lived down there, and we'd go surfing in the mornings. But we were just wasting money.

MATT: This was right at the tail end of when there was money to waste.

JOBY: I think that was the end of it, yeah. It was just insane. I had never seen anything like it. We rented all these amps and drums and microphones and compressors, and there were guys coming in and out of the studio to work on our guitars and tech the drums. We had no idea what was going on. But it was one of the best times of my life and I'm really glad that I got to experience that ridiculous lifestyle.

MATT: How was it working with Michael Beinhorn?

JOBY: When you make a record with Michael Beinhorn, you're going to make the record that he wants to make. And I think it was difficult on Matt [Caughthran] because he tracked his vocals for months; Michael made him sing his parts again and again and again, trying to get that magical take. That's what Michael is really good at. Still to this day, Matt says that's the best vocal performance he's ever given. Then we went to some big pro mixer guy named Mike Shipley, who mixed all Mutt Lange's stuff. He did all the AC/DC and all the Def Leppard records. And I was just this wide-eyed kid who couldn't believe it. But right before the record was about to get released, it basically got shelved because Island Def Jam switched presidents, and it turned into a pop label, and all the rock acts went away.

MATT: That's such a common story isn't it? If the one guy who's fighting your corner is gone—

JOBY: Yeah, it was over. But we've figured out what works for us through experiences like that. So for the next record I called up our A&R guy, and I said, "Listen, you guys spent $275,000 on our last record. For half of that, I can buy a studio and make records forever. This is what you guys need to do for bands—and yourselves." So they did, and we bought a recording studio and gear and all that stuff. Then we got dropped.

MATT: But you got to keep the studio and all the gear?

JOBY: Yeah. We recorded the third and fourth Bronx records there, and a bunch of the Mariachi [El Bronx] stuff was done there as well.

MATT: That's fucking great, man. That's punk rock.

WALTER SCHREIFELS—*GORLLIA BISCUITS, YOUTH OF TODAY, QUICKSAND, RIVAL SCHOOLS*

MATT: Did you always want to make music your career?

WALTER: No. What kind of psychopath would start their career in the worst sounding type of music ever? I was doing it so I could play CBGB; I was doing it so I could affect other people in the same way that I was being affected; I was doing it so I could make people mosh the way other people were making me mosh. I just wanted to create an atmosphere where people would stage dive and freak out. I really didn't see any potential beyond selling out CBGB.

MATT: When was the turning point when you realized you could make a career out of it? Was it with Quicksand?

WALTER: Yeah, I guess maybe toward the late eighties. The scene got very popular with kids coming from the suburbs, and that went hand in hand with the gentrification of the Lower East Side. Like I told you earlier, when I first went to CBGB, I was scared to go in. Even just the neighborhood was scary at that time. And then the word got out that you could survive—it could be done. So a lot of kids from the suburbs started flooding in.

MATT: Was that a good thing or not?

WALTER: I thought it was really cool. Just from a musical standpoint, there was more people to play to. From my point of view, it was great because the scene was getting more popular. And as a result of that, we could go and play in Connecticut and New Jersey, and other places further afield. Then we started going on tour, so we weren't around as much, and a lot of great bands started coming up. But the scene just kind of lost its wind—the wind went out of the sail. And even though a lot of those newer bands were great, there wasn't enough to get a third wave out of it. A lot of people found out about it that weren't good, too. And a lot of violence came into the scene. I remember at the last Gorilla Biscuits show that we played, a guy got stabbed within an inch of his life. So things kind of splintered out after that.

There was a movement at ABC No Rio, which was a little art space on Rivington Street where all the nerds went, and I felt more related to that crew than what was happening at CBGB. So I started a band called Moondog, where I was the singer, and that quickly morphed into Quicksand. Then we got Alan Cage, who was the drummer, and we started to write fresh songs. I think we really benefitted from all that great power of the CBGB scene, combined with the desire to do something out of the bounds of what that hardcore formula was, because I think hardcore does have a very conservative streak.

MATT: Yeah, there's only so much you can do musically before people say, "That isn't this anymore!"

WALTER: And, "We hate you now!" You know what I mean? So you're not allowed to progress too much. And Quicksand felt like a band where we could write off having to stick to that formula and just do something new. But we were still informed by our history of our experiences in this really cool scene. So we took that energy and went and tried something totally different.

DENNIS LYXZÉN—*REFUSED, THE (INTERNATIONAL) NOISE CON-SPIRACY, INVSN, FAKE NAMES*

MATT: For me, what's always been so fascinating about Refused, is the music has always been an embodiment of the radical ideas that are contained within the lyrics. And the two elements serve each other.

DENNIS: Yes.

MATT: What was the reaction from within the punk community when you guys went off the cliff and started experimenting with the sound to such an extent? Because we both know, with all due respect, that the punk and hardcore community can be quite close-minded when they want to be. And God forbid bands try to progress their sound in any way.

DENNIS: For sure. That's definitely one of the things that we felt early on with Refused—it was a clean slate, and we could try anything. But when we did *The Shape of Punk to Come*, a lot of the people in the scene didn't like it, and a lot of people thought we were a bunch of pretentious fucks, which is, of course, true—we were. We were very much like, "We're intellectuals," in an asshole kind of a way. But we made this album that we felt was really good because it was different, and we were trying out new things. And a lot of the people in the hardcore scene were like, "Fuck these guys!" So when we broke up in 1998, we had this sense that things hadn't really gone that well, and that record had kind of flopped. But here we are twenty-one years later, and *The Shape of Punk to Come* still outsells all our other records.

A lot of people didn't like the album when it came out because they thought it was too weird and pretentious and political. That's why we broke up. Then the record came out in the States like a week later, and it took off. We were all sat at home, like, "What the hell is going on with this record?" We had done two Scandinavian tours and two European tours to promote it, and we did a bunch of festivals. But we weren't getting any response. Everyone was like, "We liked the last record better." I remember the tour premiere for that whole album cycle, and there was no one there. It was horrible.

MATT: Was it a miserable experience touring that album?

DENNIS: Yeah, it was. And when I listen back to live stuff from '98, it sounds pretty awesome. But the experience of touring the album was miserable: we didn't like each other at all at that point, and the crowds started getting smaller and smaller. We were playing these really ambitious songs to about twenty people in the crowd.

MATT: That must've been so disheartening.

DENNIS: It was certainly not what we hoped it would be. Everybody was burnt out on touring, and we were burnt out on each other. I think everybody wanted something different from music at that point, too. So it was not a great time. There were some fun incidents along the way, and we tried to make the most of it, but on the whole that six-month period of touring the record was not great.

MATT: When it ended did it end badly?

DENNIS: Yeah, it was horrible. I think it took about two years after we broke up until David [Sandström] and I actually sat down and talked to each other again. There was a lot of bad blood for a long time. It wasn't good. But when we sat down and talked again, we were like, "Oh, we do like each other." It took another six years or so before we could actually start making fun of who we were back then. And nowadays it's a complete laughing matter because there's enough distance to where we can joke about it and make fun of the jackasses that we were back then.

MATT: After Refused broke up, was there a period of time where you didn't want any association with the band name or the music that you made in that group? It must've been hard for you to find peace with the legacy of that band and the way that it ended.

DENNIS: Yeah. I started The (International) Noise Conspiracy the week after Refused broke up, and we started writing music and playing shows right away. I felt so disheartened by the whole Refused experience, I wanted to start a band that wasn't part of any scene. I wanted to do something that was completely our own thing. But when we started touring, everyone was like, "I love Refused." Every single night, it was like, "That was a good show. I love Refused so much." I couldn't escape it, and that was annoying. But over time you soften, and I started to look back at that record and think, "It's a pretty good record." Then you let that sink in and you start to say, "I can live with this." But it definitely took a while to get to that place where I was okay with it.

WALTER SCHREIFELS—*GORLLIA BISCUITS, YOUTH OF TODAY, QUICKSAND, RIVAL SCHOOLS*

MATT: Why did you break up Quicksand at the peak of the band's powers in 1995?

WALTER: We'd just been touring so much and doing the major label grind.

MATT: Did that take all the joy out of it?

WALTER: Yeah. I found it really hard to recognize the success of what we were doing. It all just got too boxed in, and we had a hard time agreeing on anything.

MATT: Was that because you were all such big personalities?

WALTER: We were all big personalities, and everyone thought they were a genius. And we all felt like if we gave in on something then we'd lost somehow. We were on the road too much, around each other too much, and at a certain point, I think we all just felt like we didn't need the grief anymore. It would've been wise for us to maybe just take off six months, and then after six months if we still felt like we had to make this dramatic statement and break up the band, then we could've done that. But for us just being young and passionate, we decided to break up on tour instead.

MATT: It was all or nothing?

WALTER: Exactly. And I'm not saying that's bad, or that shouldn't be an ideal for people. I think it's fine and cool to be that principled. But we didn't do ourselves any favors not giving ourselves a bit of space. We'd played about three hundred dates in a year.

MATT: It's the age old story, isn't it? Nobody from a managerial side is going to take a band off the road and give them some time to breathe, because they want to keep you out there making money.

WALTER: Yeah.

MATT: So for them, it's like, "Let's get you out on tour. Then as soon as you're back, let's get you in the studio working on the next album. And then you have to go back out on tour again." And repeat. But maybe every once in a while, bands should just hit pause and the people who work with them should support and encourage that decision.

WALTER: Yeah. I remember constantly looking at SoundScan numbers, and if you're not touring then your SoundScan goes down and the record label's not happy. And these people who used to love you are now disappointed in you and all this kind of shit. I got to the point where I was like, "I don't need this garbage in my life; I'm not getting paid enough to deal with this grief." And this was all during a time when I was as successful as I'd ever been. But it was cool to go out on a high point in that regard.

MATT: Commercially and artistically speaking.

WALTER: Yeah, we had done great shit. And I didn't know for certain at the time, because you never can tell, but I had a good sense that the music we made in Quicksand would travel well and stand the test of time. I really thought that it would.

MATT: And it has.

WALTER: And I'm really happy about that. Then at a certain point in time we got involved in the Revelation Records twenty-fifth anniversary show, and my friend who's friends with all of us made the move to get us all to play together for this one-off show.

MATT: Was Gorilla Biscuits on that label as well?

WALTER: Gorilla Biscuits was on Revelation, yeah.

MATT: Was that like the Roadrunner Records of the hardcore world?

WALTER: Yeah, for sure. They had a run of about twenty records that were all solid. So we played their anniversary show, and it was just stunning. And it was really cool to reconnect with those guys with enough distance in the past to not be pissed off about some insignificant thing.

MATT: Enough water goes under the bridge, and you forget what you fell out about in the first place, right?

WALTER: Yeah, it's often like that. And after that show we were all like, "Shit! That was amazing." We wound up touring together about a year later. And that was amazing, too. So we took those experiences from the shows that we played, and we wrote a new record. And we used the money that we made from them to pay for it. So we kind of just sprung it. And the response was amazing, and it allowed us to go back out on tour and be contemporary. And I'm super proud of us for taking that leap and going for it. We've all come to really appreciate each other, too. We're really good friends now.

DENNIS LYXZÉN—REFUSED, THE (INTERNATIONAL) NOISE CONSPIRACY, INVSN, FAKE NAMES

MATT: How did the Refused reunion come about?

DENNIS: Someone in our crew asked me about that yesterday, and there's so many little things that lead you to a certain place. One of the things with us was that we were all living in the same city. When we broke up, we were scattered all over the world doing different things and getting into different projects. But by 2011, everyone was back living in the same town. David and I had a hardcore band together called AC4. And David, Kris [Steen], and Magnus [Flagge] had a project together. So we were all moving in the same circles, and 2012 was a year when no one had that much going on. Then we got the offer to play Coachella that year. All of a sudden, we were like, "Maybe we should do this again." And that's how it happened.

MATT: Was your first show back at Coachella in 2012?

DENNIS: The first show was in Umeå at a really small place [Scharinska] that holds maybe two hundred people, and we had a guest list of about two hundred people. There was a line outside of about five hundred people wanting to get in. It was wild. And the payday from Coachella was pretty good; it enabled us to take a few months off work. So we practiced for three months straight—five days a week, from nine-to-five every day, just to get in shape. We were fully aware of the unreasonable expectations that people had because most people had never seen us live before.

MATT: And Refused had obviously been mythologized to high heaven by this point.

DENNIS: Exactly. And it's difficult to combat that myth of who you are. People would say, "Refused are legendary." And that's a lot of pressure to put on a person. But that opportunity gave us the chance to really do our homework, and really dig in and ask ourselves, "What kind of band are we?" Because we had to make the leap from being a DIY hardcore band that played in basements and record stores and coffee shops and squats, to being a band that played Coachella. The last show we'd played was in Harrisonburg, Virginia, in front of forty-five people. And our next show was at Coachella fourteen years later. We had to figure out a way that our music could work at that level.

MATT: Did you feel like you'd grown as a vocalist and a performer in those intermittent years, working on all those other projects?

DENNIS: Yes, very much so. For a long time, I felt inadequate compared to the rest of the guys in Refused. But during those fourteen years of constant touring, I caught up to their level and became a much better singer. And that gave me the confidence to believe that we could actually do this for real.

MATT: What a trip! There's not many bands that have been separated for that long and then reconvened and created new music together.

DENNIS: It does happen. A lot of bands break up and then get back together after ten years or so. But where we're different is we completely missed the rise of our band, because Refused became popular after we'd already broken up. We could see our band creating its own legacy, but none of us were a part of it, and that was strange. I think that's what sets us apart from a lot of other bands. When we got back together, we were at a completely different level, and we weren't the same band or people that we were fourteen years ago. So where do we go from here? *Freedom* was us trying to reconcile that and figure out our identity as a band. And that was an intense experience. It was difficult because there was a lot of pressure, especially from ourselves. We knew that whatever we made people were going to say, "It's not *The Shape of Punk to Come*." And we could create a record that was ten times better, but people wouldn't have that same emotional connection to it.

MATT: That's half of music isn't it?

DENNIS: It is. We were just talking about that today. Kris said, "We can't fucking recreate people's childhoods for them." And that's the magic of music. Someone came up to me yesterday and said, "I was thirteen years old, and I was into Korn and Limp Bizkit, then I heard Refused, and it blew my mind." No matter how good the music that we create today is, we're never going to blow that guy's mind again—at least not in that way. So it was a tough process. But I think that record is great; I think it's a bold and daring record. I also understand that it's not the record a lot of people were expecting us to put out. But that's also the process of being an artist. You have to ask yourself, "What do we need to do to move on?" And now we're onto *War Music*, and this record makes complete sense to me. But without *Freedom* there wouldn't be *War Music*, which is a super exciting record. And we're super excited about moving forward.

WALTER SCHREIFELS—*GORLLIA BISCUITS, YOUTH OF TODAY, QUICKSAND, RIVAL SCHOOLS*

MATT: Your musical journey is such an interesting one. There's been so many projects, and they're all held in such high regard. And there was never that one band that eclipsed all the others, so you've been able to remain creatively free.

WALTER: Yeah, there's people who love Gorilla Biscuits that don't even know I'm in Quicksand. And there's people who love Rival Schools and have no idea I'm in Gorilla Biscuits. And there's people who follow the plot through all of the bands that I'm in. But I don't know if it's been the best career strategy; I think it might be better to brand yourself in one project and keep knocking away at that.

MATT: But would you be happy doing that?

WALTER: I just never thought in those terms. And maybe that came from hardcore, because hardcore bands generally made one or two records and then they broke up. So I just always thought that's how you do it.

MATT: With every single band that you've been in.

WALTER: You know what I mean? It was only after Rival Schools that I was like, "Oh, shit! Maybe it helps to stay with one thing." But it was kind of too late at that point. So I guess this is just the career that I've got. But it's afforded me the space to take chances and work with lots of different people, and that's been really cool. They've all been really meaningful relationships and experiences, and I've been able to keep it real. So I feel very happy and content about that. I'm still thinking about new shit to do as well. There are so many projects that I still want to do.

DAVE FORTMAN—*UGLY KID JOE, PRODUCER*

DAVE: I was in Hawaii with a record company executive one time—on acid. I was fucking tripping with this dude who was the vice president of Mercury Records. We were sitting there watching the ocean in Hawaii, and he got a call about a guy playing "Cats in the Cradle" back in Denver—or something like that. This could all be wrong because I'm old.

MATT: A DJ, you mean?

DAVE: Yeah, in Denver or Nashville or somewhere like that, this guy had just elected to play it because he liked the track off the album [*America's Least Wanted*]. And he got so many phone calls about the song, the next thing I knew we were on our way to make a video, because it was obviously going to be a hit. And that was a surprise to us. We didn't think of it in that way at all.

MATT: Was it originally done just to pad out the album and complete the track listing?

DAVE: It was. Wow, you've got some cool teeth, man. Let me see those teeth! Those are bad ass! You could fucking kill somebody with those fangs.

MATT: No one's ever noticed my front fangs before—you're the first. You're an observational guy, Dave.

DAVE: I am. But yeah, our producer Mark Dodson was really the reason why that song ended up on the record. He was so rad—he's still such a great guy, and a great producer. He really pushed us to make that song great. He could hear it, you know? We were just like, "Whatever!" We didn't even think twice about that song being as big as it was or carrying us into platinum status like that.

MATT: What are your memories of making that album? Were you all pretty wet behind the ears back then?

DAVE: We'd all been in studios before for various reasons, but not under those conditions where we had to follow the EP [*As Ugly as They Wanna Be*], which was then platinum, for fuck's sake. It was the largest EP release *ever*. But luckily Mark was a really great producer. He was definitely a large influence on me becoming such a big producer.

MATT: Was the experience of working with him when the cogs first started turning in your head?

DAVE: It was one of them. But we were all so young back then. I was baked all the time—we were partying it up, man. We were fucking tearing it up, raging like a mother fucker, just getting crazy. But the experience of working with Mark—the arrangements in particular—I remember well. I don't know if I took it all that much to heart at the time, but seeing his ability to look at the pocket of the song and get everything to where people were really playing together, I learned a lot from that. And then Garth—

MATT: Is this album number two now? *Menace to Sobriety*?

DAVE: *Menace*, yeah. Garth [Richardson] was really influential, too. He was sort of the other side of the whole thing: he was more about capturing the vibe. He let us set up like he had done Rage Against the Machine, so we got in the big living room of this giant mansion and set up a full PA, and we recorded the drums with all that shit live in the room. That album has become our *Paul's Boutique*, man.

MATT: I love that album. There's some great songs on it as well. And you obviously had Shannon Larkin in the band by that point.

DAVE: Right. Over time it's become such a cool album. People love "Milkman's Son." And "Jesus Rode a Harley" people like now, too. It's a trip, man. "Cloudy Skies," we sung last night, and people loved the fuck out of it. It's a weird sounding record as well. I've never heard anything that sounds like it in my life, and I study that shit now because I'm a producer.

MATT: Did Garth Richardson encourage you to become a producer?

DAVE: I'd been doing the demos for that record, and Garth came and pulled me aside. He said, "Man, you really ought to produce. You're basically producing this record." And I took that as an insult. I was like, "What? Fuck you! I'm an artist. I'm not gonna be a producer. Fuck that shit!" Then Whit [Crane] said the same thing during *Motel California*, and I took that as a total insult, too. I thought, "This mother fucker doesn't think I'm good enough to be an artist anymore." I was like, "Fuck this shit! Fuck you! I'm an artist, dude." But in hindsight, of course, after thirty million records sold, I'm guessing they were right.

JOHN FELDMANN—*GOLDFINGER, PRODUCER, SONGWRITER, A&R EXECUTIVE*

MATT: At what point does being a producer and an A&R guy eclipse your interest in Goldfinger?

JOHN: I think it was when I heard Bert [McCracken] sing on the cassette [*Demos from the Basement*] that he gave me in Utah. I knew right away that he was going to be much bigger than I would ever be because of his voice—his voice alone—without even seeing them perform. When I first met him, he was just this annoying drunk kid who didn't really know anything about Goldfinger. His guitar player and drummer were huge fans, but he couldn't give two fucks about my band. But I knew there was something stylistically different about The Used; they were so different to any band I'd ever heard. And I knew that his voice was unparalleled and untouchable—I'd never heard anything like it. It felt like my duty as a human to nurture this kid and take what he had and try to grow it.

I felt like Goldfinger had already peaked by this point, too. And it wasn't like a defeatist attitude; I was just being a realist. I'd given it my wholehearted attempt, and we had little moments and breakthroughs, but it never felt like it sunk in, and we were on to the next level. So it just felt like we were grinding it out. And in the beginning it was super fun, but by that point we were eight years into it and still grinding away, barely making a living. And I never thought about the money. If I ever thought about the money, I wouldn't be here talking to you about my success. The money was never important to me. It was always about having fun, and how passionate I was about developing these artists, and taking what Bert had at an incubated level and growing it into what The Used ended up becoming.

After pop punk the next big thing was emo, and to me Bert was the forefront of that whole movement. Of course you had Poison the Well and Refused, and these OG post-hardcore bands like AFI, but nobody sang like Michael Jackson like Bert did. And nobody had these soaring, anthemic, super melodic choruses that were like pop music, but with this kid screaming. I remember going to all these A&R meetings and meeting all these high-end executives, and they were all saying, "If only he didn't scream so much. If only he just sang the whole song, it would connect with so many more people." And I was like, "That's not the point. This is the new punk rock." And Bert's aggression is what people connected with the most about the music.

MATT: Is Maverick the label that you started out working for?

JOHN: Yeah.

MATT: And was that Madonna's label?

JOHN: It was Madonna's label and Guy Oseary ran it, who now runs Live Nation and manages U2. He gave me my first break as an A&R executive. I signed a band called Showoff to him, who were like a mini Green Day, and then I signed Mest, who were like a mini Blink-182. Mest had a gold record in Japan, but neither of these bands took off. And Guy was done with me. He was like, "We've given this a shot, and neither of these bands have really done anything." So he was about to let me go, and then I found The Used. But he didn't get it at first. He was one of those guys, like most of them, that just thought it was too aggressive and screamy, and he just didn't get it. But his boss, Tom Whalley—because Warner Bros. owned Maverick at this point—was like, "I understand this, and I want to sign them." So we ended up working it out through Guy, and that's how I found Story of the Year and signed them to Maverick. But it was touch and go for a moment. I thought I was going back to selling shoes again. Luckily it all just connected, one thing after another, and that's the thing about life: you just keep fucking going.

MATT: Slightly off topic, but who was the band that Madonna sent naked photos to while trying to sign them to Maverick? And is that a true story?

JOHN: It's true. It was Rancid.

MATT: Incredible. And she still didn't get them. Hard luck, Madonna.

DAVE FORTMAN—*UGLY KID JOE, PRODUCER*

MATT: Tell me about "Bring Me to Life" by Evanescence. How did that song come about?

DAVE: We had an opportunity to put the song in a movie, *Daredevil*. It was originally just going to be a song in the middle of *Daredevil*, and we were stoked about that. I was like, "Wow! I've got a song in a movie." I was freaking out. And I basically just went in and did the same thing that I always do. The bridge that exists now was an A and a B section bridge, and the A section was on every chorus. I told them, "This sounds like we're going to the bridge every time we finish the chorus, and I think that's a little offsetting, so let's take that out then go right to the break and hit the verses. Then we need to build a better outro."

They were really receptive to all that. Considering they're as talented as they are, they were probably one of the most receptive bands that I've ever worked with. And that was a good thing because I was on fire with my arrangements at that time, and that song was about to change the world. I could feel it, man. I would sit out in my car at like six in the morning, and my wife at the time was like, "You can't be doing this shit, you're going to wake all the neighbors up." There was just something about the song. I didn't know if anyone would buy it, but I couldn't wait to play it for my musician friends because I knew they were going to be blown away by this fucking thing.

MATT: What's it like having that kind of momentum behind you and knowing that you're on the cusp of something great?

DAVE: It's nothing like having it go to radio and nobody will play it because that's what happened. We went through like twenty different stations and nobody would play it.

MATT: Because it was so different and out of step with what was going on?

DAVE: Yeah. They were like, "We're not playing a goth chick and a fucking orchestra. No way!" I think one person played it in Denver— or somewhere like that, again—and it just started to take off. Then the Clear Channel research came back on it, and it was one of the biggest songs they'd ever researched. And then it was on. All of a sudden, it was like, "This motherfucker is a *hit!*" But it wasn't like it was this magic fucking thing right out of the box. Somebody had to finally play it, and the public was ready to receive it in the way that I felt like they would. I felt the fuck out of it, man.

We had a party to jam the album at Mad Dog Studios, and Todd Sullivan and Tony Ferguson came by. One guy signed Weezer and the other guy signed No Doubt, for fuck's sake—two big A&R dudes. We sat them both down and played them "Bring Me to Life"—straight out the gate, "Bring Me to Life," motherfucker. Todd turns around and says, "I don't like the song that much. But I *really* don't like the singer." And Tony was like, "I just don't get it." Me and my manager were like, "What the fuck is going on here, man? What the fuck is wrong with these people?" They both didn't like it, and it's about to be the biggest goddamn thing in the world. So you never can tell, man.

MATT: Has that been your experience over the years: you can never tell what's going to take off?

DAVE: Success ratios are so small; you can't really fucking know anything. You can love something to death and think that it's going to blow up, but if people don't fucking respond, then you're fucked. That's just the way it goes. Trying to determine what the general public likes is a fucking disaster—it's a nightmare. If they knew then we'd all have hit records every single time.

SCOTT SHIFLETT—*FACE TO FACE, ME FIRST & THE GIMME GIMMES, VIVA DEATH*

SCOTT: There's so much politics in the music business, my steadfast stance on things has often alienated me from the business side of things. Everyone always used to say to me, "It's so important that you know what's happening with your career. You need to be on top of every little thing." But quite frankly, I found that it made me a miserable asshole. I didn't start playing music to get rich or to get girls; I did it because music moved my soul. And I didn't do it to be an asshole to other people. If your band is doing well, that's fucking great. I'm not in competition with you, whether you're a small band, a medium band, or a big band; I'm just here to do music, man. I'm not your enemy or any of that shit. To me, when you've gotten to that point, you've been poisoned.

At a certain point I just decided, "Fuck this. I'm out. You guys can steer this ship any way you want, and I'm going to handle what

I handle best: I'm just going to write, produce, and perform to the best of my abilities, with as much love and passion for what I do as possible, so that when I go to my grave, I'll know that I left a lot of blood, sweat, and good tears on that stage." So many people are reaching for the proverbial brass ring in this business. They don't get it. They spend their whole life blowing off what they really wanted to do in order to succeed. And they still don't succeed.

MATT: They don't find happiness either.

SCOTT: Right. Life is short, and it moves real quick. Trust me. I can't even believe that I'm here now. Sometimes it feels like I've been alive for a thousand years. And sometimes it feels like last week that I first picked up a bass. So I'm just trying to honor the desires of that sixteen-year-old me.

ALAN ROBERT—*LIFE OF AGONY, COMIC BOOK CREATOR*

ALAN: When we first started, we were literally playing on two ping pong tables in a place called Twin Lights, and there wasn't even one light in the whole place. They were just little hardcore shows in front of our friends. We played the basement of a pancake house in Pennsylvania once. The power kept cutting out, and Mina said, "Come on. What's going on with this place?" They finally got the power back on, but she was really annoyed, and she was like, "I want to see you motherfuckers tear this roof down." And they literally did; they started punching the sheet rack ceiling and the whole roof fell down in this pancake house. The owners were this elderly couple, and they came down and said, "What did you do to our place?" To this day, we still get people asking us to sign pieces of that ceiling. That's where we come from, and we don't forget it. We've gotten to play with so many of our heroes as well: we've played with David Bowie, we've played with Black Sabbath, we've played with Metallica, Slipknot, and so many other great bands. And we're still in awe of the experience, even twenty-five years later, because we know that we played the pancake house. It's hard to accept that evolution, even after all these years. You have to pinch yourself, like, "Wow!" It's pretty amazing.

CASEY CHAOS—*AMEN, CHRISTIAN DEATH, SCUM*

MATT: Are you happy with where you're at in life? Do you feel at peace?

CASEY: Yeah, I definitely feel all right. I'm always all right. I'm just grateful that I've been able to have the opportunity to do what I've done. And hopefully it will continue. We'll see what happens. I'll make some more noise if people want it. And if they don't, I'll still make some fucking noise.

MATT: I like the way you say, "I'm always all right." Do you feel like there's nothing life can throw at you that you can't overcome?

CASEY: Well, I've died twice. And I've definitely led an interesting life. I'm not afraid of anything. I was given a death sentence when I was sixteen, and they said I wouldn't live to be past twenty-one. So I'm pretty grateful. But at the same time, it's a double-edged sword: you just don't give a fuck. You just have to do what you're going to do and whatever happens, happens. I live in total gratitude. I'm just here to ride this fucking thing—whatever it is—to the fullest.

BEN OSMUNDSON—*ZEBRAHEAD*

BEN: Before every show we play, I always think, "I wonder if anyone is going to show up today?"

MATT: You surely don't still think that at this stage?

BEN: I never take it for granted. We'll do festivals in mainland Europe on Friday, Saturday, and Sunday, and I'm telling you, I'm nervous every day. It always ends up being great, but I always feel, like, "Make sure you appreciate this, because it could be your last time." So whenever we go out on tour I always go sightseeing. I've been to Paris thirty times, but I still go to the Eiffel Tower every time, because I always think, "This could be the last time, so I'd better go." You never know when people are going to stop caring about your band. And I have no idea how people hear about us. We don't do press or anything.

MATT: Do you think it's literally just old-school word-of-mouth?

BEN: Yeah, I guess people tell their friends, or they see something on the internet—

MATT: With all due respect, you guys don't really post much on the internet. Your shows are fucking insane every day, but you're not posting videos of them for all to see.

BEN: We don't really care about that stuff. We're lucky if we post a photo from the show—that's about it. We're not very good with the whole internet/social media thing. We're kind of old-school. When we first started touring, we didn't even have cell phones. We used to play clubs all over the world, and we'd sneak into the promoter's office when they weren't around to use their phones to call home—it didn't matter if it was Russia or Europe or Japan. I don't know if younger bands know this, but it's so goddamn easy to tour nowadays.

MATT: Yeah, it makes me laugh when musicians complain about how hard it is to be on tour, like that isn't exactly what you signed up for when you started a band.

BEN: Exactly. Get a real job, then you'll know what tough is. You clearly hate your life. People come to your shows, and they sing the words, and they care about what you're doing, and you think that's tough? Really? Go work a real job where you're working for minimum wage. This is the luckiest job there is. It's crazy to think this has been my only job for twenty years now.

MATT: Do you ever feel snubbed by the music press? Because they don't seem to write about Zebrahead *at all*. And for me, as someone who's toured and played loads of shows with you guys, you're one of the hardest working, most entertaining bands around. You play Slam Dunk Festival nearly every year, and you always draw some of the biggest crowds. But no one ever writes about it. Does that piss you off?

BEN: A lot of people back home often ask me that question, but I don't feel bummed out at all. I get to play music all over the world, and people show up and enjoy it. To me, that's winning. I get paid to play shows and travel the world with my friends. I win. If the press doesn't cover us, or people write us off as this ska-punk-rap-whatever band that they can't take seriously, I don't care. I don't need it.

MATT: And you genuinely feel like that? You're not just saying it?

BEN: Seriously, I've been playing music for twenty years, and it's been my only job. I've already won.

JESSE HUGHES—*EAGLES OF DEATH METAL, BOOTS ELECTRIC*

MATT: The last time I saw you guys in London, Iggy Pop, Duff McKagan, and Alex Turner were all at the show. How many other bands would bring those three people together?

JESSE: And Iggy was going nuts. It was unreal. That, to me, was like winning an award. It was almost better than winning a fucking Grammy. I love the people that I look up to. I love them dearly. And when they show me any kind of requitement—if you will—I'm tickled to the toes. I love what I do. I love this job. This is the greatest fucking thing you could ever do—ever, in a million years. Even the worst days are better than most of the best days in a regular life. It's a blessing and a fucking gift to be able to do what I do. I haven't had to do anything at all but rock 'n' roll for the past twenty years. That's a fucking gift. And if the shithouse all goes up in flames tomorrow, I'll be able to say that I left a mark on the walls of the pantheon of rock 'n' roll. What more could you fucking ask for? What more could you possibly ask for, except for the validation of your peers, which I have.

JESSE LEACH—*KILLSWITCH ENGAGE, TIMES OF GRACE, THE WEAPON, STOKE THE FIRE PODCAST*

MATT: Why did you leave Killswitch Engage in 2002?

JESSE: I think if I were to be completely honest with you, I was chicken shit. I was depressed; I was nervous; and I didn't have a lot of confidence as a singer. I didn't have a lot of confidence as a human being either. And I didn't have the wherewithal to ask for help. The only thing I knew how to do was hide, which is what I would do.

We'd be travelling around on tour in a van, and my seat would be way at the back, so I'd roll up in a ball before the set and have a panic attack, then go up on stage and do the best that I could to look at people while I performed. Then I'd go back to the van, crawl back up in a ball, and wait for the guys to be done drinking and having fun before the van started moving again. I literally just couldn't cope with people. I had this disorder, but I didn't know what it was yet, and it got to the point where I was fucking ready to take myself out. It was after the last show in Seattle on that tour when I called my brother, and I said, "Get me the fuck out of here!" So my brother came and picked me up and helped me not kill myself.

After that, I flew home, and I worked three different jobs while I tried to rediscover who I was. And I wrote the band an email telling them that I quit. I was too chicken shit to look them in the face. I said, "Don't try to find me; I'm off the grid, and I'm done with music." I got a job at this organic bakery in Jamestown, Rhode Island—it's still there, it's a great bakery. Then I hid out and worked the graveyard shift at an antique window refurbishing company. So I didn't sleep much. And I finally had a total mental breakdown, which I wrote a song about: "Lay My Burden Down" by my band Seemless. That's when music saved my life again. I found a reason to keep going through that band. They were the reason I fell back in love with music and touring again.

Killswitch skyrocketed at that point in time, but I was ignoring all metal music because I didn't want anything to do with it. I was like, "Blues music is where I'm at now," which I'm really glad that I did because it taught me a lot about singing and scales and all that stuff. But they invited me out to a show after I'd gotten a little better, I'd say around 2009, and I went to see Killswitch Engage open for

Slayer in Connecticut. I was sat back row VIP watching the show, and when they played "My Last Serenade," Howard [Jones] held the mic out and everyone in the crowd finished off the sentence. I'd never seen that before because I just wasn't paying attention. I was like, "These people know the song?" My friends were like, "No shit, asshole! Where the fuck have you been for the last five years?" I had tears in my eyes, dude. I was like, "Holy shit! People know this stuff that I wrote, and they still care." That's when the lightbulb went off, and I decided I should continue to do music, which led me to Times of Grace.

MATT: How did you end up back in Killswitch in 2012?

JESSE: The backstory to that is they'd asked me to rejoin Killswitch *way* before I did, and I said, "No." You know why? I wanted Times of Grace to be the next thing. So selfishly I was like, "No, Times of Grace is everything." Then the label dropped us and Adam [Dutkiewicz] was like, "I've got a new Killswitch album to write. Bye." I was in New York working as a bartender, and I was like, "Shit, dude. What the fuck just happened?" I toured the world with Times of Grace and all of a sudden it was over, and Adam was like, "Good luck." And I don't blame him at all for that; Killswitch is a career band, and you have to keep that going. But at the same time, Howard Jones wasn't fit to write for that record, which became *Disarm the Descent*.

I remember working at the bar and thinking to myself, "Times of Grace, Times of Grace, Times of Grace." I wouldn't let it go. Then one day I got a text from my friend, and he was like, "Did you hear that Killswitch are doing auditions for a new vocalist?" And I went, "Oh, no! They're fucking doing it. They're actually going to do it." In the back of my head, I was thinking, "Do I want some other asshole doing this? Fuck no!" Plus third singers, do they ever work out? Not so much. So long story short, I text the managers and asked, "Can you put me on the list to try out?" I was the last guy on there, and I walked into the room at the end of the day when they were all exhausted. They were like, "This asshole?" I still have the recordings on my laptop of me auditioning. I sound shit. But they thought it was good enough, and just like that I was back in the band.

GREG HETSON—*REDD KROSS, CIRCLE JERKS, BAD RELIGION*

GREG: Bad Religion is the most dysfunctional band I've ever been in. But somehow it works.

MATT: Did the tension feed into the creativity?

GREG: It was just tension.

MATT: From day one?

GREG: No, not always. Overall, it was a great experience.

MATT: Did you enjoy it more or less than your time in the Circle Jerks? Or was it just different?

GREG: The difference between Bad Religion and Circle Jerks is the Circle Jerks wanted to be a full-time band. We didn't care about anything else; we were going to go out on tour and kill ourselves, and that was fine. Bad Religion was everybody's hobby to begin with because everybody was doing other shit. I was in the Circle Jerks, Brett [Gurewitz] had his record label [Epitaph], and Greg [Graffin] was in university. So we only did limited touring. It just kind of happened that ten years later we became really huge and popular, whereas Circle Jerks were consciously trying to build that from the start.

MATT: Was it fun being in Bad Religion to begin with?

GREG: Yeah, it was a fun little side gig that ended up being my main gig. I can't complain; I went from a band that was disintegrating, with the Circle Jerks, to a band that was up-and-coming. So I got lucky.

MATT: How was the nineties punk explosion for Bad Religion as one of the bands who laid the foundation?

GREG: All these punk bands were getting signed to major labels, and we got lucky because we were able to ride the coattails. We weren't quite as successful as Green Day, The Offspring, and some of those other bands. But it was still kind of cool.

MATT: So you enjoyed that period of being in Bad Religion?

GREG: Yeah, because at that point we were pretty established and selling a decent amount of records on an indie label [Epitaph], so we were able to dictate the terms of our major label deal and retain complete artistic control, and a really good royalty rate, which smaller punk bands who were just coming up probably weren't able to do.

MATT: When did you tap out of the party scene? When did that get too much for you?

GREG: About six years ago—six years and change.

MATT: Was there one defining moment, or was it a buildup of moments?

GREG: It was a buildup. Then eventually the guys in Bad Religion said, "You've got to get sober." And I said, "Yeah, okay, you're right." Then they said, "Take some time off." And now we'll get to what happened with Bad Religion. It's a nice segue.

MATT: That's how I roll. So what was your poison? Was it booze; was it coke? What was it?

GREG: It was pills. Benzos, opioids, Vicodin—stuff like that.

MATT: How did it start?

GREG: Anxiety. And I think I just had that predisposition; I guess I have the "ism" and disease lurking inside of me. The self-centered selfishness that I didn't realize that I had manifested itself in the form of alcoholism and drug addiction, and I became a mess.

MATT: Do you think if you were doing a different career you could've dodged that bullet?

GREG: No. When you go back and you go through the process of the therapy and the rehab and all that stuff, it all starts to make sense. I've always felt like I'm not good enough. So the band came to me and said, "Dude, get sober, we've got your back." And I'll make the long story short—

MATT: Don't make the long story short. Make the long story long.

GREG: Okay, well they said, "We've got your back, bro. We'll take care of you—we'll pay for this and that."

MATT: And they did?

GREG: They did not. And I was just trying to get my head straight. I had a marriage that was falling apart at the time. Then maybe five months go by, and I finally called up Greg and said, "You guys haven't been taking care of me like you said you would." And he was like, "Really?" And I knew he was being genuine. He said, "I thought everything was cool?" And I said, "No, I'm getting the runaround from the business manager. But I didn't want to bug you guys." And Greg said, "I'm going to be seeing them tomorrow. I'll see what's up." Then he called me up the next day, and said, "Well, I've got some good news and some bad news. The good news is we're going to take care of you. But the bad news is two of the guys said they never want to play with you again, so you're being kicked out of the band." I was a few months sober at this point, and I'd just filed for divorce.

MATT: It must've been a crushing time.

GREG: It was. And they still didn't pay me, so I had to sue them and take a mediation. It was a nightmare.

MATT: Here's my problem with situations like this—for what it's worth. You weren't the first person in that band to go off the rails and have to get sober. Brett's problems with drugs have been well documented.

GREG: Jay [Bentley] and Brian [Baker] both had to get sober, too. But here's the thing: Brett writes songs, and he plays on the records, and he plays select dates, but he's not really a band member anymore.

MATT: So he's not involved in any of these decisions?

GREG: No, he's not involved in those decisions.

MATT: So it's two *other* guys who don't want to play with you anymore?

GREG: It's two other guys.

MATT: Who didn't have your back?

GREG: Who didn't have my back.

MATT: Have you made peace with those guys? Is that something you'd like to do?

GREG: I run into them occasionally, and I'm cordial, and they're cordial. But what can you do? They don't call it show friends, they call it show business. Right? I was pretty crushed, but I was not surprised.

MATT: Why weren't you surprised?

GREG: Because I'd been in a band with them for twenty-nine years! I knew the deal.

MATT: Do you think there's any way they would ever make it up and do right by you?

GREG: That's up to them. There's a book that the band is compiling, and they asked me to participate. I said, "Can I get a cut? I was in the band for twenty-nine years." And they said, "No." So I refused to participate in the book.

MATT: You're not going to have your say?

GREG: No.

MATT: That's a shame.

GREG: I didn't even specify a number. And there's no money in books anyway.

MATT: But it was the principle?

GREG: Yeah, it was the principle. After everything that we've been though...come on guys! But I'm not on bad terms with them or anything like that. Business is business at this point.

MATT: Do you then say to yourself, "This business is fucked, and I don't want any part of it."

GREG: No, because I can understand why they got sick of my shenanigans. I did bring some chaos into the band.

MATT: Do you think you were the most chaotic member in the history of that band?

GREG: No. Actually, I don't know. That's hard for me to say. But I was pretty bad.

MATT: Everybody is capable of redemption though, right? That's what helps keep us alive.

GREG: That is true. And the fact that they didn't give me the chance to redeem myself was kind of lame, but whatever. I only have a slight resentment toward them now. I'm almost over it.

MATT: I don't think I could get over a betrayal like that.

GREG: It's hard.

JESSE HUGHES—*EAGLES OF DEATH METAL, BOOTS ELECTRIC*

MATT: How do you stay sane in this business?

JESSE: I do a lot of drugs.

MATT: But that's been the downfall of so many before you?

JESSE: Yeah, but I guess it'll be the up-fall of me. If I'm the anomaly, so shall it be in all things. This is the only job where you're supposed to do drugs. Sleep when you die. Drugs are terrible, and they're supposed to fuck you up. If I'm high on a drug, and I'm getting potentially paranoid about cops, I'll stop myself and go, "Wait, I'm on drugs. So everything is normal." And I stop worrying about it. When you're on any kind of drug that's illegal, technically all cops are out to get you anyway, so don't worry about it. I've never been paranoid; I've never fixed VCRs that aren't broken. Some people just have the constitution for it.

JESSE LEACH—*KILLSWITCH ENGAGE, TIMES OF GRACE, THE WEAPON, STOKE THE FIRE PODCAST*

JESSE: Drugs is a word that's been used by the establishment to make us feel guilty about taking things that actually help us. I'm not talking about heroin or cocaine or the stuff that ruins your goddamn life. But marijuana is a fucking plant: it's a seed that you put in the ground. And it was there before it was ever called a drug. It's medicine—it's our ancestor's medicine. Psychedelic mushrooms are our ancestor's medicine, too. They go back thousands of years. Granted, if you're doing them all the time to numb yourself, then that's probably not the healthiest or best idea. But in small doses they can be a medicine; they can take some people off those little white pills that they give you to balance your brain out, that are actually fucking poison based on a multibillion-dollar corporation that's feeding off the habit that they've given you in the first place—all in the name of healing you.

The medicine that you need is actually in nature. It is. I've started to speak openly about this and some people are like, "You're fucking crazy. Fucking hippy." But mark my words, the revolution is happening *now* with medical science. Medical marijuana and CBD are very valuable. They've helped me a lot. And low dose psychedelics have changed my life. Unfortunately, we live in an archaic puritanical society where these things are still illegal. I have friends who are serving prison sentences because they believe that this medicine works. The fact that our governments keep it illegal, there's a reason for that. Some of you might be thinking, "This guy's a crazy mother fucker." But micro dosing psychedelics and medical marijuana work across the board, if diagnosed properly by someone who knows what they're doing. There are guerrilla-style doctors and therapists out there who treat people with these things. I've met them. They saved my fucking life.

GREG HETSON—*REDD KROSS, CIRCLE JERKS, BAD RELIGION*

MATT: Are you able to look back on your time in Bad Religion with a sense of pride and accomplishment? Or has it all been tainted?

GREG: No, it's all good. If it wasn't for that band, I wouldn't be sober. So that's a huge positive. And I wasn't happy in the band for a long time anyway, and I don't think they were happy with me. So it might all be for the best. Who knows? Only the gods know.

MATT: Do you believe in God, Greg? Are you a spiritual guy?

GREG: I don't know about any of that, but I call my higher power "Lord Stanley" because I'm a hockey fan and Lord Stanley donated the Stanley Cup, which is given to the winners of the championship of the National Hockey League each year. But when certain things happen, I just don't question it. Something might be out there looking out for me. Or it could all be coincidence. I don't know. But I don't question it.

MATT: When you're having an awful day, how do you pull yourself out of a slump?

GREG: Drugs.

MATT: You're sober now, Greg.

GREG: Shit!

MATT: That's over. It's done.

GREG: Ah, man. They didn't tell me that.

MATT: How do you get out of that negative headspace now that you are sober?

GREG: You call a fellow crazy person in the program, and they can talk you down. It's a great support group. There are people who don't understand AA [Alcoholics Anonymous] and knock it down, or call it a religious cult, or this or that. But it's not. I thought it was too, until I got involved. I was like, "Fuck that shit! I'm not going to hold hands and say the Serenity Prayer or any of that crap." I wasn't interested in finding God—"Good orderly direction" is one of the corny things for the agnostics.

MATT: That need is inside all of us, I believe. The reason I do this show, and why I like sitting down and talking to people, is I'm looking for connections and meaning in my life, and also guidance and inspiration. I feel like there's nothing that a good conversation can't solve.

GREG: Right. And I couldn't have any of that until I was sober.

PERRY FARRELL—*JANE'S ADDICTION, PORNO FOR PYROS, LOLLAPALOOZA*

MATT: As far as the drugs go, were they important to your creative process, or were they more about personal growth and the desire to go to different places?

PERRY: I would say it was incidental. There I was in Los Angeles, and those kids were messing around with really hard drugs. 1984 was when they were starting to bring in crack, and Oliver North [retired US Marine Corps officer and former President of the NRA] was trading drugs for weapons with the Nicaraguans and the El Salvadorians, and that was all exploding in Los Angeles. So we had that. Then, of course, there was all the tar heroin down in Mexico. And all the musicians were shooting speedballs and doing a lot of speed.

MATT: Drugs were just rife then?

PERRY: Yeah. I also looked up to William S. Burroughs and Lou Reed, so that stuff almost felt like a rite of passage—to go through it and understand and write about it. There was Jim Morrison before me, and Darby Crash, and those men were my heroes.

MATT: There's been a lot of casualties over the years, but you've always managed to weather the storm. Why do you think that is? Did you always know your limits?

PERRY: I'm very fortunate because I can't say I was ever very restrained. But this is something that I've learned, that I'll pass onto you—it's mysticism. They say that in life we all have our own things to overcome, whether it's an eating disorder, or alcoholism, or drug addiction. And the mystics say it will take you forty years to overcome them. So don't be too disheartened or feel too bad if you got into it in your twenties, and you're still struggling in your thirties. I'm sixty years old now.

MATT: You look amazing by the way.

PERRY: Thank you. And it's kind of easy for me now because those years are behind me. I'm not one hundred percent sober. I'm just into living and doing the things that I want to go about doing. Part of it for me was that I really enjoyed ducking out more than I enjoyed the world and seeing what I had to face out there. I would just get disheartened and overwhelmed. And that's all excuses, right? But I'm just letting you know that I'm not as amazing as you might think. It's taken me sixty years to overcome what's been biting me.

MATT: But you're in a good place now?

PERRY: This is something that's fun and interesting—it's more mysticism. As we cross the Messianic Threshold, heaven will come down and God will live among man, and we will all come to know God equally. And that "we" is very important, because you're not looking to point fingers or push people away. You're looking to include and educate people and bring people together. You have to operate on that premise—we're all going to start to know God better, from a different place. A lot of people try to understand God from their head, and I don't think they quite get it. If you can, try to understand God from the innermost dimension of your heart, and you'll start to understand things from a different perspective, and that will lead you to understand that we're all brothers and sisters. God's waiting for everybody to get it. And there'll be a certain amount of people that won't, and those people will perish. But the rest of us, who are the meek, we will inherit the earth.

GREG ATTONITO—*THE BOUNCING SOULS*

MATT: As a father, do you worry about the future of the world?

GREG: In theory, worrying doesn't get us anywhere. It doesn't do anything. Those feelings definitely come at me stronger than they used to now that I'm a father, and I have someone that I really care about who's going to be in the world after I'm gone. As opposed to just thinking, "I'm going to do what I can while I'm here, then see you later." But I practice meditation to alleviate those concerns.

MATT: Do you do that on tour as well?

GREG: When I can.

MATT: I imagine it's tough trying to fit stuff like that in on the road—even finding a quiet room can be near impossible sometimes.

GREG: Yeah, but it's loose. And to me, meditation isn't about striking a pose and all that stuff. It's a minute-by-minute practice, and you can live your whole life in meditation.

MATT: A lot of punk rockers that I've spoken to recently seem to be getting into this stuff.

GREG: When you break it down, it's not that strange at all; we don't want to do what everyone else is doing; we're trying to find what's different and what's real. So, where do you go to seek that out? You've really got to go inside and observe your environment, then process that information and ask yourself, "How is this working for me? Am I just going to get blown around by all this bullshit?" Money is probably the biggest obstacle that we all face because we're all scrapping to survive and pay the bills. And those things can consume you.

MATT: I guess that's why it's called consumerism. I'd never thought about it in that way, but that's it—be careful what you wish for because it just might eat you alive.

GREG: Right. I think that's the challenge, and this is how I zero myself out when it comes to my son. Against all the odds, I've managed to make a life for myself by following my creative and whacky ideas. And my parents were supportive, but they certainly didn't actively encourage me to follow my dreams. My dad was like, "Greg, you have to go to college. You can go ahead and do that band thing for a while. But let me know when you're ready to go to college, and I'll help you out." And he wasn't negative about the band, which I give him credit for. And now he's an extremely proud parent, which is an amazing feeling. But without sounding too corny—and this has nothing to do with religion—I have to have faith in where following my heart and my own intuitive feelings has led me and trust that my son will do the same thing. I believe that he has the power in his heart and soul to create his own world within this madness, because that's what we did. I truly believe everyone has that capacity. And you understand that because you're a self-creator: you have your own podcast.

MATT: That's exactly what I've tried to do with this show: dodge the rat race for as long as possible, stay free and be happy, and live my life on my own terms. We all have to work to live. But you can also enjoy what you do, right?

GREG: Right. And there's no getting around having to be responsible and paying your own way in life. But you can do it on your own terms, like you say.

MATT: What's the best thing about being in The Bouncing Souls?

GREG: Having something in my life that's been so meaningful on so many levels; I've been able to create music, learn from all these extended experiences, see the world, and have meaningful relationships everywhere I go. It's also helped me have a better marriage and become the person that I am today. It's so deep, I don't even know how to describe it.

TOMMY LEE—*MÖTLEY CRÜE, METHODS OF MAYHEM, SOLO ARTIST*

MATT: How did you feel when you saw *The Dirt* film for the first time? It must've been a trip!

TOMMY: First of all, I was like, "Wow! I can't believe there's a movie that's been made about my life." That's overwhelming and crazy enough, right? Then you start getting into everybody's life and how this all happened—the story of how these four guys fucking did this. We started out putting up posters from my van, and we went from

200-seater shitty little clubs to playing stadiums. So there was a lot of feelings watching it for the first time, watching everybody's fun but also their struggles. At the end of it, I was like, "How the fuck are these four guys still alive?" I think about that often, and I do pinch myself, like, "How the fuck did we all somehow fucking squeak through and all make it out alive?" Because we shouldn't be.

MATT: What was your favourite scene in the film? Was there one stand-out moment?

TOMMY: The opening scene—I can't believe Jeff [Tremaine] just went ahead and did that. That opening scene with the squirter says so many things at once. First of all, no one is afraid to make that the first thing that you see. And if that is the first thing that you see, what the fuck is coming up?

MATT: What about the flip side to that? Were there any moments that were particularly hard for you to watch back? Because it's all in there isn't that? And that's what made *The Dirt* such an amazing book: you didn't pull any punches.

TOMMY: Yeah, there's a lot of those moments, you know? From Nikki's overdose to Vince's child dying, there's a lot of shit in there. And it's even more enhanced when you're watching them being recreated and go down. It just makes it even heavier—as if it's not already fucking heavy enough. That movie really is a rollercoaster of super fun, cool, crazy, dark, sad, terrible, amazing moments. It's fucking all over the place.

MATT: Much like your life, my friend, it's been one hell of a ride. How old are you now, Tommy? Fifty-eight?

TOMMY: I'll be fifty-eight in October, yeah. Crazy!

MATT: Not only do you look amazing for your age, but you also still seem so excited by life in this eternally youthful way. What keeps you so engaged and excited?

TOMMY: I don't know if there's a secret, man. It's just in my fucking DNA. I'm still very childlike; I get excited about the dumbest shit. I'll see an ant ripping across the floor carrying some stick that's way too big for him, and that will just make my day. I guess I'm just still young at heart.

MATT: Is that because of the way you were brought up do you think? Were you always encouraged to be an enthusiastic kid?

TOMMY: Yeah, I mean, I had a really nice upbringing. And I've always been very grateful for that. Gratitude is really important to me. Not a day goes by where I don't say to myself, "Fuck!" There's luck, there's talent, there's timing—there's all these things that have happened in my life that I'm really grateful for. And I think when people lose that, they start to lose a lot. So that keeps me young, because I'm really fucking happy to be here. Somehow this is what I do; I get to make music and have a blast. That's a lucky mother fucker right there. You have to have talent, sure. But you also have to be grateful for that stuff. And this is what I get to do for a living—basically just have fun.

MATT: Ego and success often get in the way of gratitude and happiness, don't they? And when you can keep that beast at bay, that's when you learn how to really wake up and smell the roses and humble yourself and be thankful for everything that you've got. It's an active pursuit, though. It's something that you need to work on throughout your life.

TOMMY: Yes. You definitely have to keep your eyes peeled for that stuff. Stop and be grateful and recognize those things that you're grateful for, otherwise they'll fly by. We live our lives at a super-fast pace, it's a fucking blur sometimes. Right? So I think it's really important to slow the fuck down for a second, several times a day, and really take in what the fuck's happening and what's going on. And be grateful, man. Be grateful!

GENE SIMMONS—*KISS*

MATT: You've mentioned the word ego a couple of times during this conversation, and I guess you get accused of being all ego—

GENE: May I say this for the record?

MATT: Of course.

GENE: It doesn't matter to me.

MATT: But I don't think in many ways you are egotistical. And what I mean by my interpretation of that is that Kiss have a very valuable and important musical legacy. I've seen and read interviews—and you can hear it in the music—where everyone from Rage Against the Machine to Weezer, and that whole nineties alternative rock generation, cite Kiss as an influence. They all say your band inspired them to start a band. But you don't seem to feel the need to go around telling everybody that.

GENE: It goes from [Dave] Grohl to the Melvins, to [Kurt] Cobain to all of them. Even Trent Reznor, who's talking trash nowadays. I welcome all of it. I love all of it. I'm thrilled that I was ever allowed to pick up a bass or a guitar, much less scale the heights. You're never going to be able to get everybody to like you or what you are.

Often, in my estimation, people misunderstand delusional self-confidence for baseless ego. Like, the guy who walks into a room and says, "I'm going to fucking to do this, and I'm going to fucking do that." If they're complete lies, that's one thing. But I remember when I was a kid, I heard this new boxer called Cassius Clay get up, pound his chest, and say, "I am the greatest." And I thought to myself, "Who the fuck does he think he is?" But actually, he knew who he was. He was just stating fact. I was unqualified or not informed enough to understand that he wasn't a braggadocio. He wasn't bragging. He was just stating the fact: he was, and maybe continues to be, *the greatest*. He is the greatest of all-time. So I accept happily that there are enough people out there who think that I'm an asshole. Listen, I called one of my solo records *Asshole*.

MATT: You did.

GENE: Thank you for the privilege of having just the best life. I accept all of it, the barbs and everything. It's fine. "What an asshole that guy is." Yeah, you're right. And the boxset over here—

MATT: genesimmonsvault.com

GENE: I'm never shy about saying, "Hey, I want you to buy this thing." I'm not going to give it away. I've worked all my life for it. And I suspect what you're doing right now, you get paid for, right?

MATT: I'm getting there, Gene, I'm getting there. It's early days, but I'm sticking at it.

GENE: But you are trying to get paid?

MATT: Of course.

GENE: I want to get paid, too.

MATT: I mean, you do it for the sheer sake of creating, of course. But you have to eat, you have to live, and hard work should be rewarded.

GENE: You just stated why communism doesn't work, and why capitalism continues to be the shining light for all humanity—the incentive to excel means you'll get more money because the guy who wins the race gets more money than the loser. That's good.

MATT: And success doesn't always mean money. Money is great, of course. But I think success is also a sense of self-worth, that you got up today, and you contributed something to the world.

GENE: I'd like to put a sidebar onto that: if you totally succeed at something and you can't pay your rent, are you a success?

MATT: Your answer would be?

GENE: No. Because you are not the definer of the entire answer; you're totally dependent on everybody around you.

MATT: What's your proudest achievement in life, Gene?

GENE: Birth is pretty good.

MATT: Your own?

GENE: Well, yeah. Once you're born, all things are possible. You're lucky if you're born in western civilization: you're *free*. You can be a human being and think for yourself, and then capitalism allows you to educate yourself. I've written books about it. I have a new one that came out last week called *On Power* [*My Journey Through the Corridors of Power and How You Can Get More Power*].

MATT: This was the book that you were supposedly bashing people over the head with on Fox News.

GENE: I'm going to tell you what I told Piers Morgan on *Good Morning Britain*, but I don't think they aired it because it was off camera. Thousands of people picked that story up, and even if you completely explain it away in interviews, the story is already out there. But I stand by every word that I said and every action that I took. You can either fight it and sue people, or you can take the high road and say, "You know what? I make a living. God bless. Move on."

MATT: Also, you're cheeky. I've been around you a few times, and you have a playful sense of humor.

GENE: I'm in a *rock band*, for fuck's sake! I'm not a priest. If you're talking about lewd behavior, turn to page three. Part of comedy—and I'm not a comedian, but I am in a band—is having a license to thrill. What's Ricky Gervais going to talk about without pissing people off nowadays?

MATT: I don't think he'll ever stop. I think he's committed to the cause, and I enjoy that about him.

GENE: Nor should he. But he better get ready for the suits.

MATT: Do you ever get flak from your wife? Is she ever, like, "Gene! You've been out there causing trouble again!"

GENE: Yeah, two days ago. She was like, "What the fuck happened now?"

MATT: It's good that she's got you're back, though.

GENE: I'm going to show you something because the lawyers are always watching your back, and they want to protect you. So I offer this, because it happens enough times, and it will happen to you, the more famous you get and the more money you make, people will come out of the woodwork. And I'm going to mention it—I just got the stink eye from someone, but I'm going to mention it.

MATT: We're going there?

GENE: Oh, yeah. So I'm doing this *Scooby Doo* voiceover a few days ago in Los Angeles, and the producer is with me the whole time. I'm in the parking lot afterward, and this woman comes out and starts screaming all kinds of stuff at me. Here's my text to the producer: "Hey...the girl who just came out into the alley to shout at me...did you see me being improper or putting my hands on her at any time? Were you with me the whole time?" That was my text to him. Now, here's his text to me. You read that aloud. Bob is the pseudonym that I use when I text, by the way.

MATT: "Bob, I saw you do absolutely nothing. I was with you the whole time in a very crowded hallway, and I was two feet away from you when she passed you. What are you talking about?"

GENE: Now, obviously there are bad guys out there. But I wasn't sexually improper with anybody. And it's not just about sexual improprieties: you can say anything you want about anybody, and unfortunately it's all down to the court of public opinion. What happened to your innocent until proven guilty? I could go on social media today, and say, "Matt Stocks went into the bathroom, and a twelve-year-old boy followed him inside."

MATT: Don't do that, Gene.

GENE: Of course not. And by the way that could be accurate: you go in first, then a twelve-year-old boy goes in after you. But it goes on social media, and it spreads like crazy, and then you get hate mail that says, "What were you doing in the bathroom with a twelve-year-old boy?" And you have no idea what went on. You finished your business and you left. You're *fucked!* Your life is over.

MATT: It's a difficult time to be in the public eye.

GENE: It's the worst time. And I'm not tugging on anybody's shirt sleeves. "You're rich, you're famous, shut the fuck up." I get it. But what are comedians going to talk about? Is Gervais going to do the Golden Globes again?

MATT: Did you see him host the last ones? He was so funny.

GENE: He was so fucking great, because he was so politically incorrect. And I know Mel Gibson well. He's a good guy, actually. He said some stupid things when he was drunk, but haven't you? I've never been drunk so I can't tell you that. But I know people who've gotten drunk and said all kinds of racist, homophobic, anti-Semitic stuff. And maybe they really feel that way. Maybe they don't. But Gervais piled into Mel Gibson and just destroyed him.

MATT: He destroyed Hollywood that night. It was amazing.

GENE: You know what? Good for him. It's comedy. But you're right: back to genesimmonsvault.com

TOMMY LEE—*MÖTLEY CRÜE, METHODS OF MAYHEM, SOLO ARTIST*

MATT: Do you practice spirituality, Tommy? Is that where you turn for guidance and support and strength?

TOMMY: Yes sir. It's a must.

MATT: Which areas of spirituality have really spoken to you or helped you out over the years?

TOMMY: Well, you know, it's one of those things that's really personal for me, and I'd rather keep that one little piece of my life private because not much else is.

MATT: I hear you, brother.

TOMMY: But thank you for asking. I do appreciate it.

MATT: No worries. Could you perhaps speculate on your interpretation of the meaning of life? Why do you think we're here on this crazy ball of water and dirt, just trying to make sense of it all?

TOMMY: I know, man. I was having this conversation with my wife the other day. It's so overwhelming to even try and begin to figure out why the fuck we're here—or how we're here. It's overwhelming. People get all fucking bugged out about shit. It's like, "Dude, do you realize you are a fucking micro-spec? It just doesn't matter." I always tell people this: "We're not here for a long time; we're here for a good time. So fucking enjoy it." Do you know what I'm saying? Because at some point, dude, not even God can stop the clock. Time as we speak is ticking and at some point, my friend, this is all over.

MATT: Amen. Death is the only certainty in this life; it's the only thing that we all know to be true. And I believe there's a great beyond waiting for all of us after this version of life is over, but while we're in this version, as you say, we've just got to make the most of it.

TOMMY: Absolutely. And I'm with you on the afterlife, too. There's got to be something after this. Maybe there isn't—maybe it's just darkness, and it's all really over. But it's nice to think there might be something else.

VINNIE STIGMA—*AGNOSTIC FRONT*

MATT: It's amazing to me how much you still love what you do.

VINNIE: Oh, yeah.

MATT: Where do you think you'd be today if music hadn't come into your life in the way that it has?

VINNIE: It could've gone a couple of ways. I could've wound up a working stiff: get up, go to work, come home, and die of a heart attack. Or I could've been used by the mafia.

MATT: Was organized crime a big thing in your neighborhood?

VINNIE: Yeah, that was a big part of my neighborhood. And I would've been dead today if I went down that road, I can tell you that right now. I've got too good of a heart; they would've had my friend kill me—because that's how it works.

MATT: You never see it coming.

VINNIE: Yeah. I lived across the street from Murder, Incorporated. You know what I mean? I lived in Vincent Coll's old apartment, and he's the guy who invented the drive-by shooting. He was a hitman for the mob. You can look him up. And I live in his apartment now. Martin Scorsese used to leave all his camera equipment there back in the sixties when he was still in film school. I've lived in the same apartment for over forty years. And I've lived in the same building for sixty-five years.

MATT: And if it wasn't for music you'd be living the nine-to-five life, or the mob life, or you'd be dead?

VINNIE: Yeah, or maybe I'd be a junkie. Who the fuck knows? I had colorectal cancer. And I had to have two operations for that, but now I'm fine. So I'm a cancer survivor. And I'm a bull fighter: I fought a bull and two midgets in South America. I was more scared of the midgets than the fucking bull. Those little cocksuckers threw sand in my face, so I kicked one of them right in his fucking ass. That motherfucker!

MATT: Hold on, how did you end up fighting little people in South America?

VINNIE: I was bombed.

MATT: Right.

VINNIE: I went to a bull fight.

MATT: Yeah.

VINNIE: And they invited me to get in the ring and try it out. I had a poncho and a big boss hat and everything. I went right up to the bull, and he turned around and looked at me. Now I know what a bull's eye means. I said, "Holy shit!" And he started charging me. So I ran away into the little area where you hide behind, and I was shaking from the adrenaline. The rest of the band were watching, and I was like, "You guys should come in here." They said, "No fucking way! You're crazy! You're on your own, Vinnie." After that I wanted to become a fire walker, so they laid out all these hot coals, and I walked over them. They had to wheel me around for about a week after that. My feet were all burnt up, and I had to play guitar sitting down.

MATT: How exactly do the dwarves factor in to all this?

VINNIE: The midgets were part of the act. And I was stealing the show. So they were getting angry, and that's why they started kicking me in the legs. I was just trying to make friends with the little cocksuckers.

MATT: You're the last of a dying breed, Vinnie. Have you got any parting words of wisdom?

VINNIE: Do whatever the fuck you want, just try to make yourself happy. We're all going to die one day anyway. So fuck it, just try to live your life to the fullest.

GENE SIMMONS—*KISS*

GENE: My piece of advice to everybody is this: to thine own self be true. Don't try to blow everybody in the room just to curry favor because it's easy to lose yourself and your soul. You're never going to please everybody. Not everybody likes Jesus, either. And I'm not Jesus. I'm just a schmuck who got lucky. But I'm not changing who I am for anybody. And in this world, you don't have to. Nor should you. At the end, when they finally drag me kicking and screaming and stick me underground—

MATT: Is that the way you'd like to go? Buried as opposed to cremated?

GENE: Well, if they try to bury me they can do it in the Kiss casket, and if they cremate me, then we also make Kiss urns.

MATT: I read that.

GENE: We also make Kiss condoms: we'll get you coming, and we'll get you going. You can use that yourself. I've used it before—enough times.

MATT: I don't doubt that.

GENE: But I do want to get serious for a second here. If you go through life and you have regrets, how sad is that? Especially if you live in a country with free speech and capitalism. I know what's going to be written on my tombstone when I die—no regrets, or I shoulda, woulda, coulda. It will just say, "Thank you and goodnight." Been there, done that, bought the T-shirt. What else can I ask for? Will everybody go thumbs up, or will some people say, "Fuck him." Cool. Then you're just like Jesus. Some liked him, some didn't, and then you die. But in the meantime, get genesimmonsvault.com

THE PURSUIT OF HAPPINESS PLAYLIST

MÖTLEY CRÜE—"LIVE WIRE"

RAGE AGAINST THE MACHINE—"BULLS ON PARADE"

HYRO THE HERO—"GHETTO AMBIANCE"

TOOL—"SOBER"

COAL CHAMBER—"SHOCK THE MONKEY"

FOO FIGHTERS—"ALL MY LIFE"

THE BRONX—"HISTORY'S STRANGLERS"

QUICKSAND—"FAZER"

REFUSED—"THE SHAPE OF PUNK TO COME"

UGLY KID JOE—"CATS IN THE CRADLE"

THE USED—"THE TASTE OF INK"

EVANESCENCE—"BRING ME TO LIFE"

FACE TO FACE—"I WON'T LIE DOWN"

LIFE OF AGONY—"RIVER RUNS RED"

AMEN—"JUSTIFIED"

ZEBRAHEAD—"ANTHEM"

EAGLES OF DEATH METAL—"WANNABE IN L.A."

KILLSWITCH ENGAGE—"MY LAST SERENADE"

BAD RELIGION—"YOU"

JANE'S ADDICTION—"MOUNTAIN SONG"

THE BOUNCING SOULS—"TRUE BELIEVERS"

MÖTLEY CRÜE—"HOME SWEET HOME"

AGNOSTIC FRONT—"OLD NEW YORK"

KISS—"ROCK AND ROLL ALL NITE"

INFLUENCE & INSPIRATION

"We're absolutely a product of it."

I*N Life In The Stocks Volume One*, there was a chapter called "The Hero's Heroes." I thought that was a solid title, even if I did steal it off my mate Chris Dean. But after the book came out, one of the guests made me see things a little differently.

When it came time to promote *Volume One*, I did a series of Instagram live chats with a selection of interviewees from the book. And I asked Danko Jones to join me online to talk about "The Hero's Heroes" chapter, since he had a great story in the book about Lemmy, and I thought that anecdote would serve as the springboard for a discussion about the chapter as a whole and heroes in general.

Now, I love Danko Jones. He's a good friend and a great dude. But sometimes he can be pretty intense, and when he feels passionately about something, he definitely doesn't hold back. I found myself on Instagram with him the week after my first book came out, and I'd hoped to talk to him about some of the stories in the heroes chapter to help get the word out to his fanbase and potentially shift a few extra copies of my book. But Danko had other plans. And maybe he didn't do it intentionally. But this is what transpired.

As soon as the live chat started—and bearing in mind this is all *live* and uncut—Danko proceeded to destroy the entire concept of a hero and explain in no uncertain terms that he didn't have any, and that the notion of looking up to someone in that way, especially in the field of rock 'n' roll, was complete and utter bullshit. Which was fine; he had a valid point. But maybe it wasn't the best time or place to instigate said debate, especially if I wanted to promote my book in any kind of positive light.

I have to admit I was sore for a couple of seconds. But I quickly reminded myself, that's who Danko Jones is, and that's what Danko Jones does. And that's why people love him. That's why I love him, too. If he behaved in any other way, or pandered to something that he didn't believe in, that would be completely contradictory to his character. And the fact remained, he'd given up an hour of his time to talk about my book. He just wasn't going to hand it to me on a plate. I was going to have to work for it. And that's precisely what I did.

I love a challenge. And my track record speaks for itself: when the going gets tough, I rise to the occasion. Check out my podcast with John Lydon for clarification, which coincidentally is an episode that Danko heard early on, and he was very complimentary about it. He also wrote me a fantastic quote for the cover of my first book. He went above and beyond, in fact. So I'm very grateful for all his support. And I'm definitely not trash-talking him here. This is all leading me to a very important point…

The word "hero" *is* problematic when used in relation to artists and musicians, for it implies they're worthy of admiration for their courage and nobility. And how many brave or honorable rock stars do you know, really? Cancer survivors are heroes. War veterans are heroes. Doctors, nurses, and first responders are heroes, as the whole pandemic has proven. Musicians, actors, and comedians, on the other hand, are not heroes—no matter how talented they are. What they can be, however, is influential and inspirational. And that, my friends, is why this chapter is called "Influence & Inspiration." Shout out to Danko Jones for instigating the amendment.

This new title also allows more space for the deeper theme to be explored, since inspiration doesn't always have to be positive to have a positive effect; people can often have a reverse impact in terms of their influence. For example, you might see someone do a certain thing, or behave in a certain way, and be inspired to do the exact opposite.

There's a couple of stories like that in this chapter—previous *Life In The Stocks* guest Steve-O is one of the guilty culprits.

You'll also read about artists as the source of inspiration, as opposed to the beneficiaries of it. Lou Koller from Sick of It All, for instance, talks about how his band inspired Korn back in the day, and how his brother is responsible for putting together Toby Morse's band, H20. And believe it or not, Goldfinger front man John Feldmann helped give the likes of Rage Against the Machine and Tool a leg up during the early days of their careers, which is crazy to think about now.

Places can also be a source of influence and inspiration. You'll soon hear about how New Jersey shaped the sound of The Bouncing Souls, and how Buffalo is at the heart of all Keith Buckley's creative output. There's a touching tribute to Anthony Bourdain coming up, too. And homages to all-time icons like David Bowie, Iggy Pop, and Perry Farrell. Even Gene Simmons has his idols—besides Gene Simmons, obviously. Here he is to tell you more...

GENE SIMMONS—*KISS*

GENE: Two years after I heard The Beatles, I started writing my own songs inspired by them.

MATT: They were the band that got everyone into music, right?

GENE: Everybody from Ozzy [Osbourne] to Alice Cooper—you name it. You hear The Beatles and your life changes. It doesn't even matter if you go into different kinds of music, that stuff is undeniable. I mean, at twenty years old, Lennon and McCartney had already written "Yesterday" and "Michelle." Even "When I'm Sixty-Four" was a song that McCartney had written during the Cavern Club days. At twenty years old, I didn't even know how to tie my own shoelaces, much less write "Yesterday," which was originally entitled "Scrambled Eggs," by the way. Did you know that?

MATT: Really?

GENE: "Scrambled eggs, she had some lovely legs."

MATT: It was just the melody that he had?

GENE: He woke up dreaming that melody, yes. When I first heard that pivotal McCartney solo record [*McCartney*], and he's engineering, producing, arranging, playing all the instruments, writing all the music, and often doing all the backing vocals, I was directly inspired by that. On a lot of the songs that I've recorded over the last fifty years, I'm doing all the harmonies, playing drums, bass, keyboards—all that stuff. And it wasn't so much that I was impressed by him, I just thought, "Wow! That sounds like he had a lot of fun." And he made the whole album at home on his farm in Ireland. How cool is that?

MATT: Do you have a home studio? Is that where you like to record?

GENE: No. There's already enough chaos at home for me.

MATT: Do you like to keep your creative space separate?

GENE: You have to be able to do that. At home, I'm having business meetings with people in suits and ties. I have a restaurant chain and a film company, and a lot of stuff going on. There isn't enough time in the day, and I don't want to be in the studio writing or recording and have the phone ring or have somebody ask me what way I want them to cut the grass.

MATT: Do you like to enter a specific headspace when you're creating?

GENE: I want to go back into the womb, where nothing gets in the way, and you can just live it and be it. You don't want a coitus interruptus kind of thing happening. These are big words like gymnasium. You have to be careful. [Puts on a cockney accent] *Do you know what I mean?*

MATT: Come on, Gene. Let's stay on track.

GENE: [Still cockney] *Come on then.*

MATT: Let's talk about Bob Dylan. Did you approach him to write music together? How did that collaboration come about?

GENE: I did. And he may be the most important lyricist of the twentieth century. I think it's fair to say that. He changed the times, and not just with that lyric, "For the times they are a-changin'."

MATT: He pushed the capabilities of what rock music could do—and be.

GENE: Unquestionably.

MATT: "Like a Rolling Stone" was so expansive.

GENE: It was so big, and so important, that Lennon was inspired by him to go and write "You've Got to Hide Your Love Away"—and lots of other songs. And everybody covered his songs, from The Byrds to Jimi Hendrix.

VINNIE SITGMA—AGNOSTIC FRONT

MATT: Were you a Beatles fan as a kid?

VINNIE: Yeah, I remember buying *Sgt. Pepper's* [*Lonely Hearts Club Band*] when it came out. But Jimi Hendrix was the one who changed me.

MATT: Did he inspire you to become a guitar player?

VINNIE: Yeah, he's the guy that inspired me to play the guitar. And Bruce Lee was the guy that inspired me to be healthy and tough. But Jimi Hendrix is still my guy to this day.

MATT: What about as an entertainer? Who inspired you to become this larger-than-life character that you are?

VINNIE: You can't buy that entertainment; I can tell you that right now. It's a hard sell. But I grab from old, like Frank Sinatra. I went to see Frank Sinatra one time—

MATT: You saw him live?

VINNIE: Yeah, I saw him perform. And I saw him in my neighborhood making a movie called *Contact on Cherry Street*. I was standing from here to where the wall behind you is away from him. I was like, "Wow! That's Frank Sinatra." I'd seen so many images of the guy. But when you see someone like that in real life, it's a different thing. Then I went to go and see him live when the first smoking ban came in, and he was like, "What do you mean no smoking in here?" And he lights up a cigarette and throws a match at the guy. I loved that. I thought that was awesome. He involved the whole crowd, like, "What do you mean I can't smoke in here?" And he threw the match at the guy. It was so good.

CASEY CHAOS—*AMEN, CHRISTIAN DEATH, SCUM*

CASEY: When it comes to the term musical artist, and artist in general, I think David Bowie is the king. For my personal taste, he's flawless. The work that he did in the 1970s alone, you just sit in awe of it: it's so massive and so genius and so brilliant. He changed so many times, and every single thing he did was just brilliant. There was some stuff in the 1980s that I wasn't as keen on, as was the case with most bands from that generation who got a little more commercial because of the MTV generation. But he still did quality work. He's one in a billion; there will never be another David Bowie; there will never be someone of that caliber ever again in the history of the world. I honestly believe that people like David Bowie, Lemmy, Iggy Pop, Lou Reed, and all these full of life characters will never exist again because of an astounding amount of reasons. I just don't think that quality of people exist anymore.

MATT: Why do you think that is?

CASEY: Back in the day there was a thing called artist development, and labels would invest into bands and artists because they believed in their vision. And musicians were able to make a living creating art. That's obviously been gone for many years now, hence it makes it more difficult for quality work to come out, just because people can't survive. And everything today is so easy with the internet, and there's no suffering for the art anymore. Of course there's suffering when it comes to pain and stuff like that, but I mean in far as anything that you want is at your fingertips now. I used to drive for *hours* just to buy one record. Now you can download it for a dollar on the internet. I like going out of my way and suffering to get something because it makes it more enjoyable at the end.

MATT: There's joy in the art of discovery, too. I remember when I first discovered punk rock, I'd read all the liner notes to see who the bands thanked, and if three bands all thanked the same band then I'd go out and buy one of their albums.

CASEY: That's exactly right.

MATT: Pre-internet, that's how you discovered new bands.

CASEY: It was.

MATT: You couldn't find out anything about them beyond what was in the *Kerrang!* magazine interview that week. Trying to get information about bands was impossible back then. Maybe one of the reasons why big stars like David Bowie probably won't ever exist again is because it's hard for them to maintain that mystique, because you can find out anything about anyone at any time now.

CASEY: And people used to put so much effort into their craft. Now they can put it all together on Pro Tools, where you don't even have to play a full song. You basically don't even have to know how to play an instrument. And I guess that's fun for some people and that's cool. But I haven't really found anything that's inspired me in that way.

MATT: Did you have some good times with David Bowie?

CASEY: Yeah, I had to the opportunity to meet him several times and have dinner with him and stuff like that.

MATT: What do you learn from someone like that?

CASEY: Most of the people that I've met who I grew up admiring, it was no wonder once I met them, it was as if I'd known them forever. I already had a connection to them because I'd connected with the individual who created that art. Nine times out of ten, these people are the most beautiful people you've ever met in your life. And sometimes you end up being friends with them and they take you under their wing. I've had a lot of that happen in my life, where these people that I never even dreamt about meeting, let alone talking to, would actually call me up and want to do something with me. In that respect, I've definitely led one of the richest lives beyond my wildest dreams. I've gotten to work with people that I truly think are the highest most elite individuals that ever created the art.

MATT: You got to work with Iggy Pop, too. That must've been incredible. What happened there?

CASEY: Well, there was a point where Ross [Robinson] was going to produce Iggy's record, and he asked me to write it. So we ended up working together on it. We met up and exchanged ideas and listened to songs together, and we made a bunch of demos. Unfortunately, the record never came to be, for various reasons, but it worked out great for me because at the end of it, Ross was like, "Dude, you've got to keep these songs. Even if this Iggy thing falls through, you've got to keep some of these songs for yourself because they're the best things you've ever done." And a lot of those songs went on to become a record we released called *We Have Come for Your Parents*. So it all turned out for the best.

MATT: And didn't Iggy's son become your tour manager?

CASEY: That's right. His son Eric [Benson] became our tour manager, and he was the most fun tour manager of all-time. He looks like a giant Iggy—he's practically seven-feet tall. And he's a real character, just like Jim. He's a really amazing dude.

MATT: Was Lemmy a friend of yours, too?

CASEY: I was friends with Lemmy, yeah. We'd always see each other. We hung out several times in LA, and there were definitely many nights out with Lemmy. He was the best. The week that him and Bowie died was one of the most iconic weeks of misery because two of my top five people who create art and music were both dead in a week. There isn't a day that goes by that I don't miss hearing their voices or look forward to seeing them again. They were both hugely important to me as individuals who created something that was more powerful and important than anything any politician has ever done. They were landmarks in history.

NADJA PEULEN—*COAL CHAMBER*

MATT: Tell me about the time you got to jam with Iggy Pop. I presume he's an all-time hero of yours?

NADJA: Absolutely, one hundred percent. He's my idol. I grew up on Iggy and the Stooges, so when that happened it seemed so surreal.

MATT: How did it come about?

NADJA: I'm really good friends with Whitey Kirst, who was Iggy's longtime guitarist back in the 1990s, and I believe through the early 2000s as well. Whitey was actually one of the very first people that I met in LA—at The Rainbow. He gave me some sort of brain massage. I still tell him it's because of him that my life turned out the way that it did.

MATT: For better or worse.

NADJA: Exactly. Sometimes better, sometimes worse. So I was home after touring with Coal Chamber for a while, and usually I get the end of tour blues when I come home. At first it's great to be home and in your own bed and all that stuff, but after a couple of days the boredom sets in. And when I get the post-tour blues, I usually don't touch my bass for a while.

It was one of those days, and I was in bed watching some television show when I got a phone call from Whitey to tell me that he was at the Swing House jamming with some dudes, and that I should come down and jam with them. But I was feeling all depressed and I wasn't really in the mood. So I told him, "Nah man, I'm in my PJs, and I'm watching Jerry Springer," or something stupid like that. And I didn't go down there. Then a little time passes, and he calls again, and he tells me again that he's down there with a bunch of guys that want to jam with me. And I was like, "Yeah, but I don't want to jam with them."

Eventually, I get a phone call from some other guy, and he's telling me that he's Iggy Pop's son and tour manager, that Iggy Pop is down in the studio with Whitey, and he wants to jam with me. So I should come down. I thought it was a prank. I was like, "No, I'm in my PJs, and I'm watching TV. And my bass has dust on it. It's not happening." I was starting to get really annoyed at this point, too.

Finally, I got another phone call, and it was Iggy. I recognized his voice right away. He said, "Hey Nadja, this is Iggy. I hear a lot of good things about you. I'm down here at the studio, and I'd like to jam with you. If you can be down here in fifteen minutes, great. If not, then fuck it." And that was it. Then we hung up the phone, and it dawned on me that it was him. And I basically shit my pants. I was like, "Holy fuck! That was Iggy Pop that just called me. I better get down there. Even though I don't know what the hell I'm doing..."

So I grabbed my dusty bass, and I went down there, and I heard them jamming when I arrived. I love Iggy Pop and The Stooges so much, so to play with him was a huge deal for me. I went in the studio, and I saw Whitey and a couple of guys that looked just like Whitey, and it turned out they were his brothers—it was a whole band of brothers. And there was Iggy Pop. One of the brothers gave me a bass, and I ended up jamming with them for a couple of hours. It was all songs that they were trying to write for a new album, and I didn't really know what they or I was doing, but it was really, *really* cool.

MATT: When he's practicing, is he shimmering around like a snake like he does on stage? What's practice room Iggy like?

NADJA: Practice room Iggy. That's funny. I mean, he was moving around a little bit, but he wasn't going crazy and rubbing peanut butter on himself or crawling around on the floor or anything like that. That did not happen. He was composed: he was singing; he was moving a bit; he was feeling certain parts. And we jammed for a couple of hours, and then I went home. I didn't play with him again after that. I ran into him on the street once, and he asked me if I was still practicing. But I wasn't going to lie to Iggy Pop. So I said, "No. I'm still in my PJs watching shitty TV." And that was it. I haven't seen him since. But that was a really cool, unexpected experience.

MATT: Was it a life highlight for you?

NADJA: Absolutely. It was definitely a dream come true. And he was so cool. I never wanted to meet him before. And I had the chance to meet him prior to that day at shows with Whitey. But I was always like, "Nope, because if the guy's a dick then I could never listen to the music the same way, so I just don't even want to meet him." But I did, and he was totally the real deal.

MATT: I met him once for about two seconds backstage at an Eagles of Death Metal show. He thought I was in the support band as we passed each other in the corridor. He was like, "Sorry, I didn't mean to interrupt you before you're about to go on stage." He was so cool. Then Josh Homme came along and pushed me to the side. He was like, "Don't worry about him, he's not in a band." And he totally mugged me off. But Iggy was the perfect gentleman.

NADJA: To me, he's the real deal, not just in music but also in person.

WALTER SCHREIFELS—*GORLLIA BISCUITS, YOUTH OF TODAY, QUICKSAND, RIVAL SCHOOLS*

MATT: Who were your main influences when you started Quicksand?

WALTER: Initially, we were definitely knocked out by Jane's Addiction. They were the one. They were a band that were rocking and doing something like The Doors or Led Zeppelin.

MATT: But then also like The Cure and Joy Division.

WALTER: Exactly. They were checking off so many cool different angles. They were the coolest band ever. Fugazi were also a massive influence. They were only just starting out at that point, but they were already leading the way.

MATT: I guess Ian MacKaye showed everyone that you could have one era defining band with Minor Threat, then go and start another that's totally different and equally inspiring.

WALTER: Yeah, and that gave us a blueprint. Jane's Addiction were from California, and they were magical, and we had no idea how the hell they figured it out. But Fugazi were bringing dance elements into their music, and this open guitar feeling where it could afford to be a little sloppier and atonal in some ways. I also loved Slayer at that time, too. I thought they were really cool. So I'd say there was an element of those three bands in Quicksand early on.

MATT: So you mixed the heaviness of Slayer with the magic of Jane's Addiction and the experimentation of Fugazi?

WALTER: Yeah, which is a really weird combination. But I think if you listen to Quicksand with that in mind, then you might take some of those pieces away from it. Also that might have been our idea, but what came out in the end was just what it is.

TOM MORELLO—*RAGE AGAINST THE MACHINE, AUDIOSLAVE, PROPHETS OF RAGE, THE NIGHTWATCHMAN*

TOM: I used to sneak into Jane's Addiction rehearsals to sit on the floor and watch them play. They really had it together. Them and Soundgarden—although Jane's was ours because they were from LA—were the two groups that redeemed hard rock music. They made it okay to be intelligent and trade in nuanced poetry, while being absolutely, uncompromisingly metal. And those two worlds rarely came together; if you were smart, you had to like new wave and punk, and if you were into metal then you had to like the devil. But those two bands dispensed with all of that in a way that was a real revelation.

MATT: Jane's must've been so dangerous and exciting back then.

TOM: Absolutely. They were my favorite band; they were like the punk rock Led Zeppelin.

MATT: They were like the Led Zeppelin of the nineties, weren't they?

TOM: Exactly. They'd have these long, beautiful acoustic sets with Perry's unique, almost child-like voice, twisted melodies, and really penetrating poetry, mixed with those big fat riffs. It was potent stuff.

JOHN FELDMANN—*GOLDFINGER, PRODUCER, SONGWRITER, A&R EXECUTIVE*

MATT: I guess a lot of people who know you for either your production work or for Goldfinger, don't know, perhaps, about the band that got it all started in terms of your professional career in music: the Electric Love Hogs.

JOHN: Yeah.

MATT: That band formed around the time as the Red Hot Chili Peppers, Jane's Addiction, and Fishbone, when the LA alternative rock scene was exploding. And you were right there as it was all kicking off.

JOHN: I moved to LA right in the middle of all that, yeah. I met Maynard [James Keenan] from Tool the day he got off the airplane; I used to work at this clothing store where he'd come visit me every day, and we would just talk about music. The Electric Love Hogs kind of bridged the gap between Fishbone and where Rage Against the Machine was headed. I was really influenced by *The Uplift Mofo Party Plan* album by the Red Hot Chili Peppers, too.

MATT: Was that the album that George Clinton produced?

JOHN: No, that was the one before it [*Freaky Styley*]. Michael Beinhorn produced *The Uplift Mofo Party Plan*, and that album sounded so good. I just couldn't get over the bass playing on it, I'd never heard anything like it. I've never been a Brendon Urie; I've never been able to sing like Freddie Mercury; I don't have the mechanics to be that kind of singer. And when I listened to Anthony Kiedis, I was like, "He's not Freddie Mercury either. So maybe I can do this—just kind of jump around a lot and people won't notice that I don't have the greatest voice."

I saw the Chili Peppers play so many times back then, and Anthony would do backflip after backflip on stage, and do cannonballs into the crowd. I was like, "This is the greatest show I've ever seen." And Fishbone as well. Angelo [Moore] would literally walk across the crowd and dance over people's heads. They blew me away with the live show, and that's when I realized the live show was equally as important as the music. And the Electric Love Hogs had terrible music. I still can't listen to that fucking album [*Electric Love Hogs*].

MATT: Didn't Tommy Lee produce it?

JOHN: Tommy produced some of it. And at that time Mötley Crüe were the biggest band in the world.

MATT: How did he get switched on to you guys?

JOHN: He saw us play at some club, and he was like, "Dude, I have to fucking work with this band," because we were so energetic live. We had a huge following in LA before we got signed, too. And Tommy came up to us and said, "You have to at least let me produce a couple of songs." So he took us to his house when he was married to Heather Locklear, and he'd get on his back and light his farts on fire. He was just the greatest dude and the funniest fucking guy I'd ever met. He's still to this day one of the best drummers ever, in my opinion. I remember the Love Hogs played this one show, and he came out and we played "Shout at the Devil" by Mötley Crüe with him. Our drummer [Bobby Hewitt] was good, but Tommy was so solid in his timing and the way he hit every drum, it was like, "This is how you're supposed to play."

Tommy's influence on me definitely brought out the metal in my vocals, and he would always encourage me to sing like Vince Neil. So there's definitely a Mötley Crüe element to that record. And it's not like I don't like Mötley Crüe. They wrote fucking great songs. But we had five dudes who all thought they were songwriters in the band, so there'd be all these tempo changes and about four different guitar solos in every song, so the album wasn't ever what I would've imagined an album that I was going to make would be. But I learned a lot from that process, like how to be a producer from the way that Tommy treated us. He was a part of the band, and he made us all laugh when shit was stressful. There was another producer named Mark Dodson involved in the process, too.

MATT: I know Mark very well.

JOHN: Oh, you do?

MATT: Yeah. He worked with Ugly Kid Joe, Anthrax, and Suicidal Tendencies.

JOHN: That's right. And we chose to work with him because he did Infectious Grooves, which was one of our biggest influences. I love Mike Muir; he was a huge influence on me. And Mark was a great, laid back, amazing engineer that got the best sounds ever. But my guess would be if he was going to list some of the hardest moments of his life, working with me would probably be in the top five.

MATT: Why so?

JOHN: I would have lists of different effects and delays and how I would want these different stereo choruses on the guitars and flangers over the drums. I'd literally have a list of about sixty things to add into the production; I was a proper little producer in training. I remember one day Mark wouldn't even let me in the studio. I want to say he was probably smoking about a carton of cigarettes a day while trying to work with me, because I was so focused on what I wanted the music to sound like.

MATT: In that group you also had Bobby Hewitt, who went on to form Orgy, and Dave Kushner, who played in Velvet Revolver. You also had Stephen Perkins from Jane's Addiction and John Norwood from Fishbone play on the record. And Tommy Lee producing it. What a lineup! You also took out a lot of bands who went on to become gargantuan, like Tool and Rage Against the Machine. What's your memories of those bands back then? Was the writing always on the wall?

JOHN: I saw Rage Against the Machine play in front of four people at this place called The Coconut Teaser before we took them on tour. Zack [de la Rocha] was already in Inside Out, so he had already established himself as kind of a legendary front man. And when I first saw Rage there was no question they were going to be huge. I saw them open for Body Count about three weeks later, right before we took them on tour, and it was a sold-out show at The Palace. Everybody was jumping, and I was like, "Fuck! This is it! This is going to be the next big band." So with Rage there was no question. But with Tool, Maynard would always have his back to the audience, he had a rattail ponytail in his hair, and he was such a unique personality, I would never have bet that Tool would become such a seminal act.

But yeah, we took Rage and Tool out on their first tours. Pearl Jam opened for us, too. We had all these now legendary groups open for us, and that was because we were so big in LA at the time because our live show was so intense. We basically had five front men in the band, which you can now see because we all started bands afterward, and we all went on to do kind of big things. But in the Love Hogs we were always fighting with each other, and that's why it never would've worked.

LOU KOLLER—*SICK OF IT ALL*

MATT: Didn't Sick of It All take Korn out on tour back in the day?

LOU: Yeah. I think they did a Biohazard tour before that as well. When we met them, they were very apprehensive. I remember the first show was in Georgia, and they were all sitting at the bar eating. I got my food, and I went and sat with them, like, "What's up guys?" And they were all just like, "Hey." But as the tour went on, we became more friendly, and it was cool.

A few years later, in 1997, we were doing the Warped Tour, and we were playing in Philly. Korn was also in town playing Lollapalooza. We were having a great show and out of the corner of my eyes I saw two guys with dreadlocks rocking out on the side of the stage. I thought they were just some Warped Tour dirt asses coming up on stage. But as we were walking off stage, I realized it was Munky [James Shaffer] and Head [Brian Welch] from Korn. They were like, "Yo! What's up?" And they started hugging me. I said, "What the fuck are you guys doing here? I thought you were playing Lollapalooza?" They said, "We had the day off, and we told them we had to come here and see you guys."

Fast-forward a few more years, and we're playing some huge festival in Belgium. We were headlining the second stage, and Korn was the main headline act. And they had this artist area. Security came through and said, "Korn is coming through to their dressing room. Everybody has to go into their cabins." We were like, "That's some rock star bullshit." So we all got in our room. Then all of a sudden, we heard the door knock. We opened the door and all the guys from Korn were there; instead of going to their room, they came and said hello to us. They were like, "Yeah, we're lifers you and us. That's how it is. You guys treated us so good."

We didn't treat them special or anything like that. We were just nice to them. But they told us horror stories, even from Biohazard, who weren't that big at the time. Apparently the bassist and the lead singer in Biohazard treated them like dicks. They treated them like shit. They even said to Biohazard, "You would've been on the Family Values Tour, but your bass player was a fucking dick." That's why we were always nice to people, because you never know.

MATT: It's not rocket science either—treat people as you would want to be treated.

LOU: Exactly. We've never been treated like shit by another band. But we've had roadies and guitar techs of metal bands that we've toured with behave like absolute assholes toward us. The first time we played with Slayer, Pete and I were all over the place. We were running up on stacks, on the monitors—everything. Then the next night, we get ready to go out on stage, and there's all this fucking red tape everywhere. And the guy was like, "You can't cross these lines." Pete was like, "Fuck that. You can throw me off the tour." And we just did our regular show. Then this guy threw a hissy fit. He had the manager come and yell at us, and I was like, "I'll fucking go home right now. I don't give a shit. But Tom Araya asked us to do the tour. Not you. And not the fucking guitar tech." After that, everything was cool. So I guess Tom spoke to the manager and told him to let us do what we wanted.

MATT: There's nothing worse than bullshit egos when you're out on tour.

LOU: Right. I remember we were out on tour with Sepultura once, and three days into the tour, us and Napalm Death were sharing a bus and a sound man, and our sound man was like, "Sepultura's sound guy keeps coming up in the middle of your sets to make me pull it down." Igor Cavalera happened to be standing in the door, and he goes, "Really? Well, you just do what you want to do tonight." So we were playing, and we were told later on that Sepultura's sound guy came up and said, "Turn it down." Then he got a tap on the shoulder from Igor, who was like, "No, no, no. Let him fucking do what he wants. We're not afraid of anybody. We want someone who's going to force us to play better on before us." And that's something that we learned from them.

In the early nineties, there was this new wave of hardcore that was coming in with bands like Snapcase, Earth Crisis, and Strife, who were more metallic and groove orientated. And they were the bands that people would go off to. We were like, "Fuck it. We're taking Snapcase out." So we did. And every night it made us push ourselves that much harder.

BEN OSMUNDSON—*ZEBRAHEAD*

BEN: The punk rock scene is like a big family; everyone helps each other, and it's not a competition. When you play with a lot of the same bands all over the world, if you treat people badly then karma is going to get you. I don't know if karma is real per say, but if you treat people badly then life is going to shit on you in return. You might get away with it for a while, but eventually it's going to catch up on your ass.

MATT: Have you ever shit on anyone and had it come back to you? Be honest.

BEN: I'm sure I have. I'm going through a divorce right now, so I'm feeling like I must've shit on somebody really bad.

MATT: Who's been the biggest piece of shit to you?

BEN: I would have to say my soon-to-be-ex-wife. That's a no brainer.

MATT: What about in the music business?

BEN: We've been really lucky. We've done shows with bigger bands like Blink-182 and Green Day, and they've all been very respectful and great to us. I can't complain one bit. We tour a lot with Less Than Jake and Reel Big Fish, as well, and they always strike their drums for us. And we would never not strike our drums for a local opening band because we want them to have a good show.

MATT: I feel like that's a distinctly punk rock attitude.

BEN: Yeah. You need to make room for everyone to have a good show, and that's one thing I've noticed they don't do so much in the metal world.

MATT: I love the way punk and ska bands watch each other's sets as well.

BEN: Yeah, I'm feeling guilty that you and I aren't watching Reel Big Fish right now.

MATT: I've been touring with Reel Big Fish for a while now, and I've seen them play seventeen times in the last year, so I feel okay about not seeing them right now.

BEN: That's fair enough. And this is nice: we have Jimmy Eat World serenading us off in the distance. If you had a table and some flowers, this would be a great place to bring a girl for a date.

KEITH BUCKLEY—*EVERY TIME I DIE, THE DAMNED THINGS, AUTHOR*

MATT: Didn't Every Time I Die play some shows with Steve-O from *Jackass* back in the day?

KEITH: Yeah, the Steve-O thing was random. I don't know how it came about because we didn't have a manager, but somehow we got a call to say that someone in the *Jackass* camp liked our demo. We were like, "What the fuck are you talking about?" So we went and opened for the *Jackass* live show, which involved Steve-O, Ryan Dunn, Preston Lacy, and Wee Man. Our thinking was, if nothing else at least we'll get to hang out backstage with these fucking maniacs that we've watched on TV. And whether you admit to it or not, if you were a teenager growing up in America at that time, *Jackass* influenced your life. It diverted your thoughts toward a much more depraved universe than you would've ever dreamed of going before.

MATT: And it combined all these worlds of skateboarding, BMXing, punk rock, and hip-hop.

KEITH: Yeah.

MATT: It was a cultural phenomenon.

KEITH: It did for skateboarding what Nine Inch Nails did for strange music, in that it made it okay all of a sudden. When *Jackass* hit, you realized that if you were a little skater punk doing stupid shit with your friends, you didn't have to change in order to make it. So people stopped adjusting who they were and just emphasized who they were. And when *Jackass* came out it was hugely influential to me, since I was a skateboarding kid with a bunch of idiot friends. We'd go into the woods with a machete and spend three days chopping down a tree. Then we'd drink beer and have a bonfire. So when the chance came up to play with them, I was like, "We have to fucking do this. I don't know what it's going to entail, but we have to be there, if nothing else just to meet the *Jackass* guys." So we went and we played.

MATT: How was the show?

KEITH: The show was fucking terrible. It was like Slayer fans but in a different world, in that they didn't want to see anything but *Jackasss*. They didn't give a fuck about music. I don't even know why they had a band opening; those people did not care about music. They just

Alan Robert from Life of Agony and actor Frank Vincent (*Raging Bull, Goodfellas, Casino, and The Sopranos*). The pair worked together on Robert's comic book series, Killogy.

Photo courtesy of Alan Robert's personal archives

Zebrahead bassist Ben Osmundson and I at Slam Dunk festival in 2016. This was the first time w̶ shared the stage together. We'd go on to become regular touring buddies and good friends.

Photo by Jodie Cunningham

Me dressed as the legendary lounge singer Tony Clifton with Chris DeMakes from Less Th̶ Jake. This is another photo by Jodie Cunningham, taken when I was on tour with Less Than Jake, Reel Big Fish, and Zebrahead in 2018.

Here I am with the hero's hero Perry Farrell outside the Karma Sanctum Hotel in Soho, shortly after interviewing him for *Life In The Stocks* in 2019. This is one of my favorite photos ever.

Photo by the legendary Gobinder Jhitta

1 wanted the best, you got the best! The hottest band in the world: KISS! The illustrious Gene Simmons and myself shortly before Kiss played the O2 Arena in London on May 31, 2017.

Photo by Sandra Sorensen

The first of two photos from the Kerrang! Radio days, circa 2011–2013. This photo is from the Kerrang! Awards in 2011, when Hyro The Hero and I presented Jared Leto from Thirty Seconds to Mars with the award for Best Single. I remember Jared Leto being very short.

From the K! Radio vault of me with old Boots Electric, a.k.a. Jesse Hughes from Eagles of De Metal. This was taken during Jesse's visit to the station on March 9, 2012. I remember the da because it was a couple of days before my birthday. As you can see, it was love at first sight

The Bouncing Souls THEN: Warped Tour, New Jersey, 2004. This must've been toward the end of the tour when the insanity and exhaustion was kicking in.

Photo by Jana Crawford O'Brien

e Bouncing Souls NOW: Brooklyn Steel, New York City, December 20, 2019. The last date of r thirtieth anniversary tour, and the last show they played before "you know what" happened.

Photo by Josh Casuccio

Joby Ford and Matt Caughthran from The Bronx pictured at the Berlin Wall some time back in the early 2000s.

A young Joby Ford and Matt Caughthran from The Bronx, feeding each other alcohol at the notorious Columbia Hotel in London. Year unknown. Photographer unknown. Basically, the less known the better.

Joey Castillo pounding the shit out of his drum kit. He's an out-of-this-world drummer and the finest human being you could ever hope to meet.

Photo courtesy of Joey Castillo's personal archives

Circle Jerks circa 2021. Joey Castillo is on the far right. Greg Hetson is seen sporting the Creem T-shirt. Also pictured is Zander Schloss and Keith Morris.

Photo by Atiba Jefferson

Dave Fortman and Amy Lee from Evanescence. Taken during the recording sessions for the band's debut album *Fallen* in 2003. That record has since gone on to be certified platinum seven times.

Photo courtesy of Dave Fortman's personal archives

The late Joey Jordison. Photographed by Dean Karr in the lead up to the release of Slipknot's debut self-titled album in 1999. Dean also shot the cover for the first record, and the cover for *Iowa* in 2001.

The one and only Tommy Lee from Mötley Crüe. This classic Dean Karr portrait was used for the cover of Tommy's autobiography *Tommyland* in 2005. This is the original photo.

Kevin Kerslake shooting the Nirvana "Come as You Are" music video
with Kurt Cobain, Dave Grohl, and Krist Novoselic.

Photo by Line Postmyr

Another behind-the-scenes shot from the "Come as You Are" music video.
Here, Kerslake is filming Kurt playing guitar for projections on the wall of the set.

Photo by Kevin's producer Line Postmyr

These three photos are from behind-the-scenes of Nirvana's "In Bloom" music video shoot. I can't thank Kevin enough for giving me them to share here.

Photos by Line Postmyr

AN EVENING WITH

KEITH BUCKLEY

(EVERY TIME I DIE)

HOSTED BY MATT STOCKS

INTERVIEW // AUDIENCE Q&A // MEET & GREET

SUNDAY 14TH JULY 2019
O₂ ACADEMY ISLINGTON, LONDON

TICKETMASTER.CO.UK

The poster for my first Live Q&A event with Keith Buckley from Every Time I Die. I didn't know it at the time, but this show would directly lead to me signing a book deal with Rare Bird. I've said it before, but I'll say it again: Cheers to you, Keith Buckley.

LIFE IN THE STOCKS & ACADEMY EVENTS PRESENT

AN EVENING WITH
JESSE LEACH
(KILLSWITCH ENGAGE)

HOSTED BY
MATT STOCKS

IN-DEPTH
INTERVIEW
STORIES BEHIND
THE SONGS
AUDIENCE Q&A
MEET & GREET

WEDNESDAY 8TH AUGUST 2018
O₂ ACADEMY2 BIRMINGHAM
TICKETMASTER.CO.UK

he poster for my first Live Q&A event with Jesse Leach from Killswitch Engage. Again, I didn't
now it at the time, but this show would eventually lead to the second podcast that I now host
with Jesse: *Stoke The Fire*. I've done well out of these two "Evening with" gigs, haven't I?

The illustrious Vinnie Stigma from Agnostic Front, photographed by me at the
Kentish Town Forum in London on January 26, 2020.

The inimitable Walter Schreifels of Gorilla Biscuits and a thousand other bands, photographed
by me at the Kentish Town Forum in London on January 26, 2020.

The delectable but deadly Nadja Peulen of Coal Chamber fame, photographed in her natural habitat looking like an absolute bad ass as always.

Photo courtesy of Nadja's personal archives

This is the infamous polaroid photo that Dean talks about in the book, of when he, Casey Chaos, and Ross Robinson spent the night in jail in Las Vegas. Thanks to Dean for letting me publish it in the book. I would've loved to have been a fly on the wall that night.

I have no idea what's going on here, but it could only have come from the deranged minds of Casey Chaos and Dean Karr—two of the craziest, most creative people I know.

Photo by Dean Karr

wanted to see a dude put a staple gun to his scrotum, and that was it. So we were young kids trying to play our songs that nobody was paying attention to, and after our twenty minute set I headed wide-eyed backstage to go meet the *Jackass* guys.

I went into the dressing room and Steve-O was just berating the other guys about the bad cocaine that he had. He said he wanted different cocaine, and that they had to go and get it for him now. I had an idea in my head of who these guys were and how they were changing pop culture, and how it must've been a brilliant meticulous formula that they'd figured out and they knew exactly what they were doing. After seeing what degenerates these guys were, I realized that nobody knows what the fuck they're doing—ever. You really don't want to meet your heroes in that way. If that was something I momentarily aspired to be, I didn't aspire to be it anymore. And that's okay.

The same thing happened to me at Ozzfest years later, where I'd see things happening backstage and the way that arrogance and ego affects bands and informs their personal relationships, and I decided then and there that I didn't want to be the kind of band that would ever get asked to do an Ozzfest again. Those kind of things make me lose a little faith in idols, but also reaffirm who I think I am.

JESSE MALIN—*HEART ATTACK, D GENERATION, SOLO ARTIST*

MATT: How did the Californian and the Washington, DC, hardcore bands influence what was going on in New York? Because you were right there on the front line for the birth of that whole scene. What are your memories of that time?

JESSE: The Bad Brains were from DC, and I saw them play in New York to about ten to twenty people. We were also getting fanzines like *Damage*, *Slash*, and *Flipside* from California, and seeing little blips of what was going on out there. But you weren't really looking for things because everyone was saying that it was over and that punk rock was dead. The Dead Boys had broken up, Johnny Thunders was half dead, and Blondie was playing pop music. So it was kind of a weird time.

The New Romantic thing was happening and people were dressing up like pirates and Peter Pan. And rockabilly was in again. But for us kids, we wanted raw music that was driven, so we'd buy records from the UK by bands like Cockney Rejects, The Exploited, and U.K. Subs. And they would hold us over. The Damned kept going too, but even they were changing with their albums *The Black Album* and *Strawberries*.

In California, the Dead Kennedys were like a bridge band because they had a punk kind of thing going, but then they also had that fast stuff, and some songs on *Fresh Fruit [for Rotting Vegetables]* that really move. Then the Circle Jerks record [*Group Sex*] came out, and the Black Flag record [*Damaged*], and we were getting that stuff from California. I loved the Germs record [*(GI)*], too. All of that stuff walked that line between punk rock and that next sound of hardcore. And after seeing the Bad Brains we wanted speed, so we'd listen to our Ramones records on the faster speed. My friend Jack Flanagan from the band The Mob would do that, and I got hooked on it as well. So all of that was brewing, and it affected my writing.

I first met the guys from DC at the Black Flag/Mission of Burma gig, which was a famous gig in New York at the Peppermint Lounge. Those DC kids—Henry [Rollins] and Ian [MacKaye]—had been out west on The Teen Idles tour. They'd seen the Huntington Beach kids and the Circle Jerks, and they'd brought a lot of that back to the east coast. I think they'd tell you that. So we were at this Black Flag/Mission of Burma double bill and there were all these people skanking—guys like Mojo and Harley Flanagan. Then suddenly all these guys from DC started doing that creepy crawl thing, and they wrecked almost everybody on the dance floor at the Peppermint Lounge. They got down low and were really getting into that other kind of thing. It was pretty wild.

Then you had moshing and what people now know as the mosh pit. And they have those barriers in front of the stage whenever you play a show, because "there's going to be moshing." I don't know who put that word out there more internationally, maybe the band Anthrax, but everybody says it now—even people's grandmothers say, "Is there a mosh pit?" But I think where that word first came from, from my recollection, was the Bad Brains. They used to bring all this reggae music to us white youth in New York and HR would say stuff like, "Mash down, Babylon. Mash down." And I think it was misinterpreted by some kids from Queens—The Mob guys like Jack Flanagan. And they started saying, "Mosh it up, man. Mosh it up." So it's funny how it then became this word as we now know it for a dance style all over the world.

Me and a bunch of friends from DC and Chicago went on TV to show the world that style of dancing on *Saturday Night Live* with FEAR, and that was pretty funny. I was in junior high school, and my teacher said, "I know where you were this weekend." And I was like, "How did this guy see that?" But thinking back now, a guy in his forties was probably home on a Saturday night in Queens watching *SNL*, and the next thing he knows he sees my leather jacket jumping off the stage. But it's all about expression. I think that whole hardcore scene was a lot of fun until it got really macho and metal, and that's kind of when I stepped aside in around 1984. I still go back to those records from time to time, though. And we really learned a lot about creating and doing stuff without any support, just helping each other. It's that whole DIY mentality.

DENNIS LYXZÉN—REFUSED, THE (INTERNATIONAL) NOISE CONSPIRACY, INVSN, FAKE NAMES

MATT: Were the British punk bands like The Damned, the Sex Pistols, and The Clash important to you growing up? Or were you more influenced by American hardcore?

DENNIS: I was definitely influenced more by the American hardcore. *The Troops of Tomorrow* by The Exploited was one of the first punk records that I bought, but then I got way more into bands like Minor Threat, Dead Kennedys, Black Flag, and Bad Brains. I remember being sixteen and hearing Sex Pistols for the first time, and I thought they were too slow.

MATT: I guess if you'd already heard bands like the Bad Brains first, the Sex Pistols probably just sounded like old fifties rock 'n' roll.

DENNIS: Yeah, but then you grow, and your tastes evolve. I've been in love with the seventies UK punk bands for a long time now. But when I was a young kid during my formative years, American hardcore was definitely something that appealed to me way more.

MATT: Was it the sound, or the message, or a bit of both?

DENNIS: It was a bit of everything. You're impressionable when you're young, and after I got into Youth of Today, I was straight edge all of a sudden. It was the same with the Dead Kennedys; their music was amazing, but then you had the booklets with all the politics in. My mind was blown. Later on, I got into The Damned and the Sex Pistols, and The Clash became a huge band in my life, but during the formative years it was all bands like DRI, Agnostic Front, Youth of Today, and Negative Approach.

MATT: How important was punk to you as an ideological framework to sustain your personal views and creative endeavors?

DENNIS: To this day, it's probably the most important thing that happened in my life. It affected everything that I am and everything that I do, and everything that I thought I knew about the world. It was massively important. When you're young, you have the whole trajectory of your life and where you're supposed to go laid out in front of you, and punk changed everything for me. I've always thought about punk as this idea that anything is possible. And it changed everything for me: the way I talk, the way I dress—everything.

MATT: Who were the thinkers that switched you on to a lot of the themes and ideas that've defined your creative body of work? Were they all musicians? Or were authors, writers, philosophers, and activists inspiring you as well?

DENNIS: It all started with music and the idea that music was a platform for you to speak out against injustice. But one of the first writers that I really got into was Noam Chomsky. After reading some of his stuff, I was like, "Wow! It's insane how everything ties in together." So Chomsky was definitely the first writer who opened my eyes to a bigger political picture. And from a very young age, I started hanging around with the local Anarchist Youth Group. But that wasn't so educational—it was more nihilistic, to be honest.

Later on, I studied [Karl] Marx, [Mikhail] Bakunin, [Peter] Kropotkin, Emma Goldman, and those famous anarchist writers, and I went all the way through to the Situationist International movement in France, with Guy Debord and Raoul Vaneigem. I've read it all, to be honest. I didn't have much of an education, and I kind of dropped out of school, so when I discovered politics I really made an effort to learn as much as possible. I actually had a couple of years during the late nineties and early 2000s where I studied political science at home. I had stacks of books by political thinkers by the edge of my bed, and I'd read them for at least two hours every day. Books by [Michel] Foucault—

MATT: I read a lot of Foucault at university.

DENNIS: I did it voluntarily because I wanted to learn about these things myself, which was a very interesting journey. And I think that's the cool thing about punk—at first it's like a gut reaction to the world.

MATT: It's purely visceral and emotional.

DENNIS: Purely visceral and purely emotional. You get the feeling that something is wrong, so you speak out against it even though you're perhaps a little uninformed.

MATT: But you're passionate about it.

DENNIS: Passionate and also very honest. But one of the things that happened to me is I would be doing interviews, and every once in a while someone would come up to me and challenge me for real. And there was a lot of things that I didn't have the answers to because I was running on pure emotion. That's why I started studying; I knew if I was going to be this guy that was going to devote my life to talking about politics, I really had to know what I was talking about.

I still read a lot of political theory to this day, so I know what's going on in the world, and when people challenge me now, I have an answer and a clearer idea of what I actually want to say. A lot of our music is very slogan-driven because we want something for people to sing along to. But behind the slogans there's been hours and hours of discussions about these topics, and hours of rewrites so that our lyrics fit the verse-chorus-verse trajectory.

GREG ATTONITO—*THE BOUNCING SOULS*

MATT: A big part of The Bouncing Souls' identity is the huge anthemic choruses, which are at the center of all the most beloved Bouncing Souls songs. Where did you guys draw inspiration from early on when developing that side of your sound?

GREG: We were really inspired by the British soccer chants. Those chants are so passionately sung by so many people. And that's powerful. I also saw Bruce Springsteen at Giants Stadium in New Jersey in 1984, on the *Born in the U.S.A.* tour, and he did ten nights in a row to sixty thousand people.

MATT: Sixty thousand people per night?

GREG: Per night. That was at the height of his fame and power. And he did this thing when he played the song "Hungry Heart," where as soon as the verse started, he didn't sing it—sixty thousand people sung it for him. That was a transformational musical experience for me.

MATT: How old were you at the time?

GREG: I think I was fourteen.

MATT: The exact right age to be experiencing something like that and having it light a fire inside you.

GREG: It was as mind-blowing as mind-blowing gets. And a few years later when The Bouncing Souls started playing together, the idea of inspiring the crowd to sing along was automatic. That was always the carrot that we were chasing as songwriters.

MATT: I think that's what makes music so special, if you want to go down that road: it can be a spiritual experience. You're gathered together in a large group, you're all on the same emotional plane, and everyone's exercising whatever shit they've got going on in their lives, and just soaking up the moment.

GREG: That's it. And doing that breaks away the disconnect that we all feel in the world from time-to-time. That was something that me, Pete, and Bryan bonded over very early on. Along with the other guys who've been in the band over the years, that's always been our main focus—to attack that.

MATT: And go full Springsteen!

GREG: Exactly.

MATT: How important is New Jersey to the DNA of The Bouncing Souls?

GREG: Pretty important. People ask me about this quite a bit, and it's one of those unexplainable things. I think where you come from is just a part of you in the way that you see things, how you speak, and your perspective on the world. And that's the same for everyone. There's definitely a sense of pride that comes with being from New Jersey though, because of New York and all the crap that New Jersey gets from New Yorkers.

MATT: Like an underdog spirit?

GREG: That's right. And on top of that, when we were coming up all the West Coast bands were becoming really popular. That's where the song "East Coast Fuck You" came from.

MATT: Assumedly, a lot of those Southern Californian bands understood what you were saying with that song, and they enjoyed it?

GREG: All of them did. Fletcher [Dragge] from Pennywise loved it. So did Bill Stevenson [Descendents]. He was like, "Nobody writes songs like that anymore." He was stoked on that song, which was amazing.

MATT: I had Steven Van Zandt on the show a while back, and he talked a lot about the New Jersey sound. Obviously you're a lot younger than him, but was that scene still impacting the local music circuit when you were coming up? Was that bar band thing still a part of it?

GREG: I think those guys lived in a different era, and it died out a bit because the world was changing. I just read an article on the history of The Stone Pony in Asbury Park, and it goes into great detail about that whole scene, which he may have talked about on your podcast.

MATT: He did.

GREG: About how they brokered a deal with The Stone Pony to play original music on a Tuesday night.

MATT: Because that wasn't the done thing at that time—they wanted Top 40 hits.

GREG: All covers, yeah. They wouldn't even let bands play original music back then. Now, by the time we started playing shows a lot of those old venues had gone. We had to rent out halls and do all-ages shows. But the vibe and the inspiration of those New Jersey bar bands was still there, so we were definitely inspired by all that music and the fact that they came right where we came from. That was enough.

KEITH BUCKLEY—*EVERY TIME I DIE, THE DAMNED THINGS, AUTHOR*

MATT: I want to talk to you about Buffalo. How has the cultural character and qualities that you associate with that city fed into your psychological makeup as both a songwriter and a human being?

KEITH: Buffalo is a very depressing place, as anybody who's been there can attest to. But there's also, when you get to the heart of it, this incredibly unique sense of desperate hope that lingers in the air. And there's really nothing to grasp onto as far as proof that anyone should be hopeful, except this weird primitive drive just to stay alive and support your family and friends. It's the kind of town where, if you're born there, then you're usually going to die there—people rarely make it out. And if they do make it out, they always come back. It's a black hole. But the people there are so accepting of who they are that you can't help but admire it. And it's a strange sort of dichotomy because when you think of people accepting who they are, especially when they're miserable alcoholics that come from dysfunctional families and are working terrible jobs, that acceptance seems like another way of giving up. And you start to think, "That's just because you're fucking lazy, or you don't believe in yourself enough." But people in Buffalo have really accepted it in a Zen-like way, like, "This is who we are. We're a city that's defined by loss."

It sounds funny, but when you're a kid growing up there, that shapes you. The Buffalo Bills lost four Super Bowls in a row. That shows you can invest everything that you have into something and will it to happen every minute of every day, as people who are Bills fans do, yet it often doesn't come to fruition because the universe is cruel and indifferent. What that does is it builds you into someone who accepts loss and doesn't necessarily see that as failure. Athletes are heroes in a sports town: they're bigger than God. And when you see them constantly disappointed and embarrassed, and you see them crying, there's really nothing left to believe in except yourself, so you do that in a non-narcissistic way. You put your head down and work because the process of work in itself is something to be proud of. And you enjoy the simple pleasures in life.

As dysfunctional as it sounds, a simple pleasure in Buffalo is going to the bar. The city was built on a steel plant called Bethlehem Steel, which closed down a few decades ago, so the city went under and lost everything. People who had been doing the jobs that their grandfathers had done lost their jobs—they lost everything. But they kept the bars open later for them. And everyone was like, "Fuck it! I guess I'll get drunk," because you always find a way to drink. So that sort of despondency juxtaposed against this weird, undefinable hope is a really unique push-pull situation that I see a lot of in this city. And it's a little depressing to talk to those people sometimes, but they're still romantic and idealistic, and they still buy Bills season passes. They're just not going to give up. That's something that I really felt needed to be explored and the music that I write is built from that. Buffalo took to the marble stone of this band [Every Time I Die] and really chiseled something out of it. We're absolutely a product of it.

LOU KOLLER—*SICK OF IT ALL*

MATT: How did Toby Morse from H20 wind up being your roadie back in the day?

LOU: Toby was a friend of ours who lived in a house with some of the guys from Gorilla Biscuits. He actually lived in the closest because he couldn't afford rent on a room. The first big tour that we did on our own was in '93, and we jokingly called it the Urban Retreat Tour because we took our friends who never left New York City along with us. So we took Toby out with us. And we didn't take him out because we thought he was a good roadie. We took him out because we thought it was funny.

Toby had to be one of the worst roadies ever. He tried—he busted his ass. But he had to be one of the worst roadies ever. Toby was in charge of breaking down the drums, and Armand [Majidi] and I would be walking out of the venue after the show, and I'd be like, "Armand, is that your hi-hat stand still on the stage? How could you miss that?" So we'd all get in the van and sit there and wait for Toby to come in, then say, "Have you got everything, Toby?" And Toby would be like, "Yeah, I put it all away." "Are you sure?" "Yeah, I got everything." "Why don't you go back in there and look at the stage?" "What do you mean?" He'd go back inside, then come out, like, "I'm so fucking sorry." He'd lose snare drums and all sorts of shit. How do you lose a fucking snare drum? He'd just leave it somewhere because he was all scatterbrained and shit.

After a couple of tours, we started doing this thing, because Pete had come up with this weird riff, which was like a droney emo-type of thing, and we'd get Toby to sing over it on stage. He'd come up and be like, "My band's called H20 because water is the purest thing that you put in your body." It was all just a joke, but people fucking loved it.

We had to fire Toby shortly after that because he was just the worst roadie. And he got kind of depressed. Then Pete [Koller] felt sorry for him, so he goes, "Look, I've got these five songs that don't really fit Sick of It All, and I want to give them to you. Get your friend Rusty [Pistachio], he's a great guitar player. And tell your hippy brother [Todd Morse] to cut his hair. Then you've got yourself a band." So Pete basically put H20 together. And he gave them five songs, one of which is their biggest hit: "Five Year Plan."

When Pete played us that song, I turned around and was like, "That's a fucking great song." But Armand and Craig [Setari] were like, "Nah, that's not us." And with Toby's lyrics it came out great. But that's a fact that a lot of people don't know: Pete actually built H20. We took them out to Europe before they even had a record out or anything. They only had maybe twenty minutes worth of music. That gave H20 a foothold in Europe like nobody else, because that was Sick of It All in their prime when we were at our biggest. We were telling everyone to check out this brand-new band that no one had heard of yet. And everyone was like, "Holy shit. Who are these guys?"

GREG ATTONITO—*THE BOUNCING SOULS*

MATT: There's a few artists that I've spoken to over the years, and I'm sure you're aware of them too, because they're quite vocal about their admiration for The Bouncing Souls. A couple that spring to mind are Brian Fallon and Dave Hause, who've both been guests on this show. Is that something that makes it all the more rewarding for you, to know that whatever inspiration you took from certain bands growing up, you've also passed it on to others?

GREG: Yeah, I feel so fortunate and have so much gratitude for that. As an artist, you're trying to express something that's happening inside yourself, and you want the world to listen to it. You want a response, whether it's positive or negative—depending on what you're saying—and when you see and hear feedback like that, it gives you great satisfaction. It's not the end all satisfaction. And you have to be okay without it. But all that stuff means a lot, for sure. And when your music helps people in their lives, from varying levels of helping them have a good time to helping them get through hard times, I can't ever overstate how awesome that is.

JESSE LEACH—*KILLSWITCH ENGAGE, TIMES OF GRACE, THE WEAPON, STOKE THE FIRE PODCAST*

JESSE: Anthony Bourdain was a punk. And when you grow up a punk, you never think you're going to make it outside of the small shitty clubs that smell like piss and beer. I never thought in a million years I'd be where I am now. And he had the same sentiment. On his shows, from where he started right up to his old and gray years before he took himself out, you see the journey of a young punk who's pissed off and trying to figure himself out, to an old man who's traveled the world and softened his heart and realized that we're all connected in some way. It's such a profound journey.

The running joke with friends of mine who are comedians, bartenders, restaurant people, and musicians is that we're all the same type of people. And I believe that most of the bar tenders and restaurant people I meet are very similar, chemically, to musicians and comedians. We all need to be treated with fragile respect, because we're all fucked up people. Anthony Bourdain brought that to light. He was one of the first people to stand up and say, "Stop treating the people who are serving you like shit." Guess what? Behind the scenes, in that kitchen that you don't see because you're sitting at your table ordering, there's chaos going on back there. It's a lot like a mosh pit, only they have knives and hot food. He really brought that to light and made me realize that I love that aspect of it. It made me want to be a bartender and work in restaurants, which I did in between Times of Grace and Killswitch Engage. And I fucking loved it; I still keep in touch with all my bartender friends.

I realized that if this fucking punk could grow and learn and become an international traveler after writing a book that exposes all the fucked-up shit that goes on in a kitchen, we can all do something similar, if we just embrace that darker side and reveal it. He'll be a hero of mine forever, God rest his soul. And it's funny how you think you know somebody because of their work or social media or whatever, but Bourdain had a dark side. He was a guy who on paper had everything, but he fucking killed himself because he had this mental illness that he didn't really know how to talk about. When Anthony Bourdain passed, it gave me even more purpose to keep talking about people who are broken like myself. And sometimes when you just say it out loud it can mean the difference between life and death that night.

INFLUENCE & INSPIRATION PLAYLIST

THE BEATLES—"YESTERDAY"

BOB DYLAN—"LIKE A ROLLING STONE"

JIMI HENDRIX—"PURPLE HAZE"

FRANK SINATRA—"MY WAY"

DAVID BOWIE—"HEROES"

IGGY POP—"THE PASSENGER"

FUGAZI—"THE WAITING ROOM"

JANE'S ADDICTION—"JANE SAYS"

RED HOT CHILI PEPPERS—"FIGHT LIKE A BRAVE"

MÖTLEY CRÜE—"SHOUT AT THE DEVIL"

RAGE AGAINST THE MACHINE—"KILLING IN THE NAME"

KORN—"BLIND"

SICK OF IT ALL—"STEP DOWN"

ZEBRAHEAD—"ALL MY FRIENDS ARE NOBODIES"

ANDREW W.K.—"WE WANT FUN"

BAD BRAINS—"BANNED IN D.C."

REFUSED—"NEW NOISE"

BRUCE SPRINGSTEEN—"HUNGRY HEART"

THE BOUNCING SOULS—"EAST COAST FUCK YOU"

EVERY TIME I DIE—"BUFFALO 666"

H2O—"FIVE YEAR PLAN"

TIMES OF GRACE—"RESCUE"

CREATIVE RELATIONSHIPS

"You are only the quality of those who you surround yourself with."

WELL, BOYS AND GIRLS, we're about halfway through the manuscript. How are you enjoying it so far? Is this book better than the last one? Is it worse? Or is it just different, but you're enjoying it all the same? Hopefully it's the former or the latter, not old *Malcolm in the Middle*. Personally, I prefer this one because I'm in a much better place in my life these days. I was out of my mind during the compilation of the first book: that entire three-month period was fueled by alcohol, insanity, and all-night writing sessions. And I was revisiting interviews from a time in my life that wasn't all that great either, and that opened up a lot of old wounds.

I'm in a much better headspace these days. And I haven't written a single character or letter of this book under the influence of anything stronger than tea. I've been one hundred percent sober the entire time. That's not to say I am sober—I write Monday to Friday, then get pissed up at the weekend. But I wanted to write this second book sober to be more present in the creative process. You'll have to tell me whether or not that's had a positive effect on the text—reach out to me online. I'm genuinely interested to know: does being out of your mind make you a better writer? I wonder if Hunter S. Thompson would've been half as good a scribe if he was straight. I guess that's another conversation for another time.

As you can see, we've had another chapter tweak here. What was once "Creative Partnerships" is now "Creative Relationships," and that subtle shift means we're no longer confined to just partnerships;

we can also explore the creative dynamics and working relationships between bands and various individuals, as opposed to just double acts. We're widening the playing field once again.

Have you ever wondered what it was like to be in Rage Against the Machine, or why that band broke up in the year 2000 at the peak of their powers? Pontificate no more, dear reader. This chapter features all kinds of insights into the unique group chemistry and interpersonal relationships that make up your favorite bands, some of which are still together, some of which aren't. And you'll find out why some bands stayed the course while other acts grew apart. If you're into all that *VH1: Behind the Music* stuff, this is definitely the chapter for you.

You'll learn about how legendary—and I do mean *legendary*—filmmakers and photographers helped shape and create a new visual aesthetic to accompany some of the most exciting and progressive bands of the last four decades. And hear firsthand accounts of working with amazing artists like Mike Patton, Billy Corgan, Scott Weiland, and Kurt Cobain. Some stories are tinged with sadness, as a couple of those figures are no longer with us, but they're fascinating and enlightening all the same.

Gene Simmons will also pop up to tell you how he discovered not only Van Halen, but also Katey Sagal from *Married...with Children*, *Futurama*, and *Sons of Anarchy*—and he's not even bullshitting you. Linus of Hollywood has some great stories from his time working with Puff Daddy. Or is it P. Diddy now? Or just Diddy? I can't keep up!

Chuck D talks about collaborating with Spike Lee on *Do the Right Thing*. John Feldmann and Charlie Paulson peel back the layers of their thirty-year relationship, warts and all. Dean Karr, Casey Chaos, and Joey Castillo all shed light on their personal connections to Queens of the Stone Age. And Dave Fortman lays it all on the line in his recollection of the recording of Slipknot's fourth record, *All Hope Is Gone*, which was the band's final studio album to feature the original lineup.

Incidentally, I find it fascinating to hear what certain bands will sacrifice and endure in order to become successful. It makes the few bands who rise to the top of the mountain and keep their original lineup intact seem all the more impressive. Rammstein are a fine example of this, and Richard Kruspe will share intimate details of their collective journey momentarily. There's also stories about Rick Rubin, Ric Ocasek, Pete Steele, and Brent Hinds.

I guess the final thing to say on the subject of creative relationships, and the key difference between where I am personally and professionally between this book and the last one is I finally found my own creative partner. You may remember in *Life In The Stocks Volume One*, I reflected pensively on my lifelong quest to find a likeminded confidante to collaborate with. I feel that's something I've been lacking my whole life.

Enter into the equation a man by the name of Jesse Leach. You'll know Jesse as the lead singer in Killswitch Engage and Times of Grace, and a staunch advocate for men's mental health. I know him as those things, too. And I deeply respect and admire him for all of his efforts in those fields. But even more than that, over the last year or so, during this whole pandemic period, Jesse has become like a brother to me. And on March 2, 2021, he and I launched a brand-new podcast together: *Stoke The Fire*.

If you like *Life In The Stocks*, you will absolutely love *Stoke The Fire*. And it's available on all the same podcast platforms, so please check it out if you haven't already. That podcast has changed my life. It's the single most enriching and rewarding project I've ever been involved in and working with Jesse is an absolute dream come true. If you're interested in interviews where the hosts and guests get vulnerable and deep, *Stoke The Fire* is definitely the podcast for you. I genuinely believe there is no other show like it, especially not in the "alternative" scene. We've already built such a beautiful and supportive community around it, too, and we're only just getting started—by the time this book comes out, the podcast will have only been going exactly one year.

Nobody has ever had my back or encouraged me quite like Jesse does, and our friendship has blossomed into something truly special over the last year. If you're familiar with *Stoke The Fire*, you'll know exactly what I'm talking about. I feel blessed. And I'm genuinely excited about the future for perhaps the first time ever. I really do feel like the sky is the limit with that show. The amount of emails that we get on an almost daily basis from listeners all over the world is mind-blowing, not to mention validating and inspiring. I've never experienced anything quite like it.

I'll continue doing *Life In The Stocks*, though—don't worry. If anything, producing *Stoke The Fire* alongside it has raised my game and elevated me as a conversationalist. So the future looks bright on both fronts. And without *Life In The Stocks*, there would be no *Stoke The Fire*. I'm definitely not blind to that fact. I've said it before and I'll say it again: aside from my family and the friendships that preceded it, literally everything that is positive in my life is a direct result of *Life In The Stocks*. And I'm eternally grateful for all the opportunities and connections that have come out of it.

Let's crack on with the next chapter, shall we? In the last book, Joey Cape from Lagwagon talked about his personal history with Me First and the Gimme Gimmes. Here, Scott Shiflett from Face to Face shares his side of the story of how the world's best punk-rock-supergroup-covers band first started. Over to you, Scotty!

SCOTT SHIFLETT—*FACE TO FACE, ME FIRST & THE GIMME GIM-MES, VIVA DEATH*

MATT: What's your history with Me First and the Gimme Gimmes?

SCOTT: Well, here's an interesting back story: pre-Gimmes, when my little brother [Chris Shiflett] was still living in Los Angeles and we were both living with Bill Armstrong, who runs Side One Dummy Records, Chris, Bill, and I had a band together, which also included Josh Freese from The Vandals. This was in the early nineties, but I go back to 1981 with Bill Armstrong. He was one of my best friends growing up, and we still talk on the phone all the time. And we had a joke idea that never came to fruition, which was going to be a band called Clown Fight.

MATT: What a great band name.

SCOTT: Right? We were going to dress as clowns, get as drunk as we could, and play punk rock covers of eighties pop songs. That was the idea. I even went as far as going out and buying a clown suit for myself, with giant blue shoes and a red nose. And I bought everyone else who was going to be in the band a red clown nose. But they were going to have to go and get their own clown suits. It never got off the ground though. It was just one of those drunken conversations that we said we would do.

When my brother moved up north, originally just to get a job at Fat Wreck Chords, I was going to move up there with him, and we were going to maybe do a side-project with Joey Cape from Lagwagon. Joey has been a friend of mine for years, and I played in bands with Joey prior to Lagwagon. But two weeks before the move, I backed out. I've never been very good at adulting, and I knew I was never going to get a job, and that I'd probably end up broke or dead if I went up there. And Chris already had an internship lined up at Fat. So I just told him, "Man, I'm staying in LA," which ultimately worked out as I wound up joining Face to Face.

Not long after Chris moved up there, they created this band where they dressed in costumes, got as drunk as they could, and played covers. It wasn't specifically eighties songs. And even though I knew they didn't rip the idea off, I always felt like I had a pre-history to the concept. I was surprised when they made that first record, too. I thought it was just going to be a local gag that they would do until their livers gave out. Then they made a second record, and a third record.

On the 2003 Warped Tour, Chris had to leave for some reason, so they roped in dudes from other bands to come up and play, and I got up and did two songs. That was my first introduction to playing with the band. Then in 2004, my little bro Chris called me up and asked, "How would you feel about doing a two-week tour filling in with the Gimmes?" He said that some of the guys who were filling in kept trying to be the guy that played on the records, and I had no such aspirations, so I was like, "Yeah, I'll jump in, and I'll cover it. I'm not out to steal the gig. You're my brother, and it's your gig. It always has been and it always will be." Ironically, almost fifteen years later, I'm still doing the gig.

LINUS OF HOLLYWOOD—*NERF HERDER, SOLO ARTIST, PRODUCER*

MATT: Tell me about working with Cheap Trick.

LINUS: I played guitar on their album, *The Latest*. It was produced by this guy named Julian Raymond. I was literally sitting on my couch in my boxer shorts watching television in the afternoon when I got a call from my friend Roger Manning, who used to play in Jellyfish and now plays with Beck. He said, "Hey, what are you doing right now?" I was like, "I'm watching TV." He said, "Why don't you come down to A&M Studios and play guitar on the new Cheap Trick album." And I said, "Okay, that'd be great." So I went down there and played some rhythm guitar tracks on the record. I was basically just hired as a session musician, but it was a pretty cool experience. I was playing Rick Nielsen's actual guitars through his amps.

MATT: They're the kings of power pop. Without Cheap Trick, there'd be no Weezer.

LINUS: Of course. They're one of the greatest, for sure.

MATT: Talk to me about Puff Daddy.

LINUS: Yeah, that was a random one. It was around 1999, right after Size 14 broke up. The manager from Size 14 managed another band called Fuzzbubble, who actually sounded a little bit like Cheap Trick. They were an amazing power pop band, and I'm still friends with the main writer [Jim Bacchi] in that band to this day. The manager guy said, "Hey, Puffy's doing this rock remix of this song, "It's All About the Benjamins." He's just getting riffs from everybody, and then he'll pick the best ones.

MATT: Who else was he getting riffs off?

LINUS: Dave Grohl. Rob Zombie. People like that. Puff Daddy was literally handed a CD with no names on it and told, "Here are fifteen riffs that people did." And he picked mine. I think I was the only non-super-famous person on that CD, and I ended up becoming his rock remix guy for the next two years. Every time he did a rock remix, which he did a lot of at that time, he would send a limo over to my crappy one-bedroom apartment on Franklin Avenue, fly me out to New York, and put me up in a really nice hotel off Fifth Avenue. He treated me great, and he paid me really good, and he was just about the biggest thing going at that time. Just to be around that energy was really inspiring and cool. He called me "Guitar Man" for two years. I don't think he ever called me by my name.

MATT: Is he a cool guy? He seems like he's very self-aware and has a great sense of humor.

LINUS: Yeah, he's super funny. And whatever the X-factor is, he's got it. It's like you really want to do a good job for him, you know what I mean? He's a really good leader, and he surrounds himself with a lot of awesome people. And he's super funny. He never gets credit for being as funny as he is. He's so freakin' funny. He only sleeps about four hours a night, too. He's a total multi-tasker, a total worker, and I don't have anything bad to say about him. He's amazing.

MATT: Did you get to go to any cool parties with him?

LINUS: Well, what was really funny is about a year or two after things died down and I wasn't working too much with him anymore, I ran into him while doing another session at the Record Plant. He pulled up, and he was like, "Guitar Man, what's up?" So I said hello to him there, and then a couple of days later, one of his people called and invited me to this "white" party where everyone dresses in white. I looked at my wife at the time, and I said, "Should we go to this thing?" And we had a conversation about it, but we decided that we'd feel really out of place. This was back when the East Coast-West Coast beef was still going on. And whenever I went to the studio and

Puffy was there, I would get frisked on the way in. There was still this feeling that any moment now something crazy could happen. It was pretty freaky. And I was just this nerdy white kid. We pictured all these hardcore rappers smoking blunts and all that kind of stuff, so we ended up not going in the end. Then the following week I picked up a copy of US Weekly and there were pictures of Gwyneth Paltrow and Brad Pitt, and all these other people who were there. We were like, "We should've gone."

MATT: You blew it.

LINUS: We totally blew it.

MATT: Always take the invite. That's the moral of that story. How did the Smashing Pumpkins collaboration come about?

LINUS: That was also a Puff Daddy thing. The Smashing Pumpkins sent the song "Perfect" to be remixed. They sent us the masters, and we got to deconstruct the song. Billy Corgan's melody stayed the same, but I changed all the chords behind it.

MATT: What an amazing band to get that opportunity with.

LINUS: Yeah, it was super fun. That's how big Puffy was at that time. I remember being in his office and sitting next to the two-inch reel of "Roxanne" by The Police because they had just sent him that song to mess around with. Everyone was sending him their stuff to remix at that time.

MATT: And you were his go-to guy—The Guitar Man.

LINUS: Yeah, it was super cool.

DENNIS LYXZÉN—REFUSED, THE (INTERNATIONAL) NOISE CON-SPIRACY, INVSN, FAKE NAMES

MATT: Tell me about working with Rick Rubin.

DENNIS: Rick Rubin was the guy who taught me how to sing. He punished me quite a lot on the singing front.

MATT: That's interesting, because I've heard a lot of people say he's not a very hands-on producer.

DENNIS: We [The (International) Noise Conspiracy] did two records with Rick. The first one was *Armed Love*, and he was super hands-on for that record. He was in the studio every day, and I did six weeks of vocals with him, just me and him and the engineer. Some days we did vocals for seven hours, and some days we did vocals for twenty minutes. He'd be like, "You sound tired, go home." He was very particular about how he wanted me to sing. And I came out of that process a ten times better singer. Then the next record we did with him [*The Cross of My Calling*], he only showed up every once in a while. He just left some notes and was like, "You're doing fine."

MATT: Is that because he felt like he'd got you to a place where he could leave you unsupervised?

DENNIS: Yeah. He also surrounds himself with engineers who really know what they're doing. So he wasn't hands-on at all for the second record that we did with him, but during the first one he was super hands-on. And the experience of working with him is something that I'll remember for the rest of my life. I wish those records had done better. But that's a part of life, too. I learned so much from making those records. It was amazing.

CHUCK D—*PUBLIC ENEMY, PROPHETS OF RAGE, SOLO ARTIST, AUTHOR*

MATT: One thing I noticed, which I love about you and Tom Morello—and I had Tom on the podcast when you guys were touring with Prophets of Rage.

CHUCK: Oh, that's great.

MATT: I noticed that you two would go out into cities at night after the shows.

CHUCK: That's right.

MATT: And you'd go into local bars and take them over, and just start having a block party inside the club.

CHUCK: Yep.

MATT: So few internationally recognized musicians do that kind of thing: go out and connect on a street level with their audience. Is that just something that's just in you that you can't escape?

CHUCK: Well, coincidentally, Tom Morello is a man of the people, and he loves to do that. I occasionally step in, but Tom Morello and DJ Lord were the ones at the forefront of going in and doing that. And every once in a while I participated in it also. I usually just turn my hotel room into an art studio and work on my art after the concert is finished. But I relished being in the same fold as the great Tom Morello. He's my guy! And we had a fantastic time in the Prophets of Rage; it was a four-year school of existence, and I felt like we taught and entertained the world. And we had a great brotherhood. We still do.

MATT: I had B-Real on the show a while back as well, and he was saying how there was two camps on the road when you guys would tour together: the camp who would, in his words, "elevate," and then those that did not. I guess those that did not would be you and Tom Morello, and the rest of the guys would be on the smoke bus getting blazed.

CHUCK: Uh-huh.

MATT: B-Real also said what an amazing full circle moment it was for him joining Prophets of Rage with you since the Bomb Squad was instrumental in getting Cypress Hill's career off the ground, with the inclusion of "How I Could Just Kill a Man" on the *Juice* soundtrack.

CHUCK: Yes, exactly. I remember it like it was yesterday: Hank Shocklee and Gary G-Wiz specifically placed it in the movie *Juice*, which was one of the seminal hip-hop films of all-time. And the placement of that song during the chase scene was perfect. The song caught on after that; it was the spark that Cypress Hill needed, and they wound up becoming one of the greatest rap groups of all-time. We take great pride in that move.

MATT: How important was the *Do the Right Thing* movie and soundtrack and moment to the story of Public Enemy?

CHUCK: Well, the beautiful aspect of that is Spike Lee put "Fight the Power" in there as an anthem, but he also placed it in the movie at least 25 percent of the time. Who does that? So he significantly made it happen for us.

TOM MORELLO—*RAGE AGAINST THE MACHINE, AUDIOSLAVE, PROPHETS OF RAGE, THE NIGHTWATCHMAN*

MATT: Talk me through when you four—Tim [Commerford], Brad [Wilk], Zack [de la Rocha], and yourself—first came together as one. Was the chemistry evident right away?

TOM: It was, yeah. The first time the four of us played together was either August 30 or 31, 1991. Tim and Zack had known each other for some time, and Brad and I had previously played together, but when the four of us finally got together in a room, it sounded like Rage Against the Machine. And nobody knew or even liked Rage Against the Machine back then. We had no ambitions of ever getting a record deal or playing a show in a club, or anything like that. There was no multi-racial, neo-Marxist, punk-metal-hip-hop groups playing the LA scene back then. No one was looking for that band, and those bands weren't selling tickets, because there weren't any. We just wrote music for ourselves. I remember the first person who heard Rage Against the Machine was a worker at the industrial complex where we used to rehearse. We saw him outside one day, and he said, "What are you guys doing in there?" I told him we were a band, and he asked if he could come in and listen to some of our music. So he sat down, and we played him a few songs. His response was, "This music makes me want to fight." That's when I knew we were onto something.

MATT: Is it true that you put out a want ad for a singer, "Seeking socialist vocalist who likes Black Sabbath and Public Enemy"?

TOM: Yes, I did.

MATT: It's safe to say you found your guy.

TOM: He didn't answer that ad—that was a couple of years before I met Zack. But it eventually rounded into shape, yeah.

MATT: And Brad had one, too? "Drummer who loves John Bonham and James Brown."

TOM: He absolutely did, and that's him to a tee.

MATT: That covers record [*Renegades*] was such a fitting end to an amazing run of albums. It also gave fans a great insight into the musical DNA of Rage Against the Machine.

TOM: Absolutely. We drew from a lot of different sources to come up with that heady stew.

MATT: Do you have a favorite record from Rage Against the Machine?

TOM: My instinct is to just say the first one [*Rage Against the Machine*], because it was made with such innocence and the expectation that no one was going to hear it. Expectations were none; we just recorded our songs. And at the time, I thought that we captured about 70 to 75 percent of what we were. Listening back to it now, it's like, "Wow! We must've been good because that record still sounds pretty great."

MATT: It's incredible. Didn't a lot of demo versions of the songs actually ended up on the final album?

TOM: Yeah, the "Bullet in the Head" demo version made it onto the album verbatim, which is pretty crazy.

MATT: It's the sound of four guys having the time of their lives playing together.

TOM: Yeah, and unapologetically melding these genres of hip-hop, punk, and metal in a way that, while it had been toyed with before, had never been harmonized in quite such a way.

MATT: In your mind, looking back now with the benefit of hindsight, why do you think Rage Against the Machine ended when it did?

TOM: It was a surprise to me that the band didn't end every Tuesday. It was merciful, in some ways, that it ended when it did, because it wasn't a pleasant time to be in the band. And while the shows never suffered, and the records never suffered, being in that band was not a great time. I always imagined myself being in the same band for my entire life, but when the dissolution of Rage Against The Machine happened it opened the doors to a lot of great things: to be in Audioslave with Chris Cornell, to have the Nightwatchman career and four Americana records that I'm very proud of, to play with Bruce Springsteen and the Prophets of Rage, and this latest *The Atlas Underground* record, all of which have been so deeply fulfilling. They've allowed me to make such amazing connections with other musicians and audiences, and I'm very grateful for all of that.

RICHARD KRUSPE—*RAMMSTEIN, EMIGRATE*

RICHARD: Making records with Rammstein is always very painful and intense. Last time, we almost broke up because of the record [*Liebe ist für alle da*].

MATT: Is that because there's a lot of people in the band, and you're all quite large and different personalities?

RICHARD: Yeah, we have six members with six totally different views, and it's so hard to bring that together. When you write and you have a vision, you have to bring that vision through five other different points of view. It's very time consuming. I would say Rammstein is about fifty percent music and fifty percent talking. And we all have a lot of respect for each other, which really helps with the understanding. I'm actually really enjoying making music with these guys right now, and I didn't expect to do that again.

MATT: I guess you've all grown a little older and a little wiser; you're not angry young men anymore.

RICHARD: We're still angry—we still have that in us. I think because of the dynamic that we have when all six of us are together there's always going to be that explosive energy. But we've also been through all the things that you go through as a band, which every band goes through, and we've always paid attention to the weakest chain in the band and tried to listen to them. That hasn't always been easy. The normal reaction is, "Get them out and get another person in." And there's a thousand examples of that all over the world. But we didn't do that; we really tried to sort things out and stay together.

MATT: To keep the original lineup intact?

RICHARD: Exactly. At the end of the day, the DNA of Rammstein is the chemistry between those six guys, and if you exchanged someone, it would be a different DNA. I'm proud that we managed to get through all that and work as a team. I always see genius in a team, not in one person. There was something about Rammstein that came together—you could call it destiny or whatever. We had a singer who sung in German and played with fire on stage, which obviously developed into something bigger and bigger over the years. The vision that our manager had was also very important; he was a big part of it; he was very visionary. And coming from East Germany, we weren't really influenced by West German or American music. So all those elements came together and formed something that was very unique.

This type of success story only happens once every hundred years. But I don't have the formula. If I did, I would give it to someone else. In the beginning, nobody cared about playing our music on the radio. Even our videos didn't get played to begin with. So the live show became our tool to promote the record. We invested a lot in our live show again and again and again, because it was the only weapon we had to bring our music to the people. And because we were singing in a different language, we had to put something in there to make it more attractive to the rest of the world. It was always important for us to combine the music with those strong visual moments to make sure people had an interesting and important time when they saw our shows.

MATT: It's such an unlikely and amazing success story. But after watching the *Rammstein in Amerika* documentary, all of you individually, and the band collectively, seemed to be so ambitious, focused, and driven from the start. Did any part of you foresee what came to be unfolding in the way that it did?

RICHARD: No. And that's the secret, I think.

MATT: You didn't set out to be the biggest band in Germany then?

RICHARD: No. We really didn't give a fuck. No one believed in us. Even in Germany, we'd go into a record company and play them a tape, and they'd say, "No fucking way. This is not going to work—*ever*." We just took the tape and walked out laughing, we really didn't care. We were so free and involved in ourselves. We had no idea what was going on around us. We were just in love with each other—but not in a gay way.

MATT: You mention the word gay there, and homoerotic visuals—and actual acts on stage—are a big part of the Rammstein live show. Tell me a little bit, if you can, about the special relationship between Till [Lindemann] and Flake [Christian Lorenz] because on stage there does seem to be a very unique chemistry between those two.

RICHARD: I guess so, huh? Beauty and the beast. The question is, who is the beast?

MATT: It's interchangeable.

RICHARD: Yes, sometimes it's the other way around. But visually it kind of makes sense.

MATT: And there's obviously real trust and respect there?

RICHARD: I don't know what they do when they're alone. They do share a dressing room, I can tell you that for sure. But I don't think anyone else would allow Till to do what he does. Flake was the only one who kind of went with it. And that's Flake, you know? He's a very strong personality, too. But he's also very giving. I remember sitting in the car with him once trying to look for a parking space, and people were driving in front of him and taking slots, and he just sat there waiting. We sat there for ten minutes, and I started freaking out. I was like, "What the fuck are you waiting for? Just go in!" He's just very giving and friendly, and he doesn't want to confront anyone—that's him.

CHARLIE PAULSON—*GOLDFINGER, BLACK PRESIDENT*

CHARLIE: I do daily maintenance of my headspace. It's real easy to isolate and not check in with people. That anger builds up quickly, and it quickly turns into depression and that gets you into trouble. So you have to keep your fucking head, and that means a lot of different things for different people. What I find it primarily means for me is to do no wrong and keep your side of the street clean. Don't talk shit. And if you fuck something up, or you fuck somebody over, fix it as quickly as you can. That helps keep your head clean. When you start holding onto that nasty shit it festers, and then you start feeling bad about yourself. Resentment can kill you—it really can.

MATT: Do you apply the tools that you learn in the work that you do to your day-to-day life?

CHARLIE: Yeah, you have to.

MATT: And does it improve your life?

CHARLIE: A hundred fucking percent. I'm back in Goldfinger because of that very thing. John [Feldmann] and I were talking about that just the other day. Like I said, you try to keep your shit together on a daily basis. But things do accumulate—it happens. And I get it out by writing shit down. You have to take stock of how you feel and where you're at, and you really call bullshit on yourself. When you've got it written down in front of you in black and white, it's the fucking truth because it's just between you and that piece of paper—you're doing it for yourself. When you really see where you're at and you hold yourself accountable, it makes it really easy for you to see what you've got to fix. I had literally just done that, and I knew exactly what fires I had to put out when John reached out to me. And at that point he and I hadn't spoken in five years.

MATT: That's how long it had been?

CHARLIE: Yeah. And I swear to God, right out of nowhere, right around that time, he text me: "Hey, do you wanna get coffee?" And my instant thought was, "Yeah. You're my fucking brother; I've known you for thirty years, of course I'll get coffee with you." So we met, and we got coffee, and we had a long talk, and it was really good. We aired a lot of shit—a lot of the reasons that we hadn't been talking and everything like that. And in addition to both of us being sober, we're both fucking middle-aged men now.

MATT: So you can both take ownership of your past mistakes?

CHARLIE: Exactly. You can embrace that and act your fucking age. I was sitting across the table from somebody that I've had many, *many* differences with over the years, but I know at our core that we both care about each other. I've screamed at him; I've gone flying over tables at him, and I've said some fucking unholy shit to that dude. And vice versa—in the heat of the moment. But when you're calm and there's no fucking static or bullshit, it's easier to be honest about that kind of thing.

MATT: How is it being back in the band and playing all those old songs again?

CHARLIE: We're both crazy people, so we've had a couple of days on this tour in particular where it's like, "I'm just going to walk out of the room." Or he'll just walk out of the room, and we leave each other alone. Or we'll just say whatever we have to say. And it's been fucking great, to be honest with you. That last record, I had nothing to do with. And when John first asked me to come back and play, I was thinking about that, and I was thinking, "Fuck that, man. I'm the original guitar player; I'm an original fucking member; I'm not playing that shit." But if Slash can get up with Axl [Rose] and play that shit off *Chinese*

Democracy, who the fuck am I? And the truth of the matter is, I dig the new songs, and they're really fun to play live. So fuck it!

JOHN FELDMANN—*GOLDFINGER, PRODUCER, SONGWRITER, A&R EXECUTIVE*

JOHN: Charlie Paulson comes from the Electric Love Hogs lineage of every man for himself. Even in the very beginning of the band, Charlie had such a strong presence. He and I were always sort of battling for stage positioning, because he had his circular thing, and he's just a big dude. And by the time he quit, him and Darrin [Pfeiffer] sort of formed a team. And Darrin ended up suing me, which is one of those things where it's hard to come back to a relationship after that. I don't know if that relationship will ever be mended—I hope so. I don't really dislike Darrin on any level.

But Charlie and Darrin sort of went away at the same time, so I just kind of assumed that Charlie would never come back without Darrin. Then we had coffee, it must have only been about three months ago, and he said to me, "This is all the shit that I wish I would've done different." And I said, "This is all the shit that I wish I would've done different." And we came to this really great emotional meeting place.

I didn't know that I was going to have him back in the band; I just thought that we would be friends again. But he was working at this bar as a bouncer, and I was like, "Why the fuck would this huge talent be stuck in Downtown LA working at a bar, when he could be on stage in Manchester tonight playing a show?" So I asked if he'd be interested, and he was like, "Fuck yeah, I'd be interested!" So now we have four guitar players, and the energy is fucking awesome.

CHRIS DEMAKES—*LESS THAN JAKE, CHRIS DEMAKES A PODCAST*

MATT: I want to ask you about this, and I've spoken to some of these people on the podcasts that I've done with them, so I'm not shit talking. But there seems to be a lot of politics in the Orange County ska punk scene. When it comes to bands like Goldfinger, Reel Big Fish, and Save Ferris, there seems to be a lot of rifts and drama behind the scenes. Less Than Jake seem to be the only band who hasn't had all these interpersonal fallouts and spats with other bands. Why do you think that is? Is it just because you're not from the same local scene, so you've dodged all the politics that come with it?

CHRIS: Yeah, for sure. We were never included in that bunch because we weren't part of that scene. We get mistakenly referred to as a Southern California band a lot, because most of the other ska punk bands are from there, but we're from the opposite coast where there's a completely different vibe. When we were playing shows in Florida in 1992, we weren't playing with five or six other ska bands. We'd be sandwiched in between the Pearl Jam tribute band and the wannabe Stone Temple Pilots band, or whatever the latest flavor of the week was. It was a way different scene. So we never got swept up in the stuff that was happening with the bands on the west coast.

MATT: Do you guys feel like you exist on your own little island then? And can that also be a lonely space sometimes?

CHRIS: It's both. There's definitely times when, because we're not part of that Southern California club, we're not invited to certain festivals, or we're playing second out of ten bands when we probably deserve a little higher billing. But that's just part of the territory. And either you let it bum you out and ruin your career, or you accept it for what it is and you move on. But yeah, we feel it.

MATT: We'll talk about Vinnie [Fiorello] leaving the band in a moment, but the other interesting thing about Less Than Jake that I want to touch on is the fact that you've had all the same members since the start. And that's another thing that makes you guys unique, because Goldfinger, Reel Big Fish, and Save Ferris are always changing band members. And I imagine you guys have your own tensions and fallouts from time to time, as all bands do. But you've managed to remain together and on good terms with each other for nearly thirty years. What's the secret?

CHRIS: We split the money evenly.

MATT: That's straight up what it is?

CHRIS: Absolutely. I've been saying that for years. When one guy is living in Beverly Hills and the rest of them are living in Compton, then you've got a real problem. It's always money that messes up bands—in my opinion.

MATT: And Less Than Jake have split things evenly since the very beginning?

CHRIS: Yeah.

MATT: What great foresight on your part.

CHRIS: We just knew. I would say we only made one right decision during our whole career, and that was it.

MATT: Only one? You're perhaps being a little bit hard on yourself there.

CHRIS: I think we made a lot of good decisions, but I don't know them to be true. I'm convinced that one was the right decision though because we're still here with the same band. And Vinnie was with us for twenty-six years. He only left last year.

MATT: What was his reason for leaving?

CHRIS: Exactly what he said in the statement that he made: that he wanted to stay home and be a father to his daughter. And he has a lot of other stuff going on.

MATT: Is he still running the record label [Fueled by Ramen]?

CHRIS: He's still running the record label, and he's still working behind the scenes for Less Than Jake. He's doing all our merchandise and social media stuff. So there's been no fallout whatsoever, he just didn't want to be out on the road anymore.

MATT: In the past, Vinnie always wrote the lyrics. Is that still the case going forward?

CHRIS: We haven't been working with Vinnie on the next record. We're all going to be writing lyrics—Roger [Lima], myself, and the rest of the band. And that's not to take anything away from Vinnie. He was the chief lyricist during all those years when he was a full-time member of Less Than Jake. But we all wrote lyrics and fit things in here and there to create the songs. There will be a void there, for sure. But it's a new time for the band, and we're embracing it. We're excited.

MATT: Do the live shows feel fresh and different now that you have Matt Yonker playing with you? He's obviously been working with the band for years as your sound engineer and tour manager, so he's already part of the family. But does it feel like a new chapter for Less Than Jake?

CHRIS: Yeah, it does. A band member is never replaceable—like our fingerprints, each one of us is unique. And if you take that energy away, it's never going to be the same. You can say, "The new drummer is better," or, "The new drummer is worse." But the new drummer is just the new drummer, and it's different. Like you said, we've known Matt forever. He started out selling T-shirts for us eighteen years ago, and when we were looking for someone to take over the drum throne, he was the perfect person. We've known him all these years, and we knew he was a great drummer.

MATT: It was too perfect!

CHRIS: It really was. And it's a totally different energy now because it's a different human being. Matt brings a totally different energy to the live shows and that's been rejuvenating in a sense because he's been encouraging us to play songs that we haven't played live in years. He's brought a sense of fire and urgency back to the band and working on the new material for our next album has been the same way. We've all been collaborating with each other in a new way and that's been exciting for all of us. And we like the new songs, so hopefully the fans will like them, too.

GREG ATTONITO—*THE BOUNCING SOULS*

MATT: How does it feel to have been in The Bouncing Souls for three decades of your life?

GREG: I just feel really proud, man. We're not the biggest band in the world, but I'm a dude from [New] Jersey, and I'm in London right now, and we sold out a club in Manchester last night. It's fantastic. But even more than that, we still just really like hanging out with each other.

MATT: That's what I wanted to ask you: is that the secret to the Souls' longevity? The fact that you guys still genuinely enjoy each other's company?

GREG: Yeah. None of us would do it anymore if we didn't. And there's been a lot of trial and error throughout the years. Touring nine months out of the year for five years straight just wore us out, and everyone kind of had different ways of dealing with that.

MATT: What was yours?

GREG: I was the only guy who was married.

MATT: So you had some anchorage back home?

GREG: Yes. But nobody likes the married guy on the pirate ship. And I don't mean the rest of the guys didn't like me, we just started living different lives.

MATT: Because you were travelling in different lanes.

GREG: Exactly. So there wasn't any animosity, but we were splitting off, growing up, and doing different things. And that was hard to deal with because no one was really connecting. And Bryan [Kienlen] and Pete [Steinkopf] were off in Wild West world, which they've talked about. So that was kind of our trial by fire for a few years—for my marriage as well, which thankfully survived, and I'm very happy about that.

MATT: Are you a father as well?

GREG: Yes. I've been a father for two years now. So that's amazing. And I'm so happy that I waited until I was almost fifty to have a child; I don't think I would've been as present as I am now during my younger years.

MATT: You, Pete, and Bryan have all known each other since you were fifteen years old, correct?

GREG: Yeah, maybe even earlier. We knew each other because we grew up in the same town [Basking Ridge], but we didn't really start hanging out until around that time. We're essentially still in our high school band together.

MATT: That's super rare. There's a few people that've done that and stayed the course, but not many.

GREG: I really value the fact that we've grown up navigating these different things together, throughout our twenties, thirties, and forties.

MATT: That's a lot of history.

GREG: It is. And the music has definitely kept us together. You see it with bands who break up, but they still keep coming back together. It's the magic of making music with people that you've known your whole life.

JOBY FORD—*THE BRONX, MARIACHI EL BRONX, ARTIST, PRODUCER*

MATT: What's the age difference between you and Matt [Caughthran]?

JOBY: Five years. My roommate at the time was friends with Matt's older brother, Jeff. They used to work together at this karaoke bar in Huntington Beach called Mr. Ks, and we would always go there because they didn't card anybody, so we could bring in anybody that we wanted. You know what I'm saying?

MATT: I know what you're saying.

JOBY: It sounds so hilarious saying it now, but they had private rooms that you could rent, so you and your friends could go in there and sing the songs that you wanted to. And Jeff was always trying to get me to go and see his brother's band, which was called Brotherhood of Death. And I was in a band called Jack Ruby, who was the guy that shot the guy [Lee Harvey Oswald] that shot one of our presidents [John F. Kennedy]. Jeff was like, "Your bands should play together."

Matt would come into Mr. Ks every once in a while, too. Jeff introduced me to him one night, and I was like, "Hey, man. You wanna sing a song? Let's sing 'Hot for Teacher' by Van Halen." So we did. And I was really impressed by how much of a good singer he was. Then I went to see his band at a place in Huntington Beach called the Liquid Den. Still to this day, some of the craziest shows I've ever been to were at that place. The security would literally beat people up, and all the shows were just fights.

MATT: Those days are gone now aren't they?

JOBY: Oh, yeah. It's over. At that time we were looking for a singer, so we'd go and watch all these bands that we heard had cool singers, and that show was the most insane thing I've ever seen in my life. I was like, "Man, this guy's awesome." I just really wanted to be in a band with him.

MATT: Just because you liked his voice? Or was the whole front man package already in place?

JOBY: Well, there were some girls at the concert who were really out of place, so Matt jumped off the stage onto their table. There were pitchers of beer on it, and he smashed all the glass and the beer went all over the girls, and it was just the coolest thing I'd ever seen. After he did that, two of his friends in the crowd picked up some tables and chairs and just started smashing them, and the security guards came over and started beating them up. So the rest of the guys in the band just laid down on stage and refused to play until the security stopped beating people up. It was just insanity.

MATT: What happens next? Do you start writing songs together right away?

JOBY: Yeah. A friend of ours had a studio, and we went down there and cut three songs that we still play to this day: "Heart Attack American," "White Tar," and "Strobe Life."

ALAN ROBERT—*LIFE OF AGONY, COMIC BOOK CREATOR*

MATT: It happened pretty fast for LOA didn't it? The response to that first album [*River Runs Red*] was insane. It was a massive album for Roadrunner Records and for that genre.

ALAN: Yeah, it was incredible. Our first show was February 11, 1990. And between 1990 and when we got signed to Roadrunner in 1992, we felt this momentum. We went from this little hardcore band to finding our own sound, to working with Josh Silver from Type O Negative, who produced our early demos and the first album. We had the same management as Type O Negative, too. So it was very incestuous. But you could really feel the swell and the popularity of the band growing. We'd go up and down the East Coast all the time, building a following until finally that record came out, and it made a big impact. Then we went to Europe for the first time on a sold-out tour with Pro-Pain, and the reaction to the band there was mind-blowing.

MATT: Before we go any further, what was Pete Steele from Type O Negative like?

ALAN: I tell you, he was one of the funniest motherfuckers I ever met. He had a truly dark, Brooklyn-style, sarcastic sense of humor. He was very warm as well, and exceptionally talented. I say it all the time: this band would not exist without Carnivore. That was one of our biggest influences. Pete's genius opened the doorways of imagination of what you could do with heavy music. And I have a lot of really awesome memories of him just hanging out at Josh's house. I was close with Josh all through making the demos and the album, and we'd hang out at his home studio all the time. Pete also lived on that block, so he'd pop in from time to time.

One time, we were hanging out in Josh's room, and I heard all this banging and clanking outside. I was like, "What the hell is that?" Pete came in, and he was wearing these knee-high tube socks, Daisy Duke cut-off jeans, a tank top, and a headband. He asked Josh for a wrench, Josh gave one to him, then I looked out in the backyard, and

Pete was building a twelve-foot tall metal cross, which they ended up using in one of their videos. And they were in this Orthodox Jewish neighborhood. It was classic Pete.

We're actually in a few of the Type O videos—in disguises. The whole band was in the "Black No. 1" video dressed as droogs. And we're in the "Christian Woman" video wearing monk robes and gas masks, dancing around a girl on a pentagram or some shit like that. It was filmed after hours at L'Amour, and they decorated the club with candles and stuff.

MATT: Going back to *River Runs Red*, did you write that whole album on your own?

ALAN: I wrote all the lyrics, but the album was definitely a group effort, and Josh played a big part in how it sounds. We recorded all the demos in standard E tuning, and Josh suggested we tune down to D, which we did. We were like, "Oh, yeah. This sounds heavier." Then he encouraged us to slow down the tempos to make it sound even heavier. He encouraged us to take another look at the song structures, too. He had a real vision for that record; he was able to see something that we couldn't see.

I was always a big Pink Floyd fan. So I always had the vision of wanting to do a concept record. I think that's where all the interludes came from. But Josh was the one who put all those soundscapes together. He knew how to use audio clips and layer them in a way that made them sound like real scenes. He was really gifted in that way, and he was able to bring those ideas to life. So even though the ideas spawned from me, Josh actually executed them in a creative way, from a production standpoint. The record was very much a collaboration in that sense. It couldn't have happened without everyone who was involved.

RICHARD KRUSPE—*RAMMSTEIN, EMIGRATE*

MATT: When did Rammstein and Jonas Åkerlund first work together?

RICHARD: I think it was the video for the song "Mann gegen Mann" that we did. Visually, he put it somewhere else, which I really loved.

MATT: Was it his idea to have all the naked men wrestling?

RICHARD: That was his idea, yeah. Another thing that made me think, "This guy is different," was the video for our song "Pussy." We just gave him the song, and he wrote us an email saying, "Let's start a revolution: let's do porn." He has a lot of crazy ideas, and I like that about him.

MATT: Did you premiere the "Pussy" video on a porno website? Is that right?

RICHARD: Yeah.

MATT: That makes sense, I guess. Otherwise, you wouldn't have been able to show half the things in the video.

RICHARD: Exactly. That was a lot of fun.

MATT: The "Mein Land" video was Jonas, too. And that's something different again; that's like a Russ Myers Beach Boys parody.

RICHARD: Exactly right.

MATT: How is it working with him? Is he a force of nature?

RICHARD: Well, he's definitely a force of editing.

MATT: I've never seen a live concert film like it [*Rammstein: Paris*] before. It's a mash-up of a live concert film and a music video. It's like he smashed those two genres together.

RICHARD: I have to say, this was the first time that Rammstein gave up control. We basically just followed his vision. When we were shooting "Ich Tu Dir Weh"—the first live video that we did with Jonas—we felt, like, "Wow! He has such great rhythm and editing." So the idea came from that video. We said, "We should do a movie like that." But during the process we sometimes felt, like, "Maybe that's a little too far."

MATT: A bit too stylized?

RICHARD: Yeah. But sometimes to do something different you have to give up control, get out of your comfort zone, and let somebody else lead you. That was kind of difficult for us because it was our first time, and when I see the film I think, "I would've done things differently." But it was important to let somebody else lead. We felt like we were basically actors in a Jonas Åkerlund movie.

MATT: Does that mean you approached the live shows differently?

RICHARD: No, we didn't do that. He saw the show a couple of times before and said, "Do exactly what you normally do."

MATT: Was there any dress rehearsal or anything like that?

RICHARD: Nothing, no. We had two shows in Paris, and those two shows were captured with, I don't know how many cameras—a lot.

MATT: There's also a lot of special effects and CGI elements, which I've never seen in a live concert film before. I liked it, but you're kind of shaking your head.

RICHARD: It's not really my taste. I feel like he overdid it a little bit. But it's different, and what I like about the movie is that it's polarized people; a lot of people love it, but a lot of people from the old days think it's too modern and a bit cheesy. But that's just the way it is.

TOMMY LEE—*MÖTLEY CRÜE, METHODS OF MAYHEM, SOLO ARTIST*

MATT: The very first episode of my podcast was with Steve-O from *Jackass*. And in that episode, which is going back about three-and-a-half years now, Steve-O regaled me with the story of how he tracked down Mötley Crüe and bagged backstage passes to your show, where he met you as a kid. Then years later, he hit you up on your message board while he was under house arrest, and you formed an online friendship with each other. Then when Mötley Crüe got back together, you reached out to Steve-O and asked him to introduce you guys at the first show back. Steve-O told me what a beautiful full circle moment that was for him. And since then, of course, *The Dirt* movie has come out. And Jeff Tremaine—who obviously directed all the *Jackass* TV shows and the movies—directed *The Dirt* as well. What a beautiful series of events. How did Jeff Tremaine become involved in that project? And how hands on were you and the rest of the band when it came to the development and making of the movie?

TOMMY: I actually just saw Steve-O maybe two weeks ago. He's doing a podcast out of his fucking van.

MATT: I've seen it. It's called *Wild Ride*.

TOMMY: Yeah. And he was doing my wife's podcast [*Worst Firsts* with Brittany Furlan], so he came by here and I did his. It was great to see him again. I fucking love him. He's a fucking maniac. And it's crazy how Jeff ended up directing *The Dirt*. I fucking love it when that happens. That kind of stuff doesn't happen all the time, so it's precious when it does.

We met with several directors, and Jeff was like, "Look, there's nobody else on this planet better suited than me to direct this film; I'm a massive fan, and I'm going to make you guys so proud. And I'm going to bring everybody right back to that time period—whether it's the phones or the cars or the clothes. I'm going to bring everybody right back to that insanity and what it was like, because I was there and I get it." We had interviewed a few other directors at this point, but we were like, "Jeff's the guy. He's going to murder this." So we went with Jeff, and he did everything that he said he was going to do.

MATT: Not only is he a fan of your band, who was there for that whole period, he's also no stranger to wrangling an all-male cast of out-of-control maniacs. So he had the perfect reference points for what was going on, because he had a similar situation doing *Jackass* all those years. He really was the best qualified guy for the job.

TOMMY: Yeah. And you have to imagine, we were like, "Hang on. This is our life's story. This isn't a fucking comedy." So we were a little sceptical at first, only in the sense that we thought, "He's so great at what he does, but this isn't *Jackass*. This is a movie about a huge fucking band with a crazy fucking story. How is he going to pull this off? How is he going to tell our story and create the drama, and all the other stuff that you do when you make a film?" So we were a little concerned at the beginning. But at the end of the day, he nailed it.

GENE SIMMONS—*KISS*

MATT: Did you discover Katey Sagal?

GENE: Yes.

MATT: For anybody who doesn't know her name, she's obviously Gemma Teller in *Sons of Anarchy*.

GENE: And she was the voice [Leela] on *Futurama*, and the wife on *Married with Children*. She actually sung backing vocals on tour with Bette Midler as well. But when I first met her, she was a waitress at a restaurant called High Pockets, which was a restaurant in LA. The idea with that restaurant was the people who would serve you would also go around and sing at your table with an acoustic guitar, or acapella. I became friends with Katey—you can fill in all the blanks—and I'd always hear music around her, so I asked her, "Do you have a band or something like that?" And she said, "Yeah, I have some people that I get together and write with." So I went down and saw the band. I said, "I tell you what I'm going to do: I'm going to produce a demo for you." Then I called Neil Bogart, as I'd already discovered Angel at this point, and got him to sign them. I said, "Neil, I've got another band for you."

MATT: This is the guy who ran Casablanca Records?

GENE: Yes. And Kiss was the first act on Casablanca Records. I said, "Neil, I've got another band for you. I don't know what their name is, but check this out." He goes, "Okay, I like it. I'm going to sign the band." So they got signed. But they couldn't think of a name. I suggested Swan, or something like that, because they had three chicks and two male lead singers, and a big band behind them, kind of like Delaney & Bonnie and Friends. They couldn't come up with a name in the end, so the album came out by The Group With No Name—that's what they settled on.

MATT: Literally?

GENE: Yeah. They had one record, thank you very much, and then it was over. But yes, I discovered her.

MATT: And you obviously discovered Van Halen. What was your first impression of them?

GENE: When I first heard Van Halen, I was flummoxed. I was stunned. I'd never heard a guitar player like Eddie [Van Halen] before. He was so technically proficient. I'd never heard a guitar played tap or run around the fret board the way he did. And somehow it was still melodic. But it wasn't blues. Years later, Eddie would profess a profound admiration for Eric Clapton, B.B. King, and all that stuff. But you can't hear it. When you hear Hendrix, you can hear the R&B and the Buddy Guy clearly. Not with Eddie. His was this other thing. It was closer, almost, to a Mahavishnu orchestra. When I found the band in a club called Starwood, I just thought, "This is the future. This is the next big band." But I couldn't get anybody else to believe in it. So I signed them to Man of a Thousand Faces, which was my company, and I produced their fifteen-track demo myself.

MATT: What was David Lee Roth like back then?

GENE: A sweet guy with no ego—that I saw. But I did take him aside one day, and we had a heart-to-heart. I said, "Look, I'm backing you guys. I'll help you, and I'll push you, and I want very little for it. But let's call it what it is: you're the lead singer and the name of the band is the last name of the guitar player and the drummer. And that's okay, if you're okay with it. But you understand that it's called Van Halen, and you're David Lee Roth, not David Van Halen? And you're okay with that?" Roth said, "Hey, man..."

By the way, as soon as he says, "Hey, man," I would later learn that's when the bullshit comes in. But initially I thought he was speaking from the heart. He said, "Hey, man! We're all for one and one for all, and I don't care what it's called." Well, later on, he did care. And there were other problems, too.

MATT: Didn't Eddie ask you guys if he could join Kiss at one point, because things got so bad in Van Halen?

GENE: Eddie did. During the making of "Jump," he was so miserable that he came down to the Record Plant where we were recording the beginnings of *Creatures of the Night*. And we had our own problems at that point with Ace [Frehley] and Peter [Criss]. We were looking for different guitar players to play on the record, and Eddie called to say, "I've got to talk to you." So he came to the studio, and he played me the demo for "Jump." He said, "The vocal's going to go here and the vocal's going to go there." I said, "Eddie, this is interesting, but why don't you put some guitars on it and let me hear what it sounds like then." He said, "Oh, there isn't going to be any guitars on it." I go, "*Really?*" But he clearly knew something. The thing that I was saying earlier about vision and having a point of view—that's priceless. And Eddie had that.

KEVIN KERSLAKE—*FILMMAKER*

KEVIN: Mike Patton is a total genius—in the craziest way. And with Mr. Bungle, especially lyrically, it's really dark and carnivalesque. The first line of "Travolta" says, "All behold the spectacle / A fleshy limbless rectangle," and that's about a double amputee. That image is so shockingly precise. Patton has a special knack for that kind of thing. My idea for the video was to do an everything and the kitchen sink kind of approach, and then just throw it all at the wall. Putting it together was sort of madness in itself; we were hanging people from hooks and there were severed heads with bugs crawling out of them. My job at that point was to step up and do something that had that same sort of visceral impact as Patton's lyrics.

MATT: How did you first meet Mike Patton?

KEVIN: I grew up with Roddy Bottum and Billy Gould. Their parents went to school with my parents, so we knew each other since we were little baby tots. They were younger than I was, so they were more friends with my brother, but we were around each other all the time because of our parents, who remained really good friends. And I was a fan of Faith No More throughout the years. But I'm sure we both felt for a while like it would be weird for us to work together, just because we knew each other so well. So I didn't push it, and they didn't push it. Plus, they were living in the San Francisco Bay Area by that point, so we hadn't spent that much time together in a while. But the lines converged when it was time for "Midlife Crisis." I was like, "Fuck yeah, I love that song." And I loved them—personally, but also as a band.

I can't remember how I came up with the idea of being quartered by horses, but it was just something that sort of stuck. And the question then was, "All right, well, how do we pull that off?" Because when you put four horses facing opposite directions, that's not in their nature. They're pack animals, so their instinct is going to tell them to go in the same direction. We were shooting above the stunt man who was on a marble plate in the middle of a quartering situation. We gave the cue and one horse reared up while the horse opposite pulled forward, which pulled that horse onto its back. It was basically about to land on the stunt man, and I was looking at all this from above, like, "Oh shit!" Luckily, the stunt man was so agile that he slipped off the marble plate and got out of there, and no horses were hurt. Thank God.

JOEY CASTILLO—*QUEENS OF THE STONE AGE, DANZIG, THE BRONX, CIRCLE JERKS, ZAKK SABBATH*

MATT: You strike me as a dude who has good relationships with everyone that you've ever worked with.

JOEY: Absolutely. I try to, man. I don't think there's really any bad blood with anybody that I've ever played with. There's always that moment of when something goes down where everybody has to kind of step away for a minute, just to let the dust settle. But the next time around when you see them, it's like, "Hey! How are you?"

MATT: A wise man once told me that nothing ends well—whether it's a friendship or a relationship, or a band mate, or whatever it is. When something ends, it's gnarly no matter what.

JOEY: And let's be honest, the word "end" is so final. It's done, it's over. And that doesn't necessarily have to be something to get angry about. But it can be sad and there can be that time. We've all been in those places, I think, where it's done and you kind of know that it's done, but you're waiting for the other person to say something before you do. And that starts to feel nasty after a while.

MATT: Yeah, that's when it starts to get mean: when people don't have the courage or the honesty to say, "It's done." And when it is done, it's the people who can't accept that it's over who struggle. You have to accept it.

JOEY: Correct.

MATT: How long did you play with Glenn Danzig?

JOEY: I think I was with Glenn for about seven years.

MATT: What was it like working with that dude? I'm good friends with Casey Chaos, and I know he's a good friend of Glenn's.

JOEY: I'm good friends with Casey, too.

MATT: I love that man so much.

JOEY: He's a sweetheart.

MATT: Actually, here's something that I want to say. Casey and Nick Oliveri are two dudes who have a pretty bad reputation around the world, because they're kind of crazy—for lack of a better word. And they've both done some pretty gnarly shit. Now, I know Casey pretty well. I don't know Nick as well, but I've interviewed him and spent a bit of time with him. And for me, they're two of the sweetest, coolest, greatest guys. They just happen to be wild animals.

JOEY: Absolutely. And here's the thing: I go way back with both Nick and Casey. I go way back with Glenn, too. And I get that question all the time: what's Glenn like? I get more questions about Glenn than anyone or anything else in my life or career. And to this day, Glenn and I remain friends. I just saw him recently at the Misfits show in LA, and it was incredible. I couldn't be happier for him. It's so well deserved and hard earned, I have to say. He's like my brother, and I love him to death. And I know that he'd do anything for me if I asked—and vice versa. He was tight with my parents, and I met his parents and his brothers. I have nothing but good things to say about Glenn. There's always ups and downs and that's with everybody, but there's nothing I could ever trash or talk shit about when it comes to Glenn. And the same goes for somebody like Nick—Nick's my brother as well.

MATT: He's a special guy.

JOEY: And that's the thing, I don't think those kinds of people are maliciously or intentionally doing anyone any harm. And people can say whatever they want, but I've never had those experiences with any of them.

MATT: Like I said, they're just wild animals.

JOEY: Absolutely. And what happens when you try to contain a wild animal? Nick's my brother. He lives down the street from me, his girl is best friends with my wife, and we have a long history together. We played together in Blast, we played together in Bloodclot, and we played together in Queens of the Stone Age. And I've always been put in situations with people that other people think are misfits, or crazy, or this or that. But I don't have any problems with these people. I love that.

MATT: From what I know of Casey and Nick, they both had pretty intense upbringings, which created a certain type of psyche in both of them where they're both a little loose and unpredictable.

JOEY: Which is awesome.

MATT: And they're not bad dudes. They're just people that have demons.

JOEY: One hundred percent. They're not bad at all; they're just wild animals. But they're not the first and they're not going to be the last.

MATT: I hope not. But I do feel that people like that are a dying breed.

JOEY: The times have definitely changed.

CASEY CHAOS—*AMEN, CHRISTIAN DEATH, SCUM*

MATT: What's been your favorite musical project outside of Amen?

CASEY: That's a good question. Well, Shannon [Larkin] and I had a little band with Josh [Homme] and Nick [Oliveri] from Queens of the Stone Age, and Twiggy [Ramirez] played bass. It was called Headband, and it was very short-lived. But fun while it lasted.

MATT: What era was that?

CASEY: That was when Queens [of the Stone Age] were doing *Songs for the Deaf,* and I was doing *Death Before Musick.*

MATT: Didn't you do one of the radio voices on the *Songs for the Deaf* album?

CASEY: I did.

MATT: For me, that album is one of the last great Californian rock 'n' roll records. It captures the landscape and the culture, and that band at that time were fucking unstoppable.

CASEY: They were brilliant. Amen did a show at The Troubadour once, and Queens opened for us under a different name. They wore masks and everything. It was fucking amazing. Those guys were good friends and good guys, and an amazing band. They were definitely a force.

MATT: Nick was on the show a while back. I loved talking to him.

CASEY: I love Nick.

MATT: He's a special guy isn't he?

CASEY: He's so unique.

MATT: He has a bad reputation for one reason or another, but I found him to be a total sweetheart.

CASEY: He is. He's an angel. And the thing about Nick that's so brilliant, is he can sing as fucking brutal as anyone, but he also has perfect pitch, so he can sing an acoustic song like an angel. He's such a unique talent. I love him. He's the best dude. He's definitely a great guy.

MATT: Are you close with Josh as well?

CASEY: Yeah, Josh and I are friends. I don't see him as much these days though. He's very busy.

MATT: I don't want to shit talk, but I think that band misses Nick. The magic of Queens of the Stone Age, for me, was the chemistry between Nick and Josh—those two together.

CASEY: I prefer the band with Nick in it, as well.

JOEY CASTILLO—*QUEENS OF THE STONE AGE, DANZIG, THE BRONX, CIRCLE JERKS, ZAKK SABBATH*

MATT: How does the offer to join Queens of the Stone Age come about?

JOEY: Funnily enough, it was through a friend of Casey Chaos, who was a photographer with Queens back in the day. My old band Sugartooth—that I was in prior to Danzig—had played a few times with Kyuss, so I knew Josh [Homme] a bit from then. And we kind of reconnected when I went out and played some shows with Goatsnake opening up for Queens in the UK, while they were still touring the *Rated R* album. So I got to see Josh and hang out a bit more then. And funnily enough, after I left Danzig I went to see Amen at The Viper Room in LA. I came home from tour, and I don't know if I'd spoken to Casey or Paul Fig or somebody else, but I heard that Amen were playing at The Viper Room that night, and I'd just got back into town so I went to check it out.

MATT: Amen were on fire at that point.

JOEY: They were fucking great. I loved them—*loved* them. During the very early stages of that band, Casey actually asked me to play drums for them, but I was busy doing stuff with Danzig at that time. So I went down to their show at The Viper Room, and I was hanging out after the gig when I saw my photographer friend Nigel. He was roommates with Josh [Homme] at the time, and he said to me, "Hey, did Josh ever get a hold of you?" I was like, "About what?" He said, "Queens are looking for a drummer." But I'd heard that they'd already found somebody. He was like, "No, there's a few people who have played for them that they've going back and forth with, but they haven't really found anybody yet. And your name came up a few times."

MATT: Was *Songs for the Deaf* out at this point?

JOEY: No. Dave Grohl had gone out and done the promo tour with them. And Dave had agreed to sign on and do the whole tour. But after they finished the promo tour, which I think was about two weeks, he decided not to do the rest of the dates. And he went and did another Foo Fighters record instead. So the *Deaf* record was dropping, the tour was booked, and everything was loaded and ready to go. And they'd been auditioning drummers for a good couple of weeks. I was just a fan of the band at this point; I was actually at the show they did at the Troubadour with Dave drumming for them.

Nigel said, "Give me your number; I'm going to give it to Josh." A couple of days went by, and I didn't hear anything—I didn't even think about it because I thought I knew the guy who thought he'd got the gig. Then I was out running some errands one day, and I got the call. I think it was [Mark] Lanegan that I spoke to, and he asked me what I was up to and if I could come down and play with the band. I was like, "I thought you guys had a drummer." He said, "No, we don't. Would you like to come down and play a little bit." A couple of hours later I got a call from Josh as well, asking if I wanted to come and play some songs. It was super casual, and there wasn't any pressure from either one of us, even though I knew this tour was literally days away.

MATT: That's the other thing with what guys like you do for a living: if you come across as too keen or pushy, it can put people off wanting to work with you.

JOEY: Absolutely. And at the same time, I was already in a band [Danzig], and I had a gig. So it wasn't like I desperately needed that

Queens gig. I was just a huge fan—I've always loved that band. And it was funny, just as I was getting ready to start learning all the songs, they sent me *Songs for the Deaf*. The album wasn't even out yet, and they sent me a burned CD with all the commercials on it, so it was just one big, long song—I couldn't even fast-forward any of the tracks.

MATT: So you had to sit through all that, "I need a saga. You can't even feel it," stuff?

JOEY: Yeah. Then a day later I got another call from Josh, and he was like, "Dude, I'm so sorry. But we're not going to be able to do this. My grandmother just passed away, and I have to go back to Palm Springs." Right then and there, I said, "No problem, dude. Handle your business. Thanks for everything. And if anything should happen, just let me know." That was on the Wednesday. Then Lanegan calls me on the Friday, and he was like, "Hey, man. I'm really sorry. But is there any way you could come and play with us." And he asked me if I could get it together over the weekend and be ready to go out on tour on Monday. I said, "Yeah. Just let me know the songs and let me know what's up."

Josh was still in Palm Springs at this point taking care of his family business. When he got back to me, he said, "See you on Sunday at noon." And the funny thing was, Josh didn't tell anyone except for Nick and Lanegan. So Troy [Van Leeuwen] had no idea I was coming in. And I knew Troy, and I knew his drummer who was trying out for the gig in Queens, so that was kind of weird. But we started playing, and it sounded fucking heavy, and raw and loud as shit. After a couple of songs, Josh stops me and says, "All right, man. Thanks for coming. I'll be right back." And he went outside to make some calls. He said, "I've got to talk to the old people and make some changes. And I need to go home and handle some business. But can we meet back here at three p.m.?"

MATT: That same day?

JOEY: Yeah, because the first show was the next day. Then all of a sudden the news was out all over LA. I was like, "Holy shit." And we rehearsed that day from three in the afternoon to three at night, just pounding a set together. Josh was like, "Can you do this?" And I said, "Yeah, of course." And the crazy thing was, the day before I had just been to a Danzig video shoot, so I was like, "Shit! Now I've got to call Glenn." And I knew that was going to suck.

MATT: You knew that in your heart?

JOEY: Yeah, I knew. But I also knew that it was time to go. We weren't really doing much, and we weren't working as much as I needed and wanted to be. But I felt bad, you know, because he's my brother. And he was a little bit weird at first.

MATT: It's that old saying again: nothing ends well.

JOEY: Yeah. But before I knew it everything was completely back to normal. I hit him up when I was on tour in fact, and Josh came with me. It was great.

DEAN KARR—*DIRECTOR, PHOTOGRAPHER*

MATT: Queens of the Stone Age.

DEAN: Oh, yeah.

MATT: "No One Knows" was one of the last great rock 'n' roll music videos from the MTV era. What was the inspiration behind that video?

DEAN: I was going for a graphic novel, comic book effect.

MATT: It came out around the same time as *Sin City*, so that aesthetic was definitely on trend.

DEAN: Yeah. It was a fairly easy shoot, too. We shot the band on green screen in England.

MATT: In England? Were they on tour? What was going on?

DEAN: It was somewhere in London. They were on tour, Dave [Grohl] was drumming with them, and I wanted to go and do like three countries with them. So after we wrapped, I jumped on the bus. It was so cool to see Dave drumming with them.

MATT: Was Mark Lanegan in the band at that time?

DEAN: You better believe it. And he's my brother from Seattle.

MATT: For me, that was that band at the absolute peak of their powers. That album [*Songs for the Deaf*] is one of the great Californian rock 'n' roll records.

DEAN: I agree. And as far as the inspiration for the video goes, I was coming home from that first college that I told you about—about six hours from Seattle. It was during the winter, I was driving solo, and I hit a fucking deer in the snow. So I pulled over, and I got out. It was nighttime, and I was trying to follow the trail of blood to see if the deer was still alive or whatever. But I couldn't find it anywhere. In my head, it was going to rise up and strike me for hurting it. So that whole story was based on my drive home from Washington State University in my 1967 Mustang Fastback.

JOEY CASTILLO—*QUEENS OF THE STONE AGE, DANZIG, THE BRONX, CIRCLE JERKs, ZAKK SABBATH*

JOEY: For me, *Songs for the Deaf* was the last real rock 'n' roll record that made a statement and an impression to where it could not be ignored. I feel like it was a weird time that was ending for rock, and this new thing was happening.

MATT: It was the end of the record business, wasn't it?

JOEY: Yeah. That record caught the tail end of it. And we'd all been playing in other bands throughout those years, keeping it raw and real, so to speak.

MATT: Then you all rode that wave of success with *Songs for the Deaf*. And rightly so.

JOEY: It was insane, man. And that lineup that we toured with—Josh Homme, Nick Oliveri, Mark Lanegan, Troy Van Leeuwen, and myself— was monster. Wherever we played, we rolled in like a gang. That was something that was never overlooked. And it wasn't intentional.

MATT: You weren't peacocking or strutting around like you owned the place.

JOEY: No, not at all. We were the opposite of that. At that point, Queens still had a lot of its underground punk rock ideas and ways that it went about doing things—our sound, our gear, how we stepped up on stage, how the show went down. We used to use this term a lot among ourselves: there was this controlled chaos to what we did. We could push things, speed and arrangement wise, and everything got pushed right to the fucking edge where it was just about to fall off the rails, then we would reel it back together. The insanity that was going on at that time as well—

MATT: Was there drugs and chaos everywhere the band went?

JOEY: I wouldn't have changed it for the world. Just like with Glenn, those guys were my brothers, and that was a time that's never going to come back. It's never going to be recaptured; it was just that time, and everybody was there together. It really was the perfect mix of everything. Everybody was having a great time, and it was a lot of fun. It was still dangerous, and it was still reckless, and it was still controlled, and it was still alive. Not that it's not anymore. But it's different now.

MATT: Nick said something interesting to me once. He said that nowadays there's people attached to that brand—and it is a brand now—that he wouldn't have wanted attached to it back in the day.

JOEY: Yeah, he and I have talked about that.

MATT: Because it was their thing, right? Him and Josh built that band together.

JOEY: Nick was the face of Queens early on. And that's not to take anything away from anyone else's creativity, regardless of how things came to an end with Josh and I—we're friends now and we're cool. It came to an end, and it wasn't exactly the best way to come to an end, but he's still one of the best people that I've ever worked with. That guy's talent is just beyond, and I feel nothing but proud of everything that I was a part of with that band, just like I was with Glenn. There's a real feeling of accomplishment there, of making a mark and leaving an impression.

MATT: And that's beyond success. It's about legacy.

JOEY: That's just it. To this day, I've never been a person that was out to capture success. I love what I do on all levels, whether it's playing to a room of ten people or a festival of twenty or thirty thousand. It's the same thing for me, and I approach them both the exact same way: to have as much fun as I possibly can and kick as much ass as I possibly can. We all know there's some stuff that's out of our hands, and some shows are just better than others, and some days are just better than others. But I don't ever go, "Man, there's not enough people here." Or, "I don't like where we are on the bill."

MATT: Or, "My dinner was shit!"

JOEY: Or, "My room is shit!"

MATT: Diva shit.

JOEY: Yeah. Give a fuck, you know? It's about the music. Everybody knows and everybody's heard it a million times, but music and the arts in general is bigger than all of us.

MATT: I'm not a religious person, but there's something about that element of being at a show: it's a communal moment for everyone who's there. It exists in that time and then it's gone. But for that one moment, you're all there and you're all together.

JOEY: That's why it's tough to get things back together, especially over the years when people either grow apart, or they don't grow as players and people. And that's not good or bad, just that everybody's not on the same path anymore. Everybody's veered in different directions, and it's hard to wrangle them all together.

MATT: That's true of friendships and relationships as well—not just band mates.

JOEY: Yeah. We all know what that's like, trying to get back with an ex-girlfriend.

MATT: Trying to recapture the old magic that once was.

JOEY: Exactly. And my time in Queens was magical, as cheesy as that sounds. It's something that I wouldn't change for the world.

JESSE HUGHES—*EAGLES OF DEATH METAL, BOOTS ELECTRIC*

MATT: There's a brilliant scene in the Colin Hanks documentary [*Nos Amis*], where you're talking about the night that you and Joshua [Homme] were driving down to the studio to start work on the first Eagles of Death Metal album [*Peace, Love, Death Metal*], and he gives you the talk. He says something to the effect of, "We're going into this world now, and bad things can happen in there, so I want to just prepare you for it."

JESSE: Yeah, and I want to write a book just about that lesson of preparedness that he gave me, almost like a rock 'n' roll bible. It's how I've taken everything in this business. I came into it so late in life, and so blessed with advantages that I only wanted to capitalize on them. I never looked at it like I was ever in Joshua's shadow; I was always in the shade. And if anyone wanted to accuse me of riding coattails, I'd be like, "Duh! It's a lot easier and a lot better on the legs." One of the proudest things I'll ever have in my life is that I'm a musical peer of my best friend Joshua. That will never suck—ever.

DEAN KARR—*DIRECTOR, PHOTOGRAPHER*

MATT: You shot the cover for the debut Slipknot album, right?

DEAN: Yeah.

MATT: It's such an iconic image. I remember picking up *Kerrang!* as a kid at school, and thinking, "Wow! Who the hell are these guys?" How did they come your way?

DEAN: Ross Robinson was producing the album, and I was spending a lot of time in the studio with him. That was at Indigo Ranch out in

Malibu. I think it's burned down since then, but Ross did pretty much all of his work out there back then. And I did almost all the covers for all of Ross's projects—even Vanilla Ice.

MATT: What was your initial impression of Slipknot?

DEAN: They were great, man. We got along famously. After we did the photoshoot, we ended up in Vegas together a couple of times, and there was a lot of chaos. But Slipknot were always really cool and professional. And they're on top of their game right now. They had to do some personnel changes, and sadly we lost Paul [Gray] on bass, but I've been shooting a lot of their live stuff lately, and it's like a photographer's dream.

MATT: Let's talk about Casey Chaos. He's coming over in a bit.

DEAN: Oh, boy. He's not coming to my house. He's gonna be in my house? He ain't coming in here!

MATT: How far do you two go back?

DEAN: We go back, man—probably twenty-six years.

MATT: Is that another Ross Robinson connection?

DEAN: Absolutely.

MATT: He came out to LA when he was super young, right?

DEAN: I didn't know him when he was so young, but I know that he was a skateboarding rat kid that lived in Florida. Then he came out here and did some pretty amazing stuff. And we did some pretty amazing stuff together.

MATT: The *We Have Come for Your Parents* album cover was another super iconic image.

DEAN: Yeah. We did two album covers and the video ["The Price of Reality"] for Amen, and the video is just as fierce as it gets. He was on fire for that one. For the album cover, we had like twenty of our rock 'n' roll friend's children naked and crusted in clay out in the desert. It was like a rock 'n' roll day care gone wrong. It was pretty cool, man.

Casey and I have known each other a long time and been in a lot of trouble together. We've had a lot of fun together, too. He's a great guy, and you guys will have a lot of fun talking.

MATT: How long has he been on the straight and narrow for now?

DEAN: He's been a good boy for a while now, not running into the neighborhood parked cars—not lately anyway. But he's great. He's working on a bunch of new projects, and I'm sure he'll tell you all about them. We just need to get them done and get that band out there kicking ass again like they like to do.

MATT: Who did you meet first, Casey or Ross?

DEAN: I honestly don't know, man. I was on a shoot with Korn in 1994 for the Ross Robinson album [*Korn*], and I think that's when I first met Ross. I went through those photos just the other day. It's crazy how young we all were—we were all around the same age. It was a funky time.

MATT: A good time to be in LA?

DEAN: Yes sir. We were on the pulse of what was going on in this town. We were like the Rat Pack.

MATT: Any fun memories from that time spring to mind?

DEAN: You can ask Casey about the time Ross Robinson, Casey, and I got arrested at Excalibur Casino and spent the night in jail. I think I have a photo of our mug shots somewhere.

CASEY CHAOS—*AMEN, CHRISTIAN DEATH, SCUM*

MATT: Tell me about your friendship with Ross Robinson. Was he the first close friend that you made when you moved out to LA?

CASEY: He was one of the first guys who was interested in my band at the time, and then we became really close friends. This was after Christian Death, which was the band that I was in when I first moved out here, and Disorderly Conduct, which was my first band—that was a hardcore punk band. Then I had this idea for a band called Amen, and we started playing around town. At that time, we were playing a lot with a band called Creep, which was Korn but under a different name with a different singer. Ross was working with them and the singer in Creep was a big fan of what we were doing, so he turned me on to Ross, and Ross was like, "Dude, I love your band. I want to record your demo." And I was like, "Cool. Let's do it." So that's the way it all began.

MATT: Weren't you telling me once that Ross asked you to think about being the singer in Korn?

CASEY: Yeah, they were looking for a singer, and they wanted to see if I was interested. But they were a funky band, and I'm not much of a funky guy. I'm more of a metallic punk rock guy.

MATT: So that never happened?

CASEY: No.

MATT: Did you entertain the idea?

CASEY: No. I was pretty headstrong in those days with what I wanted to do. For me, music was always about expression, and I felt like they already had their expression. They had their writers and a band of friends who had been together for a long time, and that was totally cool. Hats off to them. I just had to do my own thing. And it didn't matter if it was going to be popular, I just had to get this shit out of me.

MATT: Let's talk about your old friend Dean Karr. Dean told me to ask you about the time that you, him, and Ross Robinson got arrested in Las Vegas and spent the night in jail.

CASEY: Oh, God. He didn't tell you about it?

MATT: No, he put it all on you. He said, "You ask Casey about it!"

CASEY: Thanks, Dean. Well, it was funny because I'd become real close friends with Dean, and I'd been friends with Ross for a long time, and it was crazy to me that they'd never met. It was just so strange. So I went, "All right, that's it. This is preposterous. We're going to

Vegas this weekend—the three of us." And we all jumped in a car and went to Vegas. Then we ended up in jail later that night. It was just some stupid bullshit, but it was funny and the cops were super cool. They were laughing about the whole thing, and they took a bunch of Polaroids of us looking all dingy on the floor.

MATT: You did a proper photo shoot playing up to the lens and everything?

CASEY: Yeah, totally—as if we were convicts in San Quentin or something like that.

MATT: Did they know who any of you were?

CASEY: I don't think so. They were just cool about it. And we weren't trying to be macho or anything like that. We were just, like, "Whatever you say, boss." They were having a good time. It was all good.

MATT: It's seems like you were right there at a time in LA with people like Ross and Dean, where all your friends were involved in the coolest shit going on.

CASEY: Absolutely.

MATT: You were right on the pulse of all of it.

CASEY: Absolutely. That's what I really love about this city: you run into people who are taking care of business and making shit happen. They were all doing so much incredible work, and I found that really inspiring.

MATT: Were you around when Slipknot were taking off?

CASEY: Yeah. Slipknot and Amen recorded our first albums at the same time in the same studio with Ross. I blew my voice out recording the Amen record [Amen], and Slipknot was booked in the day after our time was up, so Ross said, "Why don't you just stay up here," because we were living at this studio [Indigo Ranch] in Malibu in the middle of the mountains. Slipknot had come up early and were hanging out with us while we were still recording, and we all became friends. And when Slipknot were done recording during the day, I would go in at night and finish off my vocals.

MATT: That's wild.

DAVE FORTMAN—*UGLY KID JOE, PRODUCER*

DAVE: "Snuff" by Slipknot was a fucking fight for my life to get that to happen.

MATT: As a single or just as a song on the album?

DAVE: Everything—to get it done at all. Corey [Taylor] was the only one who was really there and believed in it like I believed in it. I had to get the rest of the band to just play shit on it, then I Frankensteined it all together. Corey cried his face off in the studio when I played it back for him—just the rough mix of it. I was like, "Dude, I told you this was something fucking special, man." And he was like, "Fuck, I get it now." He was freaking out.

The record company didn't see it either. So then I'm fucking tripping with Monte Conner [former Senior Vice President of A&R for Roadrunner Records] on email because he's trying to use some stupid B-side from the studio where Shawn [Crahan] and some other guys in the band were recording. I was like, "What the fuck is going on?" Then they tested the song, and he came back and apologized to me. He said, "Sorry, Dave. You saw it. We didn't see it." Then it becomes three times as successful, commercially, as anything the band's ever done. "Snuff" was the reason that album [*All Hope Is Gone*] went platinum in America. But I really had to go to war for it.

MATT: Was that record the last Slipknot album with the original lineup?

DAVE: Yeah.

MATT: Put us in the eye of the storm: what was it like making that album with that intense mix of personalities?

DAVE: They split camps on me. And maybe that was partly my fault, but I wasn't feeling the fact that you had these core dudes who wrote the history of the band—Corey, Paul [Gray], and Joey [Jordison], who'd done the demos, like they always do—and now there was this opposition over here who wanted to write as well. I wasn't all about any of that shit. And they got mad that I didn't want to entertain that idea, so they went and built another studio next door. And when they put "Snuff" on their board, that's when I fucking lost it. I was like, "Corey, follow me. You're laying this down right now on a click, and I'm going to develop it tonight. Trust me."

MATT: It wasn't without its troubles then?

DAVE: It was a disaster. It was a total nightmare. Me and the core people who made that band happen in the first place got along famously; Me, Joey, Paul, and Corey are responsible for the band's success on that album—hands down. Jim [Root] and Shawn are responsible for complaining a lot.

Shawn came in to play percussion, and he'd never even heard some of the songs. That's how much you respect your band? You don't even know the fucking demos. Sid [Wilson]—what a nightmare! He didn't know a single fucking song when he came in to perform. Then he gets on VH1, and when they asked him how it was working with Dave Fortman, he says, "He didn't really do anything." *Really?* You weren't even fucking there, dude. Those guys were so fucking disrespectful.

Jim fucked with my career. He couldn't wait. He slagged the shit out of me in the press. It stayed on Google forever—I got rid of it eventually. They asked him, "So, how was it working with Dave Fortman?" He basically said straight up, "He made me appreciate Rick Rubin. He couldn't do what Rick could do: get nine people in the room together and on the same page." You know what? That's not my fucking job at this point. I've got the demos that I need, I've got the people who wrote them, and I've got the fucking rock stars who will make it happen for me.

I don't give a fuck if you're friends or not with these people. It's your band, you guys are all millionaires now, go figure out how to be friends again. I don't want to be a fucking psychologist for a nine-headed fucking monster; I've got what I need, and I don't need him complaining about it. But they wouldn't come to practice, and they wouldn't do shit. Joey started playing the drums for the songs he wrote, just playing them. Then I went and got Shawn and Jim individually, and I made them listen to the drum tracks. I asked them, "Is this fine? Is it okay?" And they were like, "Yeah, man. Keep going, bro." They gave me permission to do it.

When Jim started playing guitar—he wrote one little transition in one of these songs that Joey had written—the transition didn't go that well, and all of a sudden, all hell breaks loose because I decided to go back in and tighten up the drums. And Joey didn't care. Then all of a sudden there's this big fucking thing about how I didn't capture the vibe, and they want to redo all the drums. Joey basically said, "Go back and tell those mother fuckers that I'm not redoing the drums. I'll take all these songs, and I'll walk out the fucking band tomorrow." So I went and told them that, and they got shut down like little kids, and they fucking hated me for it.

But the battle was on, and we were always going to win. Right in the palm of our hands, we had this album that was going to crush people, and as it started to grow they got more and more mad. Jim didn't want to use any of the music. He called a dinner with me and Corey, him and Shawn, and their management. Corey spoke up and said, "I just spent all this time writing the lyrics to these demos and I think they're great." I said, "I think they're fucking fantastic, too."

So you had a guy that was trying to eliminate all this shit that had just got written, that was about to become the biggest per capita fucking singles they'd ever had, and he was trying to flush it all down the toilet based on his own ego. It was really fucking douchey of him to do that. I will give him this though, he did come back in the press later on and say that it wasn't really my fault, that they themselves were in an inner turmoil. And the sweet part of that record was seeing them on fucking Jimmy Kimmel playing "Snuff." I was like, "You motherfuckers. I told you!"

MATT: In moments like that, does all the hard work, struggle, and grief pay off?

DAVE: Fuck yeah, it pays off. It still pays my bills. The song was bigger than the band and sometimes I can see that. So you have to fight to the death to make it happen. Corey gave me the demo out of a Garage Band recording, and I couldn't even drive my car without driving off the road because it was so intense. I was like, "Fuck, this song is amazing." But nobody else was feeling it. Paul was actually the first person to speak up and say, "This is the kind of song that could make the band go platinum." And he was right.

MATT: Was Paul a good dude?

DAVE: He was the sweetest guy ever. Me and Corey talked when the song went to number one, but I called him. Paul was the only guy who called me directly. He said, "I know it was hell to go through. But it was worth it. You did a fucking great job, man."

MATT: Do you think the band can still be Slipknot without Paul and Joey?

DAVE: They can be a version of it. But the songs will never be there because the main songwriters are gone. Name any Slipknot song that you love from the past; one of the those guys either cowrote or wrote it—period. The musical body of "Duality" was written just like it is in Joey's mom's basement, by Joey, then Corey wrote lyrics over the top of it. All that shit, man. "Dead Memories," what a beautiful song. Paul wrote all that music. "Psychosocial" was Joey—all of it. There's not going to be that shit happening ever again.

KEVIN KERSLAKE—*FILMMAKER*

MATT: Talk to me about working on the "Cherub Rock" video with Smashing Pumpkins.

KEVIN: That song is really trying to kick indie rock impulses in the teeth. It was aimed at the indie rockers who sort of wanted to be coddled and insulated and not really grow up—in Billy's eyes. So lyrically, it's a song that takes a negative approach toward something that I hold really dear, because I think so much amazing music came out of that culture. One of the things that I wanted to do, which I don't think Billy [Corgan] really got at the time, was to shoot in a format that was pure indie rock, and that was Super 8. You can tell by the next videos that they did off that album [*Siamese Dream*] that they wanted a lot more polish. "Cherub Rock" was probably a little dirty for them.

MATT: We obviously have to talk about Nirvana. You shot four videos for them, right?

KEVIN: Yeah.

MATT: Which one was first?

KEVIN: We shot "Come as You Are" first. Then "In Bloom." Then "Lithium." Then "Sliver." We were doing a film after that, as well; it was supposed to be about the Nirvana experience from the inside and out. We were at the stage where it was sort of the outward look in, with a lot of live performances and stuff, and Kurt [Cobain] died right in the middle of that.

MATT: How did you wind up working with the band in such a close and intimate way? They could've obviously worked with anyone and done different videos with different people. But it seemed like you were their guy. Was it just a personal bond that you shared with each other?

KEVIN: I think so. And Nirvana was a funny one. To be in that bubble—and this is just a third person's perspective on Nirvana—from literally living under a bridge to then all of a sudden having the world at your feet, that's abrasive in so many ways. So Kurt was really protective about who he worked with. I've been told they didn't have a great experience on "Smells Like Teen Spirit," and that was the first video off the album [*Nevermind*]. When it came time to do the second one, they wanted to work with somebody who carried the same aesthetic. And I'd seen them tour with Sonic Youth, who they had opened for on several tours. But the first time I met Kurt properly, he said to me right off the bat, "You've done my favorite video in the world."

MATT: Which was?

KEVIN: "Halah," my first video for Mazzy Star. And it was pretty funny because when you meet people like that, the praise typically goes one way.

MATT: It's outgoing.

KEVIN: Exactly. So that was pretty disarming. But we connected, and we talked for a long time, and it felt like we shared that sort of bond. So when it came time to shoot the "Come as You Are" video, Kurt said he wanted to work with me. And his only note to me was, "I don't want to be in the video," because he was on the front of every magazine cover in the country by that point. His image was ubiquitous. Actually, all of Nirvana's images were ubiquitous; they were sick of themselves. And I knew I was going to have to walk the line with that because the record company wasn't going to like it. So my job was to come up with something that served both masters. That's why there's so many images in that video that sort of obscure the band's identity.

MATT: Tell me about "In Bloom." That's my favorite song by Nirvana. And you address the subject of fame and celebrity directly in that video.

KEVIN: Originally, I came up with an idea that ultimately became part of "Heart-Shaped Box." That was about a kid growing up in a [Ku Klux] Klan family, then seeing them for what it was and pivoting out of it. There was a lot of abstract stuff and some *Wizard of Oz* imagery in there too. It was a very ambitious idea. But the record company didn't have the time to develop it. So the idea was basically to do something just riffing off Ed Sullivan and how we like our pop stars, and we went down that road with our tongues-in-cheek.

MATT: It fits well with the song, which seems to be having a dig at people who were jumping on board the alternative rock band wagon.

KEVIN: Sure, and liked the band for all the wrong reasons. It's funny because that song showed up on the album that made them popular, but they weren't super popular when they wrote it. It's almost like it anticipated that fame.

MATT: I was watching the "In Bloom" video the other day, and it's funny how in character Dave Grohl is. He's fully in the zone. He's obviously well-known for being funny in all the Foo Fighters videos nowadays. But you must've seen it first-hand, even back then, that guy's a comedian.

KEVIN: Completely. He was super hammy. Krist [Novoselic] was too, actually. That video is only four takes: two in suits and two in dresses. And every single one of those takes, you could've just taken that one and released it as a video.

MATT: Just as one shot?

KEVIN: Yeah. They were all super funny guys.

JESSE MALIN—*HEART ATTACK, D GENERATION, SOLO ARTIST*

MATT: What was it like working with Ric Ocasek? As well as The Cars, who I adore, he obviously did those early Weezer albums, and he produced albums by Suicide and Jonathan Richman.

JESSE: And the Bad Brains.

MATT: Of course.

JESSE: I didn't realize he also did that Romeo Void track, "I might like you better if we slept together." ["Never Say Never"] I used to hear that in clubs as a kid. But we had a major label record deal, and we met with all these producers because our A&R guy really wanted to get it right. We got dropped from EMI after our first record [*D Generation*], and we got another chance at Columbia Records, so we met with everybody. We were getting fat from all the dinners and the beers on the record company budget.

MATT: How old are you at this point?

JESSE: I was in my mid-twenties.

MATT: A good time to be getting wined and dined.

JESSE: Yeah, it was good. But we wanted to get back on the road and make this record. The A&R guy was holding it tight to do it right, you know? And some of the people in the band could be very disrespectful, and we could be rough with people. But here came Ric Ocasek, who we met at a place called The Coffee Shop on Union Square, and everybody just listened to what he had to say. He'd worked with the Bad Brains and we'd heard stories about how difficult HR could be. They were an intense, volatile band, and we figured if he could deal with HR and the Bad Brains, then he could deal with our little band. So we got together with Ric, and we loved him right away. We did it at Electric Lady Studios where we'd done the other record.

MATT: Is that studio gone now?

JESSE: It's still there: 52 West Eighth Street. It's one of the few things we have left in New York. And recording *No Lunch* there was just a great experience. Ric brought Alan Vega from Suicide in to sing on the song "Frankie," and that was when I first connected with Alan. And I would see Ric in New York until recently. He lived on Nineteenth Street and Gramercy, and he'd always walk around the neighborhood. I miss that. There were these characters as I grew up in New York that you'd see, like Joey Ramone, Howard Stern, and Paul Stanley. You still get a little bit of that, but that generation is changing and dying out. And whenever I would see Ric, he'd always come over and be very sweet. He'd put his hand on me and see how I was doing. And I got to interview him years later for the Bad Brains documentary [*Bad Brains: A Band in D.C.*] that I did with Mandy Stein.

MATT: I didn't know you worked on that film?

JESSE: I did the interviews.

MATT: Right. I didn't know that.

JESSE: I get an Executive Producer credit because they didn't know what to give me, but I did all the interviews from the past with people like John Joseph, Anthony Kiedis, and Ric Ocasek. Then the filmmakers followed the band around in the present.

MATT: It's a great documentary.

JESSE: Yeah, at the time there was so much going on around it—endless energy—and it was a heavy time. But now when I look back and watch it, I really get to enjoy it. Mandy Stein makes great films. And it was great to sit with Ric again. He's such a sweetheart, beyond being a great artist. And that first Cars record [*The Cars*] is amazing.

MATT: I think it's the best new wave album ever made.

JESSE: It's just a great rock record. And Roy Thomas Baker produced it, so you hear all those vocal things that he did with Queen on there. "Good Times Roll" has all these voices layered. Whenever those songs come on the radio nowadays, they still sound fresh. That record was so ahead of its time. It still holds up and most people still haven't reached that level now. It's one of those records where every single song is good.

MATT: It's perfect.

JESSE: So great. His solo stuff was really cool, too. And he produced some of my favorite records. I'm going to miss Ric a lot.

JESSE HUGHES—*EAGLES OF DEATH METAL, BOOTS ELECTRIC*

MATT: Where does your friendship with Brent Hinds from Mastodon begin?

JESSE: Well, it begins in the American south. He's from Georgia, and I'm from South Carolina, and my momma is from Georgia, so we immediately connected from jump street the very first time we were at a festival together. We hung out together because we were the only two hillbillies, and there was just a natural affinity there. On top of that, he's one of the finest fucking individuals I've ever known. He is one of the most unparalleled, finest fucking men I've ever known in my life. And he's one of the most gifted guitarists and songwriters of our generation. All that together provides one monster of a human being. I loved him immediately. There was a wildness in him.

MATT: There is a wildness in him, I can see that.

JESSE: There is a wildness in him, and it's completely real. It's completely legitimate, and it's terrifying. It's also beautiful and precious. I feel very lucky to be in a peer group and a generation that has such people in it. I really hope the next generation has it—we'll see.

MATT: It's a continuation of the community that first emerged during the sixties and seventies, where you had these groups of guys making music together, and they were all like brothers.

JESSE: They were true peers and friends, yeah. And they also understood what they do in this rock 'n' roll world, and the moments that are possible in show business. Every time Brent comes onstage with us, it's fucking magic. He's come out on stage and played with us in a clown outfit before. It was just a hilarious statement to the bands. The crowd probably didn't get it, and they didn't need to, just the fact that he felt comfortable and safe enough to be like that with us, those are moments that you couldn't ask for, and couldn't write.

I hope one day to make an album with Brent. I'd kind of like him to produce parts of my next solo album. I think when he's unchained from the constraints of heaviness, the places that his mind goes and the music that he loves is so vast, it's ridiculous. In fact, I think I'm going to make that an order of business right after this interview. I'm going to call him up—I'm not even fucking around.

ALAN ROBERT—*LIFE OF AGONY, COMIC BOOK CREATOR*

MATT: Was it 1997 when Mina left Life of Agony?

ALAN: Yeah. *Soul Searching Sun* came out that year, and that's when she left.

MATT: Was it evident when you were making that album that things weren't great, and that it was going to play out in the way that it did?

ALAN: No. In fact, making that record was a lot of fun, and I felt like we were actually in a more positive place. Even the artwork on the record was more vibrant and colorful and hopeful—in a way. Even though there was some really dark lyrics on that record, the vibe and the production was very uplifting. So I think we were in a better place as a band. But Mina was battling her own demons with her sexuality and identity issues. And I believe she said to me along the way that she didn't want to be a success as a man. So she just had to leave before that happened, because we all felt like it was going in that direction.

MATT: So it wasn't like the creative well was drying out? And it wasn't like the band wasn't functioning or progressing or anything like that?

ALAN: No. In fact, we had more opportunities with that record than ever before: songs like "Weeds" were doing well at radio and that was opening a lot of doors for us, even on different continents. We had plans to do Australia, New Zealand, and Japan on that album cycle. But we were forced to cancel those tours because she left the group.

MATT: That's must've been tough.

ALAN: I'll never forget, we were on the front cover of *The Aquarian Weekly*, which was the local New Jersey entertainment music paper, and in the back of the paper we had a want ad for a new singer. So we were on the front cover, and we had a want ad for a new singer in the back. That was the crazy time that it was. And when Mina quit, we were locked in to do a video for the song "Desire." Everything was all set and Roadrunner were like, "We need you to do the video anyway." And we didn't want to lose momentum because we'd worked so hard on the album. So we just had a bunch of characters mouth the words. Then I think it was Scott Ian and the Anthrax guys who said we should try out Whit Crane from Ugly Kid Joe.

MATT: I know Whit very well. He's a dear friend, and on paper his voice is the perfect fit for LOA. There's not many people out there who can hit those notes.

ALAN: That was the problem: people couldn't hit those notes. They couldn't pull off the *River Runs Red* stuff.

MATT: Whit's such an underrated singer.

ALAN: Yeah, and I really wasn't that familiar with Ugly Kid Joe or how differently they were perceived from us. We just wanted a singer who was a confident front man, and Whit walked in with this confidence and the pipes. He also had experience with large crowds—he'd been playing arenas with Bon Jovi—so we were like, "Let's see if this can work."

We were offered the Megadeth tour at that point, and we didn't want to turn it down. So I wrote down all the lyrics on these giant oak tag papers for Whit. If you were up on the balcony, it must've looked like there was a bunch of cue cards on the floor. But he pulled it off, and I give him a lot of credit for that. He learned a lot of material in a very short amount of time. And we rocked some really big crowds that year. We did Ozzfest '98 with Incubus, System of a Down, and Limp Bizkit, and Fred Durst would come out and jam with us. So we were like, "Maybe we have a shot at continuing what we love to do," even though Mina had left.

MATT: Was it a painful breakup when Mina did leave?

ALAN: It's funny, our last show together was at Irving Plaza in New York City. She called me the next morning, and said, "Al, I just can't do this anymore. I'm gonna have to quit." And I said, "That's cool." The last thing she said was, "I'm just in too much pain to continue." I accepted it and that was it. But I was upset because I didn't understand why she was in this turmoil. It wasn't until she came out, which she needed to do to be happy, that I understood.

MATT: When Mina came back into the band after she'd transitioned, did you feel reignited as a group? Did it feel like a new chapter and a fresh start?

ALAN: I think when we came back out on stage with Mina as Mina for the first time in 2014, we didn't give a shit what anyone thought. I was so proud of her: what a brave thing to do in such a masculine genre. We were just like, "Fuck you, if you don't like it." That was the attitude we took everywhere that we went. In terms of making new music, that was just something that we had to do, because it had been twelve years since *Broken Valley*. It wasn't like we had this epiphany to write new music. We just *had to*, you know?

MATT: Did it feel like you were working with someone new?

ALAN: Not at all. It's my old friend from childhood. If anything, it's just cool to see her happy. Nothing is holding her back anymore, and I feel that in the live situation too. She's really come out of her shell. In the early nineties, she was very shy on stage, and almost hid behind the microphone. She was battling her own issues in her own mind and that's kind of where we went with the *Ugly* record—more introverted. But now she's right in everyone's face with the new stuff and the old stuff, and it's a different live show. It's kind of like back to when we were kids, before she got lost along the way. And she may have always been battling that, even as a young man, but it didn't show as much. Now she just wants to play the songs, and celebrate the music and celebrate life, and she's put all that darkness behind her. She really connects with the audience in a way that she never did back then. And that's awesome to see. It's inspiring to me.

JESSE HUGHES—*EAGLES OF DEATH METAL, BOOTS ELECTRIC*

MATT: Tell me about being in a band with Jennie Vee, the magic and the power of that woman, and what she's brought to the Eagles of Death Metal.

JESSE: I expect a lot from the band members in Eagles of Death Metal. And because my mother is my hero, and because I champion and I love women—I genuinely love women so much—I expect a lot when a girl comes into this band, just because I know that they're up against a lot. They're in a boy's club, and they're up against a lot of shit that isn't fucking fair. That being said, no one is a boy or a girl when they join the Eagles of Death Metal. They're whatever instrument they're playing—that's it. You're either good, great, or whatever.

MATT: Or out of the gang?

JESSE: Or out of the gang. And Jennie joined the band when it was a very difficult time to replace Matt McJunkins. Every band member that's gone on, it's difficult to even consider the possibility of having to replace them, so I've learned not to. You can't replace McJunkins, so why try? Let's just find a bass player. And when Jennie came in, the possibilities of what can happen in this band were immediately enhanced, and what I thought we could pull off live as a band just jumped. And that was exciting. It was really fucking exciting. Our bare minimum bar has been raised so much higher, and it's even more exhaustive now. Everyone's challenged everyone and everyone's exalted themselves.

Now, we're not only a band who came through something crazy, we're just one of these bad ass bands of rock 'n' roll that won't ever be stopped. There's a difference between vanity and conceit: one is informed by reality. And the version that's informed by reality makes me as proud as a shiny red fucking boner in the middle of a snowstorm to say, "I'm in a bad ass rock 'n' roll band," because of these guys. And Jennie Vee is magic. She's an angel to me; she's one of my dearest friends.

You could point at any one of my friends in my peer group, and I'll tell you they're one of the finest individuals I've ever known. And it's always true, because they all are. You are only the quality of those who you surround yourself with. And you're only as strong as your weakest link. All of these clichés make sense. When you surround yourself with a certain type of person, those qualities will attract similar qualities. It's pretty simple. *Life* is pretty simple. But that doesn't mean it's fucking easy.

KEVIN KERSLAKE—*FILMMAKER*

MATT: Would you say you worked more with Scott Weiland than anybody else?

KEVIN: Probably, yeah.

MATT: You did "Interstate Love Song" and "Vasoline" for Stone Temple Pilots.

KEVIN: A couple of others too. I did "Days of the Week," and a couple of live shows. I also did a video ["Mockingbird Girl"] for Scott's side-project, Magnificent Bastards. And then, obviously, Velvet Revolver.

MATT: So, around seven or eight projects in total?

KEVIN: Yeah.

MATT: Was the relationship there one of purely creative understanding, or was there a personal friendship between you two as well?

KEVIN: Both. It wasn't dissimilar to my relationship with Kurt, to be honest. There was a trust there that was born early on in both of their careers. And as they became more popular, they were looking for normalcy. I think that's something that you seek out when you're in that place: you need someone you can trust and something that you know.

MATT: Were you one of the first people to find out about Velvet Revolver?

KEVIN: Other than the label, yes. Scott called me and asked if I'd be interested in doing a video for them.

MATT: And you based the "Slither" video on a party in the Catacombs of Paris?

KEVIN: Yeah.

MATT: Did you shoot the whole video in Paris?

KEVIN: No, we actually built a set in Los Angeles because Scott couldn't leave the country at that point. I don't think he could even leave the city. He was dealing with some legal issues, so there were definitely some restraints on him. But in Paris, there are miles of these Catacombs that exist deep underground, and the idea behind that video was to recreate them. For me, the video for "Slither" was about going to that primordial spot where your love of music and your love of creating music exists— that primal element. And the guys in that band were all rock gods, so how could we deify them anymore? All those Guns N' Roses videos are so bombastic, and I can't stand that aesthetic.

MATT: You didn't fancy filming Slash from a helicopter while ripping a solo outside of a church in the middle of the desert then?

KEVIN: Exactly. So instead of doing that, let's have them go underground and connect to something that's much more primal. I didn't want anything that was evocative of a business calculation or an entrepreneurial venture with the biggest musicians on the planet. And we had to deal with these legal problems that Scott was facing. The challenge was, how do you create the Paris Catacombs in Los Angeles? So we built them.

MATT: He really looks like a combination of David Bowie, Iggy Pop, and Mick Jagger in that video.

KEVIN: There's a little Peter Murphy [Bauhaus] in there, too.

MATT: He was such a fucking rock star.

KEVIN: Yeah. It's funny that you say that too, because when you saw Velvet Revolver perform live, Scott would have two songs that were sort of Bowie, two songs that were sort of Iggy, a little Bryan Ferry, Mick Jagger, and some Peter Murphy. It was almost as if he channeled those guys for one or two songs each. It was head to toe, even vocally. So it's really funny that you say that.

MATT: Have you seen the "Fall to Pieces" video recently?

KEVIN: No.

MATT: Have you seen it since Scott passed?

KEVIN: No.

MATT: It's so heartbreaking.

KEVIN: Yeah.

MATT: It almost seems to foresee what happened to him. It was very brave of him to expose and present himself in that way.

KEVIN: Yeah.

MATT: Did you work on the concept together?

KEVIN: Yeah. We'd done "Slither," and I'd been traveling with them filming a couple of live shows. Then Scott called me into the dressing room one night and said that the next song he wanted to do was "Fall to Pieces," which was about his struggle. And he wanted to be honest about it. He said, "You're the guy to do it because you were there, and you saw the ups and downs of all of it." At that point, you just have to be faithful to that mission and really strip it down to the loneliness and unreliability that a problem like that delivers to your various walks of life, whether it's your marriage, your band, or even yourself. And the counterpoint to that is when you crack it and you have those flourishes of genius. So I wanted to make sure we covered both sides of that coin. It was raw. And Scott relived a lot of those moments again when we shot that video. We shot a lot of it here actually.

MATT: In this house?

KEVIN: Yeah. And we shot some stuff on the beach out in Santa Monica. His wife, Mary [Forsberg], was in it, too.

MATT: Wow! That's real.

KEVIN: Yeah.

MATT: And so rare in this day and age, to see that level of fearlessness, honesty, and vulnerability.

KEVIN: Yeah, it was brave. He used to write a lot, so I asked him to do a journal leading up to the video so we could show some of the writing in it, and even put photos and things like that in there. He took that very seriously.

MATT: Like a method actor?

KEVIN: Completely. He came in with a journal that had a lot of pages filled, and that had to be hard for him because he was rehashing a lot of stuff. But a lot of it was also romantic, like, "Wow! I was doing all this stuff, and it resulted in some great music." So what does that do with your head? You start to undercut your own message at a certain point. But he just felt like it was something that he needed to do.

VINNIE STIGMA—*AGNOSTIC FRONT*

MATT: The thing that I love the most about *The Godfathers of Hardcore* documentary is it shows how at the heart of this legendary band are two very different, very opposing figures: you and Roger [Miret]. How did you two first meet?

VINNIE: I used to see him at CBGB. I'd go in the pit, and he'd go in the pit, and we moshed together. He was a fair guy in the pit, too. He didn't go in for any dirty shots. I don't go in for any of that shit either. We're here to have fun. So, I enjoyed his company in the pit. Then one day I just walked up to him, and I said, "You're in my band now." And that was it. He'll tell you the same story. That's how I got all of my guys: you had to be part of the scene. I wasn't after amazing musicians.

MATT: You weren't holding auditions or anything like that?

VINNIE: The audition was, who shows up at the show? Are you part of the scene? That's the audition. You've got to believe in it because I've got to travel with you; I've got to eat and drink and sleep with you.

MATT: You have to go to war together on tour.

VINNIE: Exactly. And you know what? When we made *The Godfathers of Hardcore* documentary, we were supposed to go to Cuba and do some filming down there because that's where Roger comes from. To me, that's maybe the greatest story in rock 'n' roll. Some little kid from Cuba who can't speak English comes to a foreign country, and about eight years later he winds up at CBGB. And who does he meet? Vinnie Stigma!

MATT: Obviously it's a brotherly relationship, but who's the big brother?

VINNIE: I used to be his older brother, but now he's like my older brother. He's matured a lot, whereas I'm still like a thirteen-year-old kid.

MATT: What was the biggest lesson that you took away from watching the documentary?

VINNIE: It made me realize how much Roger means to me.

CREATIVE RELATIONSHIPS PLAYLIST

ME FIRST AND THE GIMME GIMMES—"UPTOWN GIRL"

DIDDY—"IT'S ALL ABOUT THE BENJAMINS ROCK REMIX"

PUBLIC ENEMY—"FIGHT THE POWER"

RAGE AGAINST THE MACHINE—"BULLET IN THE HEAD"

GOLDFINGER—"MILES AWAY"

LESS THAN JAKE—"LOOK WHAT HAPPENED"

THE BOUNCING SOULS—"HOPELESS ROMANTIC"

THE BRONX—"WHITE TAR"

TYPE O NEGATIVE—"BLACK NO. 1"

RAMMSTEIN—"PUSSY"

MÖTLEY CRÜE—"KICKSTART MY HEART"

VAN HALEN—"JUMP"

MR BUNGLE—"QUOTE UNQUOTE"

DANZIG—"MOTHER"

QUEENS OF THE STONE AGE—"NO ONE KNOWS"

AMEN—"THE PRICE OF REALITY"

SLIPKNOT—"SNUFF"

NIRVANA—"IN BLOOM"

THE CARS—"LET THE GOOD TIMES ROLL"

MASTODON—"BLOOD AND THUNDER"

LIFE OF AGONY—"DESIRE"

EAGLES OF DEATH METAL—"FAMILY AFFAIR"

VELVET REVOLVER—"FALL TO PIECES"

AGNOSTIC FRONT—"I REMEMBER"

CULTURAL COMMENTARY

"We have to start thinking outside of our own
boundaries and backyards."

IF YOU CAST YOUR mind back to *Life In The Stocks Volume One*—sorry to keep throwing back to the first book, but I'm a sucker for context—you'll recall the penultimate chapter, "Life & Death in the Stocks." For those who haven't read it, that chapter encompassed everything from mental health and suicide to gender dysphoria and the #MeToo movement, via sexism, feminism, drug addiction, and 9/11. The heavy stuff. But the stuff we need to talk about. And the stuff that, I believe, makes my show different to other interview-based podcasts.

Most band interviews are conducted around album release schedules and touring cycles, which is why you so often hear the same questions—and indeed the same answers—being recycled over and over and over again. But ever since I launched my podcast on January 31, 2017, I've made a point of rarely asking artists about their new record, or how the tour is going, unless it pertains to a wider discussion about culture, politics, society, spirituality, mental health, or other more interesting talking points than simply, "So, tell us about the new album." There's enough of that out there to fill a thousand podcasts. And I get it: people want to promote their product. There's a time and a place for it, too. But *Life In The Stocks* is not it.

There was a chapter in the first book called "Politics & Religion"—no prizes for guessing what that one was about. This chapter, "Cultural Commentary," is like a hybrid of that chapter and the one that I mentioned a moment ago, "Life & Death in the

Stocks." And I genuinely believe it's the best one out of both books. But don't just take my word for it. Read on, brothers and sisters. Read on. The segments coming up in this section are thought-provoking, eye-opening, life-affirming, and inspirational.

Jesse Hughes from the Eagles of Death Metal talks about the Paris attacks that occurred on November 13, 2015. Perry Farrell reflects on the time he freed slaves in Sudan, which is a story so incredible it has to be heard to be believed. Rappers Chuck D and Hyro the Hero discuss race issues and police brutality in the United States. (It's interesting to note that my interview with Hyro took place two years before Black Lives Matter movement blew up, which shows it had been bubbling near the surface for a while.) And Dennis Lyxzén discusses the power of knowledge, love, and unity in relation to politics, society, and technology.

These are the cultural debates that I live for. And whenever I'm worried that my listening figures aren't high enough, or that I'm not making enough money from my podcast, these interactions help motivate and inspire me to keep doing what I do. They're the big topics. The stuff of life. And we're going to kick off with an in-depth dissection of religion, faith, and the nature human existence, courtesy of Dustin Kensrue from Thrice.

Parenthetically, Dustin also hosts a podcast called *Carry the Fire*, which is strangely close in both name and content to *Stoke The Fire*. I'd like to point out that neither party plagiarized the other one, though. Great minds just think alike, and clearly Dustin, Jesse Leach, and myself all feel like the world needs podcasts like these now more than ever. I genuinely believe that we do. And I'll continue to keep making them for as long as it feels vital. Just don't call it "content." Selfies are content. Throwaway Instagram montage reels and god-awful TikTok videos are content. These conversations are something altogether different and infinitely more important. Even if I do say so myself.

I'd like to express my deepest gratitude and utmost respect to all the great minds who've contributed to this chapter. Thank you for stoking my fire and inspiring me to be a better person. It's a crazy world out there, and we all need to take better care of each other. Love and light to all—even the haters. I'm surrounded by love in my life. I can take a little hate every once in a while.

DUSTIN KENSRUE—*THRICE, SOLO ARTIST, CARRY THE FIRE PODCAST*

MATT: I'd like to talk to you about your podcast, *Carry the Fire*, if that's okay?

DUSTIN: Sure.

MATT: It's fairly new, right? I checked the other day, and there seems to be five episodes.

DUSTIN: I'm five episodes in, yeah.

MATT: What was the initial idea behind the podcast?

DUSTIN: I don't remember where the idea first came from, but once it solidified in my head it just stuck, and I realized that I had to do it.

MATT: Not enough musicians host their own podcasts.

DUSTIN: Really?

MATT: Yeah, and I think more of them should. When you compare music to comedy, it seems like every comedian in the world has a podcast.

DUSTIN: They're used to talking though.

MATT: True.

DUSTIN: And they're probably more entertaining on a podcast. I had that feeling: everyone has a podcast, so why do I need to do one? But this idea just stuck with me, which was to look at the big questions of life through the lens of the good, the true, and the beautiful. And that's just to say that I'm trying to humanize the "other"—the person that's different from you, whether it's a different religion or background or whatever. I really wanted to hear people talk about the things that really hold value to them through their specific slant on things, whether they're a scientist or a musician or a philosopher. I'm trying to make it really broad. So far I've had on a Muslim who's trying to run for State Senate in Virginia, and I just had Gerard Way from My Chemical Romance on the show.

MATT: That's the one that I heard. It was a great chat.

DUSTIN: Thanks. I also had on this guy Brian McDonald who's a story expert, and Hillary L McBride who's a therapist and researcher. So I'm trying to make it really broad.

MATT: I was just chatting to Dennis [Lyxzén] from Refused on the stairwell about this. Right now, the world seems more divided than ever; it feels like we're so splintered and fractured. And I think it's really important to get back to what unites us all as human beings, regardless of what religion or sexual orientation or gender you are. Because there's way more similarities than differences between us.

DUSTIN: Yeah, and I think that's the one common thread that runs throughout my podcast; everyone is not going to agree on everything, but I'm trying to have people on the show who are themselves open to the "other," and are engaged with humanity in a loving way.

MATT: What kind of a role has faith played in your life and outlook on the world?

DUSTIN: The way I see it, everyone has a worldview and a lens through which they look out at the world, because life's too complex for us to not have a framework to put it in. Our brains just naturally do that, even if you think you don't have a specific worldview, we all have something that we're working with. So for me, having some sort of faith and a belief in God—and I grew up in Christianity—has always been a part of that lens. But it's also been blended with a bunch of other things; I look at my formative growth as this mix of messages that I was getting in Christianity and messages I was getting in punk rock.

MATT: That's a heady mix.

DUSTIN: Yeah, and it's been corrective in certain ways because it made me look at some of the stuff in the music scene that I was in, and say, "I don't think that's great." And then it made me look at Christianity and pick out things that I think a lot of people around me weren't seeing. For instance, there's anti-imperialism throughout the Jewish and Christian scripture, and anti-imperialism is about taking care of the weak, and everyone banding together in a beloved community. I was able to see that stuff better because punk rock was saying a lot of the same things. So I look at faith as part of a lens that's being crafted at any moment for how I'm seeing the world. And I've had various points of deconstruction and reconstruction, the largest one being in the last five years or so, and that's been a really positive process for me. I'm in a really good spot right now. And I'm much more comfortable with not knowing a lot of things than I ever was before.

MATT: I think that's part of the crux of spirituality and true wisdom: the idea that the more you know, the less you know. We never truly find what we're looking for.

DUSTIN: Yeah, so next week on my podcast is Dr. James Carse, and if that idea interests you then you should definitely check that episode out. He talks about this idea of there being systems of inquiry, and he argues that religions are essentially that—as well as science. Systems of inquiry are grappling with the mystery of everything that is. And they're doing it in different ways—science does it differently to religion, for instance. But essentially they're all grappling with the same mystery: life.

But what happened was these systems of inquiry spun systems of belief, and those systems of belief are closed and claim to have all the answers within them. So science spawns scientism and this idea that everything we need to know can be found within science, and that creates a closed off version of something that was initially comfortable just wrestling with trying to figure out the mystery but knowing that ultimately it can never truly solve it. And in doing so, it turns into this very rigid and ultimately dead system of beliefs. And I think that's a really helpful way of looking at it because it helps you to not make the same mistakes as a lot of the new atheists, like Richard Dawkins and Sam Harris, who see religion as purely bad. But religion isn't the issue: it's the fundamental mindset where you become closed off to other ways of thinking and the data at hand. I think that's really dangerous.

MATT: Where do you stand on your relationship to God? Do you still identify as a Christian?

DUSTIN: I do. And there are a lot of Christians that take issue with me saying that, just because I view a lot of that stuff differently than I did. I think a lot of Christianity has become very obsessed with accenting certain doctrinal statements. That's the core of it. And I'm just not interested in that. I'm much more interested in the process and motion of living and talking about things and being able to hear other people's thoughts. I've always been kind of a theology nerd, and I've recently been opened up to whole new worlds like liberation theology, which focuses on people from different races and cultures who've not been allowed to tell their story for a long time, which comes back to that idea of anti-imperialism. So there's a lot of interesting stuff going on right now.

Culturally speaking, it feels like we're moving past a moment in time where it was hard to talk about faith because it was broken up into boxes where everything you said had to fit in those boxes, and that led to people saying, "Well, I don't want to be put in that box, so I don't have faith." Now it feels like there's a large movement happening where people are like, "The mystery of everything that is happening has to be something. Right? So let's talk about that." We all live in the same world, and we're all experiencing whatever this mystery is. Even if you're a strict atheist, you're still experiencing whatever the mystery is, so let's just talk about what it means to be human and not be afraid to talk about spirituality. There was definitely a time when spirituality wasn't taken seriously by either side, but that doesn't seem to be the case anymore. And maybe that's just because of where I'm swimming. But it's exciting to be able to engage with all these different types of people and talk about what all of this might mean.

MATT: Do you think God exists up there or in here? Is he all around us or inside all of us?

DUSTIN: Outside would be classic theism, which is the dualistic idea that God is out there and the world is in here, and He breaks into the world from time to time. Then you have pantheism, and a lot of Hinduism would be traditionally thought of as pantheism, where God and the universe are essentially the same thing. I would roughly describe myself as a "panentheist," which is kind of a paradoxical term, but the idea is that God is somehow more than the world and the world is somehow more than God. So the world exists inside God and God is inside of everything. And that leaves things open for a personal relationship in some way, and it leaves room for God to act in the world without impinging or intruding upon the natural order of things. So there's a lot of ways to look at that.

MATT: What's fucked up to me, and maybe you have some thoughts on this, is in the sixties you had hippieism, counterculture, and the psychedelic movement; in the seventies you had punk; in the eighties you had hardcore and hip-hop; and in the nineties you had alternative rock. And that seemed to be the last era of politicized and outspoken musicians operating within mainstream culture with something to say. Whereas in more recent times, although the world that we're living in is still in complete bedlam, songwriters aren't addressing these issues in their music as much they've traditionally done throughout history.

DUSTIN: I think that's true, and I don't totally know why.

MATT: But you have noticed it?

DUSTIN: Oh, yeah.

MATT: It's weird, isn't it?

DUSTIN: It is weird. The producer that we worked with on our last two records [*To Be Everywhere Is To Be Nowhere* and *Palms*], Eric Palmquist, really encouraged me to use more nouns. He said that rock has gotten so airy and ephemeral, and no one is saying anything anymore. Words are happening but no one is communicating a whole lot.

MATT: Also, bands seem to spend all their time talking on social media about these issues rather than actually writing songs about them. And you can send all the tweets you want, but it's unlikely to change anything. But I'd like to think that a great song can perhaps still change the way people think and engage with the world.

DUSTIN: I really like Twitter for a whole bunch of reasons, even though there's a lot of bad things that can happen on there. It's helped me to see a lot of different viewpoints on the world that I would never have been able to see otherwise. And I'm super thankful for that. But I can write tweets—and I have—that are trying to say something specific about something that's happening, and it's going to piss some people off. And other people are going to agree. But it's not going to change a bunch of people's minds about anything. Songs can go a lot deeper; they can get past people's defenses in a different way, if you do it well. And I believe that a good song can have a lasting effect on how someone perceives the world. I definitely try to write in that way.

MATT: And music lasts forever. But a tweet gets lost in the ether after about a week. Unless you tweet something controversial, and then it resurfaces and you lose your job over it. But music lasts forever. And I still believe it can change the world in a positive, tangible, meaningful way. Do you still believe that?

DUSTIN: Yeah, I do. I believe that stories are super powerful, and I think that musicians are storytellers—or at least they can be. When you look back at ancient tribes, you had shamans who gave context and helped shape meaning in these cultures. We have a very different set up now, but I still think that's what musicians and other creators can be.

TOM MORELLO—*RAGE AGAINST THE MACHINE, AUDIOSLAVE, PROPHETS OF RAGE, THE NIGHTWATCHMAN*

MATT: Do you think you can still be original working within the rock format in this day and age?

TOM: I think you can never say never to that. People are often counting rock and electric guitar music out, but they haven't been right yet, so I suspect they're not now. One of the things I hope *The Atlas Underground* record serves as is a Trojan horse that can introduce a radical poetic perspective and searing electric guitar to places where they currently don't exist: the dance floor and the charts. One of the things that frustrates me today is that a lot of young people are only reaching for the laptop and Ableton, rather than practicing four hours a day on the guitar, which is why there's no guitar on the top two hundred songs in the charts. Hopefully, by working with Marcus Mumford and Portugal. The man, but without compromising one iota with regards to the heaviness or the politics of the music, I'm able to sneak the Trojan horse through the gate and let people know that there's more to the picture than meets the eye. I want to show people that it's possible to rock and think at the same time, both in the mosh pit and on the dance floor.

MATT: It's interesting, because when you look back through time, during the 1960s, '70s, '80s, '90s, and even the early 2000s, everything that was going on politically fed into popular culture.

TOM: Sure.

MATT: Even pop music would often be radical and thought-provoking.

TOM: Sure.

MATT: But it just seems like the popular music of today is brainless.

TOM: I think that would be an accurate assessment.

MATT: Why do you think that is?

TOM: Well, there's certainly plenty of music being made that isn't brainless.

MATT: But it's not in the charts.

TOM: Right. The most that you can hope for in regards to that is an anti-suicide song or something like that, which is very worthwhile, but you so rarely get thoughtful commentary on contemporary events wrapped up in great songs, which popular music has often been about in the past.

MATT: And let's be honest, both of our countries are arguably in more of a mess now than ever before.

TOM: Exactly, which may perhaps explain a turn toward escapist music. But escapist music also accelerates the problem by providing bread and circuses. As to why there's been a turn toward the vapid, I honestly don't know. But what I do know is that I have a greater commitment than ever to turning that tide, at least within my own world, by making records that go beyond the confines of where my music has been before. And I feel challenged and excited when I do something that doesn't feel safe. Pushing myself, both as a guitarist and an artist, is what it's all about.

HYRO THE HERO—*RAPPER, SOLO ARTIST*

MATT: I love that new tune "Let The Snake Show."

HYRO: That's me calling out these motherfuckers, you know what I'm saying? I wanna call them out and let it be known that I hate everything about them. "I hate your fucking smile, motherfucker. I hate the way you talk, motherfucker." I'm just letting it be known. And if you listen to it, you'll know who I'm talking about—because of the situation and the time that we're in, you're going to know who I'm talking about. You'll listen to that song and go, "Ah, okay. He's talking about *him*."

MATT: It's refreshing to hear. I hear so many artists say stuff, like, "We're taking on some really important issues with this album, and we address this and we address that." And then you listen to the record—

HYRO: They're not doing it. That's why you don't really see me talk too political or too crazy online; I'd rather spit it through my music. You feel it better that way, and you know that's what I'm about. I can talk or write it or whatever, but that just leads to more conversation, and then I'm that person outside of music and it's a whole different image of me that you're going to get. So I just put it in the music and let you vibe with the music. I have a lot of opinions on things. But I'll let you listen to them in my music. I don't want to just type that shit out because then I'm typing while a million other motherfuckers are all typing their shit and chiming in. And if I put it in my music, you can't scream at my song in disagreement.

MATT: In my experience, there are two types of people in the area of cultural commentary. They're either super sociable, and they're out there all the time making connections with everyone that they meet. Or they're lone wolves that keep themselves to themselves, keep their head down, observe the world around them, and document what they see.

HYRO: That's me right there. I'm more of a lone wolf documenting what I see. I'm never really out with a bunch of people doing all that other stuff.

MATT: Have you always been that way?

HYRO: I think so. I'm a bit of a mixture, though. I'm from the hood, so there's always been a part of me that wants to roll with the crew and be with the homies. But I've also got a message that I'm trying to send out, and while I might ride for something, other people might not ride with me. It's like, if you were in a fight, I'm the type of person that would fight for you. But if I fight and you don't have my back if some motherfucker's trying to jump me—

MATT: You're never fighting for me again?

HYRO: Exactly, bro. I'm one of them kind of people. I'm a loyal person. I'm a little too loyal at times. But I go by a certain G code and a certain rule book that I feel we should all rock with. I've got my rules of what I think my life should look like, and I stick with it. But a lot of people don't do that, especially in this day and age. Some people sell out for a bunch of bullshit, you know what I'm saying? They have no integrity. But I ain't like that, man. So I think that makes you a lone wolf, in a sense.

A lot of rappers have crews and all that stuff, but that also builds jealousy and all kinds of shit like that. It's in the news right now: Kevin Hart is the center of this big scandal because he's been cheating on his wife or whatever, and he came to find out that his main homie was the one extorting him—his right-hand man. And he put him in movies and all kinds of stuff. I look at situations like that, and people from the past, and I like to stick to myself, you know? Tupac [Shakur] used to roll with a bunch of people, and then you watch his jail interview, and he says, "Just stick to yourself. The mistake I made was being with all these people. If I could tell you one thing, it would be to stick to yourself." That always stuck with me.

MATT: Tupac's your guy, right?

HYRO: Oh, yeah. Pac is the homie.

MATT: What did he teach you?

HYRO: He was a voice of the people, and he taught me to not be afraid to say anything. When he did "Hit 'Em Up," and he talked about Biggie [The Notorious B.I.G.], as a young person I was just shocked that he said his name. And then he said his wife's name, too. I didn't know you could do that; I thought there was rules against these types of things. So he always struck me as a person who spoke his mind and used his voice, like, "If this is how you feel then let it out because the best way to live is to be free." And people think that they're free, but they're not because they still hold back on certain things. Even I hold back on certain things, especially in this politically correct era that we're living in.

MATT: I'm the most liberal person you could ever meet, and I have a real problem with left-wing people who tell other people what they can and can't say. That's the same as fascism to me. I hate that imposition of regulation and collective guilt bullshit.

HYRO: Me too. One art form that I respect a lot is stand-up comedy because it's the last free art form. And they don't have any music behind them, they just go on stage with a microphone and make you laugh.

MATT: And they make you think, too—if they're good.

HYRO: Yeah, and that's tough as fuck to stand up there with just a mic and no beat to move the people. And now people are trying to silence them. But you can't shut that down with all this politically correct shit. You have to be allowed to speak your mind, and in this day and age, I fully respect anybody who does so freely and says what they feel. You might have to deal with the backlash that you get with it, but fuck it.

NADJA PEULEN—*COAL CHAMBER*

NADJA: Rock 'n' roll isn't dangerous anymore, and that's why it's boring. You have the same bands every year at all these festivals, and I've seen all these bands about fifty times.

MATT: Yeah, even the dangerous ones aren't dangerous anymore.

NADJA: No.

MATT: They haven't been for a long time. And I don't find many of the younger bands to be as exhilarating in the same way.

NADJA: Me neither. But then I start thinking, "Do I just sound like an old bitter person that's not excited about stuff anymore?"

MATT: There is that. But I feel like you can't really get away with saying or doing anything too provocative anymore. Careers can end overnight now because of the internet and the way that the popular opinion of a person can change so quickly over the smallest thing.

NADJA: Yeah, exactly. You're not allowed to say anything anymore. And everybody is offended by nothing.

MATT: And everything.

NADJA: And everything, yeah. It's a strange generation right now: judgmental, entitled, and a lot of big mouths hiding behind a computer screen where no one can see or confront you. It's so annoying.

JOBY FORD—*THE BRONX, MARIACHI EL BRONX, ARTIST, PRODUCER*

MATT: I feel like if you express your opinion about *anything* online, and somebody doesn't agree with it, they'll be the first in line to tell you why you're not allowed that opinion just because it's different to theirs. That, to me, is fascism.

JOBY: Exactly. Everyone's a throttle jockey. I heard a quote one time, and I think it so pertains to what you just said about the internet in general: "The internet's greatest strength, by connecting all these people and ideas, is also its greatest weakness." And I try to teach my kids to use the internet in a positive way—as a tool. Anything you want to know how to do, you can look it up on YouTube, and there'll be an instructional video on how to do it. And I sound like a curmudgeon saying this, but when I wanted to learn about something as a kid, I had to go to the library and check out a book.

MATT: Dinosaur!

JOBY: Yeah.

MATT: So you do believe the internet can be a positive force?

JOBY: If people use it as a tool to further their education—absolutely. But how often does that actually happen?

KEITH BUCKLEY—*EVERY TIME I DIE, THE DAMNED THINGS, AUTHOR*

KEITH: I think I was lucky to get into music before the internet. So much of what you do now is dependent on the reception that you get. If you played a show and you felt good about it, you'd go home and there was no checking posts to see how other people felt about it. There was no positive or negative reinforcement back then. It was just the gut: that was everything that would guide you to the next step. I think it's really sad now: people's tendency to be mean and disingenuous is really deterring a lot of talented but shy people away from it. Artists by their nature are often quiet and aloof, and they express themselves in different ways. So when the feedback that they see online is negative, then it hits them harder.

The reason I enjoy Twitter maybe more than any other form of social media is because everyone there is writing; it's all writers who are coming together to express themselves with the written word. And that's an awesome thing. But when someone turns the written word into a weapon, it cuts deep. And there's not a lot of people who are very resilient anymore because they didn't evolve from that period of time before the internet when you would build up this callousness—and almost ignorance—to what other people were saying. You just didn't know what people were saying back then, so you trusted your gut.

I think coming from that era was very important, and it got me to a place where once this did come into play—once Facebook, Twitter, and Instagram came into play—I was already used to not looking at it for feedback. So I just kept going. But I do know it deters a lot of people, and that's sad.

MATT: I think if you're on a public platform then you should be prepared for criticism and feedback.

KEITH: Absolutely.

MATT: But obviously the internet gives voice to everyone, and like you say, some people are just plain mean.

KEITH: Yeah, and it's hard because you shouldn't necessarily have to vet critics. It's kind of like how I look at self-publication, in that I could've easily put out a lot of books and stories that I've written by publishing them myself, but I needed to know that I met the standards of someone who knew more than I did. And I appreciate the impact of people who know more than I do. I don't think that I'm the final say on anything that I do: I'm constantly looking for input and advice. I don't take it as a threat to my identity either, and I don't shun it because of my ego. I welcome it, and it changes me for the better.

When you self-publish, none of that is there. It's just you, and you're going into the world and putting yourself out there. So while it may be easier to get yourself published, it's also very unfortunate because you're not prepared for the world of critics. And a lot of critics are going out into the world now without ever being hired by a company, or ever writing an article, or doing anything that qualifies them as critics. They're just in front of their keyboards more. And that's fine. That's just the way the world is nowadays—you have to get used to it. But it does offset the balance in a very destructive way as far as art is concerned.

CASEY CHAOS—*AMEN, CHRISTIAN DEATH, SCUM*

MATT: Do you try and remove yourself from social media as much as possible?

CASEY: Yeah. I mean, I think it's amazing that people want to communicate with each other and stuff like that, and I try to do it as much as I can. But I was talking about this with a friend of mine recently: I didn't get involved in music to be a social butterfly. Not that I don't like people. The people that I get to meet through what I do are amazing people. I'd love to hang out and do more things with them. But it's impossible. It's like, do I want to create, or do I just want to hang out and communicate on a friendly basis? Like I said, I do try and do both. But it's increasingly difficult for me with the phone going off every five minutes.

If your phone is on, it's impossible to write a song, and it's impossible to write lyrics. It takes you right out of that moment, and whatever you were thinking or whatever vibe you were on is destroyed the moment that phone goes off. I don't have that big of a brain, I guess. I just can't get back to that path that I was on before the phone rang.

MATT: Do you know one of my least favorite things in the world? The automated phone service messages, where you call up, say, your bank, and you just want to talk to another human being. But you end up on the phone for about ten minutes listening to this computer-generated voice, saying, "Press number one for this. Or press number three for this." I'm like, "Just put a human being on the phone." We could've solved my problem in the time that it's taken me to listen to all these different options. It's fucking infuriating.

CASEY: That's my favorite thing in the world right there. When I'm in hell—when I go to hell—that will be my hell; I'll be stuck on the phone the entire time; I'll be in a line of people talking really loud about nothing at all, and they'll have no consciousness of personal space, so they'll keep bumping into me. Meanwhile, I'll be on the phone the whole time trying to pay a bill, like I did the other day; I had to pay something for my car, and I was on the phone for over an hour. There were no human beings on the other end of the line, and it was just impossible. I felt defeated afterward.

DENNIS LYXZÉN—REFUSED, THE (INTERNATIONAL) NOISE CON- SPIRACY, INVSN, FAKE NAMES

MATT: Do you remain optimistic about the future of the world?

DENNIS: Most days I do, yes. I believe there's a power in all of us that can transcend the mundane madness of what goes on around us. To a certain extent the world looks kind of fucked, but I still believe in us. I still believe that we can do good, and that people want to do good. Without that feeling it would be impossible to get up on stage every night and talk about radical ideas and radical change. So I have to believe. Some days I do think to myself, "This is all too much." But then you look at what's going on right now with the whole environmental movement and Greta Thunberg, and it's amazing. She's such an inspiration.

MATT: She's like a modern-day Martin Luther King [Jr.]. She feels like that much of an important figure in the world right now.

DENNIS: Yeah, she's amazing. And she gives me hope and inspiration. If there's young kids like her around, maybe the world will become a better place. I saw an electoral map of America recently, and I think there were three states that were Republican if young kids got to vote today. There's also a whole generation of rich white privileged men who are dying out, which is a good thing. And I think if the planet itself can survive then there's hope for the future.

MATT: I guess during every period in history the people who are living through it feel this way, but I feel like this very moment in time, as well as being the most terrifying, is also the most exciting and significant period of potential change—or catastrophe.

DENNIS: Sure.

MATT: Everything somehow feels more vital than ever before right now—not just in terms of environmentalism, but also culture and politics.

DENNIS: I agree. I don't think the world has ever been this divided, either. And that's of course a tool to keep people at each other's throats, as opposed to looking at the real problems and issues that we face. But then we've also made huge strides with feminism and environmentalism. And I've been vegan for twenty-six years now, and it's the best time in my lifetime to be a vegan.

MATT: How easy is it to be a vegan nowadays!

DENNIS: It's so easy. It's not even a challenge anymore. So we've made some great strides and some great progress. But then there's other areas where we're actually slipping and things are getting worse. And the economical divide is getting bigger and bigger, especially in the western world. So there are definitely things that are better, and there are definitely things that are worse. I think it's interesting to see where all that will lead us.

MATT: Technology's a trip isn't it? The irony of the internet is it was designed to help people communicate and bring them together, but I feel like it's having the opposite effect. Would you agree?

DENNIS: Yes, completely.

MATT: There's obviously many wonderful things that the internet affords us, such as freedom of information. But I do feel like the interconnectivity of the human race is dissipating at a rate that's both scary and alarming.

DENNIS: I think political discourse has completely corroded, too. Most people spend their time communicating on platforms like Twitter and Instagram, and the way that we communicate on there is very black and white, and without depth or understanding of the complexities of the issues being discussed. It's also become a battleground to attack people. So it's very divisive.

MATT: It must be an exciting time to be in a band like Refused, though. There's obviously no shortage of things to sing about. It's an important time to be touring and travelling the world as well. I've done a bunch of tours as a DJ over the last few years, and the beauty of being on the road, for me, is you get to see how there isn't as much divide as the news and social media would have us believe—from city to city, country to country, and continent to continent. When you break those barriers down—and you're obviously in the ultimate profession to do that—you see that human beings are pretty much the same wherever you go.

DENNIS: Yeah, most people just want to get on with their lives and look out for their friends and families. But we get told constantly that we're all so different, and we can never bridge this gap. That divide is there for a reason: if we're too busy attacking each other then we're not going to hold capitalism as an idea accountable. And a lot of people find it hard to criticize capitalism because it's an abstract social construct, and they fail to see how it's a real problem. It's a lot easier to say, "This guy only just came into the country, so maybe he's the problem." But at the end of the day, most people just want to live a good life.

I think one of the main problems with capitalism as an idea is that it can't provide that for people anymore. I don't think it's ever been able to provide that for people, to be honest. The western world has always been in a privileged position because it's used the rest of the world by exploiting other countries for their resources. But that's starting to catch up with us, and we're plagued with mental illness these days. That's because we're living in an unsustainable system that places too much pressure on people to succeed in a game that's stacked against us.

PERRY FARRELL—*JANE'S ADDICTION, PORNO FOR PYROS, LOLLAPALOOZA*

PERRY: More than anything else, I think of myself as a globalist, a humanitarian, and a goodwill ambassador. These days, to be so small-minded as to think of yourself as a nationalist as opposed to an idealist, at the very least is short-sighted, uneducated, and unaware. I'm definitely not a nationalist, although I do love America.

MATT: We're living in crazy times, aren't we?

PERRY: Yes. And thinking about putting up borders and walls is the last thing we should be thinking about; we have to start thinking outside of our own boundaries and backyards. We need to start considering the atmosphere and the ocean, because that affects the water and the air. Another thing that affects us all is the idea that people would be coming into your country as immigrants. If you're not thinking about their country and why it is that they have to come and stampede into your country—

MATT: With nothing, and no promise of a secure future of any kind.

PERRY: Right. They're essentially running for their lives because they want to find a better world, and that's okay. That's what my great-grandparents did, too. You have to be considerate of that, and you can't just shut them out. As for putting up a wall, are you kidding me? You don't think people can scale your silly wall?

MATT: You clearly care about the world, and that's the fascinating thing about you; you're interested in music and the joy that it brings, but you're also all about the bigger picture.

PERRY: My audience is a global audience. That's maybe why I think about it so much. Here I am in London, and I want to make the people in London happy. I also want to go to the Middle East, and I want to make them happy. And I want to go to India and make them happy, too. So my audience is a global audience. But I'm not a politician or a president or a dictator of some place. I'm an entertainer. And my job is to make everybody happy. So I have no borders.

MATT: And business is booming all over the world because people need entertainment right now.

PERRY: They do need it.

MATT: Has your awareness of a need for that increased more with age?

PERRY: Yeah, and I'm glad that I've lasted sixty years—so far. It really does give me insight and a widening perspective of the world that I didn't have when I was younger. When I started out, I was just a kid. I didn't know how big it was going to become or how far we were going to reach. And I add ideas as I go. It's kind of like I travel through time, picking up new ways and means to operate as I go. But I wasn't raised like Michael Jackson to do this thing.

MATT: You weren't a born star?

PERRY: No. I did have an innate ability to entertain people, but I certainly wasn't thinking I was going to become what I've become. So I look around, and I pick things up along my journey that will come in handy in the future. That's how I do it. And I'm a sub-culturalist; I'm not a pop icon by any means; I resisted being involved in pop culture. But now I feel, like, "You know what? Pop culture could actually use some help."

MATT: I think so—again, now more than ever. And it's funny because there's so much going on in the world right now, yet the artists who are mainstream don't seem to be saying anything.

PERRY: Yeah, they're afraid to stick their head up above the sand.

MATT: Why do you think that is?

PERRY: Because it's difficult to know how to navigate being an entertainer and a humanitarian, and an outspoken environmentalist, and how to mix all that together. People are afraid that if they speak out there'll also be adversity and people speaking up against them. But the way to do it is to be educated and informed. You don't have to go to Harvard, but you do have to read books and keep yourself informed about what's going on. As an example, if you were going to go against me right now, and say, "There's no such thing as global warming," without having to pick a fight, I could sit you down and explain to you that, "Yes, there very much is global warming, and this is what we need to do about it." And then we could have a rational and informed discussion without hatred or aggression. I would come at you with love and kindness and education.

This is what I've done for the last thirty-five years of my life. I took my time. And I didn't corner myself into being this silly pop icon who's looking to not ruffle any feathers. I think there's a bigger calling than that in my case, and I think in everybody's case. The world should not let the powers that be—these autocrats and strawman—get away with it. If they were going in the right direction, fine, lead us there. But they're not leading us in a good direction; they're leading us in a direction where their buddies and them can make money. And in the meantime, they're destroying the environment, and they're not looking out for the poor or the weary. They're not looking out for women either. They're looking to make money with their oil friends. I don't know who their damn friends are, but they're not my friends, obviously. My friends are the common man and the working-class. I also have rich friends, and they're good people too. I'm not exactly against the rich. But I am against the autocrats and the people who would destroy the environment, and I'm against the people who try to repress the poor.

MATT: You obviously lived through that time, not just in the music industry, but also in politics, when both of those domains—and indeed the whole world—were infiltrated by accountants and businessmen, and the priority switched to profits over people.

PERRY: Yeah, it came during my lifetime, that's right. And I'm not about to let it happen again. But the good news is, I can see a way through this. And I think if we hang on to ourselves, by 2030 things are going to be great. And by 2050, I probably won't be around, but it's going to be really good.

MATT: So you're still an eternal optimist?

PERRY: I am totally an optimist. If I wasn't, I would just off myself. But I don't do it, because I'm excited about the future, and I'm excited about my children's future. I refuse to sit back and let the likes of Donald Trump and his buddies take over the world. And I'm also not alone.

MATT: I was reading that when Jane's Addiction originally got back together in 2001, and you did the Jubilee Tour, you raised something incredible like $120,000.

PERRY: And I went into Sudan as an abolitionist.

MATT: And you bought all the slaves to free them?

PERRY: I did. What happened was, we did the tour, and I put a dollar surcharge on all the tickets. Then I went into Sudan, and I met with slave owners. I transferred all the money into Sudanese currency. I was dealing with dudes who had machine guns, and I laid down my stacks of cash on blankets. There were hippopotamuses in the river and people of human bondage, and I bought their freedom. Then I returned them to their villages. I gave some of them scholarships into American colleges, too. And I returned their freedom to the rest of them.

MATT: What an amazing thing to do.

PERRY: Yeah, and we did it through the power of music. I want to do it again.

CHUCK D—*PUBLIC ENEMY, PROPHETS OF RAGE, SOLO ARTIST, AUTHOR*

MATT: One of the things that you mention in your book, *Fight the Power: Rap, Race, and Reality*, is the Million Man March. Before reading your book, I'd never heard of that demonstration, and I wasn't at all familiar with its significance. I wonder if you could talk a little bit about that event and what it meant, and perhaps why it isn't as widely known as it should be.

CHUCK: It's not as widely known as it should be as it occurred in 1995, before social media. A million men gathered in Washington, DC, in front of the US Capitol building, and also the White House and the Washington Monument, to demonstrate the solidarity of black men who were ostracized from society and looked upon as being a threat and a deterrent. It was organized by the Nation of Islam and Mr. Louis Farrakhan, who coincidentally is getting ready to speak this July Fourth. There was a lot of anticipation in the lead up to that day: will a million men show up? Well, not only did they show up, they also expected there would be some unrest, and there wasn't a sound or a peep. There wasn't even the drop of a hat.

MATT: It was completely peaceful?

CHUCK: Yeah, and that's why it got whitewashed from history. That's what happened there.

MATT: You raise so many interesting points in your book that I was so blind to. I appreciate the schooling, and I can't recommend it enough. Another thing you discuss is how a lot of African American athletes and entertainers, historically speaking, have been given the platforms to show off their skills, but when it came time to expressing their opinions and voicing their concerns, they often got sidelined. I wanted to get your take on how you think that might have changed in more recent times with the advent of social media, because you obviously wrote the book in 1997, before social media was a thing. And I often struggle to find the positives in social media, but as I was reading your book, I thought to myself, "Maybe that's one positive right there; it's given a voice to people in the public eye and allowed them to connect with an engaged audience and express themselves in ways that they weren't given the chance to before."

CHUCK: Right. Nowadays, you have athletes and entertainers dealing directly with their "fanbase," if you want to call it that, but they're also issuing their point of view and displeasure with what they see in society. People use social media to say whatever they like. And with everything that's going on right now, you have athletes speaking directly to the cause. And it's very important that you have the top athletes coming out and saying these things, because there's no such thing as being white-balled out of sports anymore. All the voices are saying it collectively at the same time, and the guys at the top can't be knocked off that perch. LeBron James is a very different leader in the sport of basketball, which ranks right alongside soccer as a world sport, and LeBron James is at the top of that world sport using his voice in sports and also culture.

MATT: What did you make of the Chicago Bulls documentary on Netflix [*The Last Dance*]? Did you catch that, and did you like it?

CHUCK: Yeah, of course. It was well put together, and it was able to fill up a good chunk of quarantine time. And a lot of people got accumulated to disseminating the myth of the Chicago Bulls and Michael Jordan. So it was educational for many people, and it was a revisitation for others.

MATT: Another thing I wanted to ask you about is the role of Hollywood and the entertainment industry in regards to representation and the lack of strong African American role models. You talk a lot in your book about how black actors have historically been regulated to these comic, one-dimensional characters. Do you feel like that situation has changed and improved in more recent times? Or do you feel like there's still a lot of work to be done in regards to the representation of black people in TV and film?

CHUCK: Yeah, of course. I'm not talking about the faces on the screen; I'm talking about every time you see a commercial. Even if you do see a black face, how often do you see a black company putting out those faces? In the areas of ownership and companies who are able to present these images, the percentage is still too low, and we need to make it a lot higher. Just because companies are throwing a bunch of black faces and symbols and images out there, if it's still the same old company that's ran by white people, then they're still owning a corner of the dictation of what's being put out there, and it's very easy to find a problem with that.

MATT: Why do you think the Black Lives Matter movement that's now in full effect has finally risen up after all this time?

CHUCK: It's just a different generation. A lot of people who were here in the eighties and nineties are no longer here, and there's also been decades of new people being born. That's the difference. And people are connected differently nowadays; if there's angst and confusion and questions that need to be asked, they're asking them themselves. So, that's what makes that different.

MATT: You know this trend of cancel culture at the moment, where everyone is jumping on people for the mistakes that they've made in the past, and demanding that they pay for them in the present?

CHUCK: Yeah.

MATT: Do you think we could take some of that energy and redirect it toward getting reparations and compensations for victims of the slave trade? It's obviously this historic thing that made so many people wealthy, and it's easy to trace all the people who benefitted financially from slavery. There are plenty of companies and individuals that we could trace and name and hold accountable.

CHUCK: Right.

MATT: Do you think we could ever bring about a movement like that, in the same way that the victims of the holocaust were compensated for their pain and torment? Because that would be an amazing thing.

CHUCK: It would. There's a lot of atrocities that've been done in the world by countries that have settled into the Northern Hemisphere, so to speak. This is a big discussion that goes way beyond the USA and the UK. Countries in the Northern Hemisphere have historically gone into lands across the world and stripped them of their resources and wealth and stockpiled it for themselves. And we can only start on a clean slate if we have some reparation and repairing for all the atrocities that we carried out in the past.

MATT: Education is obviously an important factor in change and progress, too.

CHUCK: Education, economics, enforcement, and environment. Black people need to look at controlling all these areas for ourselves.

MATT: In your book you talk about your trip to Ghana, and what an eye-opening, educational, and in many ways heartbreaking, but also inspiring experience that was. How many times have you been to Africa?

CHUCK: I've been to Africa four times, and each time it transformed me. But out of the many countries and territories that I've been to, in essence all men and women want the same thing: a good quality life and the quantity of living and gaining years. That's what most people want: to take care of their family and let newer generations know that it's viable.

HYRO THE HERO—*RAPPER, SOLO ARTIST*

MATT: You're spitting some pretty hardcore stuff in the song "Closed Casket."

HYRO: I'm speaking about real shit, bro. This is my feelings about wanting to fuck people up. A lot of these fucking cops are killing black kids and getting away with it. If that happened to someone in my family, I'd have to find that person, and we'd have to fucking fight. I couldn't care less about the consequences. You know what I'm saying? And that song is my feeling toward that whole situation and these police who are doing what they do. It's a scary thing when we can't even walk around the neighborhood without feeling threatened by the police.

In a situation where if my people didn't do anything wrong, and you shoot them for no reason, *you're* the one who should be scared as fuck to walk the street. But a lot of these police kill people of another color and then get fucking money instead; they get a GoFundMe to help them out and all kinds of stuff like that. That's the weird situation that we're in right now. We have to sit back and look at it, and ask, "What's going on?" So that song is my hardcore feelings on this shit, bro. Don't fuck with me on no shit like that.

MATT: It's mad, isn't it? You look back to the Rodney King incident, which was over twenty-five years ago now, and in many ways we still haven't progressed.

HYRO: We've progressed in the sense that people's minds are more open to this stuff, and everyone has woken up to it.

MATT: That's one good thing about the internet.

HYRO: Yeah. Everyone is seeing video footage of what's going on, so you can't deny it. You can make excuses, but you can't deny it.

MATT: But the people who commit these crimes are still being protected aren't they?

HYRO: Yeah, but that's on us at the end of the day. I respect people protesting and everything like that, but we've been protesting for a long time. We might have to find a new way of going about it. And I'm not saying go out in the streets to fight and riot. But we need to find a way of bringing justice upon these people who commit these acts. You get what I'm saying?

MATT: I hear you, man.

HYRO: These cops feel like they can get away with it because we don't do nothing. A lot of them kill somebody then just pay off the family or some shit like that. And because the family have a bit of money, they say, "Okay, we'll forgive the cop who shot him." Fuck that shit! Fuck the forgiving of the cop, and fuck the money! The problem is much bigger than that. We have to figure out a way to get justice within the system.

MATT: I think when you speak about issues like this in music, the aggressive songs with the vivid language are the ones that hammer home the message the most strong. When you think about the acts that've historically done that—from NWA to Rage Against the Machine—there's a lot to be said for powerful, violent imagery in music.

HYRO: Exactly. And listen, I'm not about to go out and kill somebody. But it's an emotion that I feel at the time for whatever situation, and the best way to get that off your chest is to speak it rather than go out and actually do it. But at the same time, especially with a lot of the injustice going on, we have to be smart about it because the police are likely to send somebody down to a protest to let off a gunshot and start a riot, so they can then say, "Look how these people act."

MATT: And they want that to happen so they can criminalize these people even more.

HYRO: Exactly. That's why you have to be as smart as them. They're ten steps ahead of us on a lot of things, man. So we have to come together as people and unify, and find a way where we can live properly together in society—the cool way. It's all about love at the end of the day.

MATT: It is, right?

HYRO: Yeah. Make love not war. I don't want people to think that I'm this political guy when they listen to my music; I'm just letting you know how I feel, and I feel that we can do this as a people. We get so caught up with having a leader, especially in the black community—we always want someone to lead us. But we just need to come together as one and handle these things ourselves. We look at people like Tupac, Malcolm X, and Martin Luther King [Jr.] as leaders, but look at what happened to them. When you take that leader away, the house crumbles. So we need to figure out a way where we can do this, and we're all on the same page with the same mindset. We need a code that we can all abide by, which everybody goes by, and then I think we can all reach farther and not have these situations that we have going on right now.

MATT: That's the dream, right? Working together toward a better world.

HYRO: That's the dream. And I don't know if it will happen just like that—overnight. But it is the dream. And these kids nowadays are woke. They're actually interested in knowing more. I'm seeing that a lot more than I am seeing dancing and foolishness and stupid stuff like that. I'm seeing them having real conversations about real topics. When something happens on the news today, they're right on it. But at the same time, we also have to see that the game that's ran on us is they give us stories, which we then get emotional about.

MATT: And distracted by.

HYRO: And distracted by. There's two sides to every story. And whoever's running this show is smart as a motherfucker, you know what I'm saying?

MATT: Yeah, you're talking about the lizards.

HYRO: That's basically what I'm trying to get to: the reptilians are running this motherfucker. You have to watch and see if they blink. I'm just fucking around, obviously.

MATT: But it's important to have a critical eye, and not take everything that you see or read at face value.

HYRO: Amen to that.

JESSE LEACH—*KILLSWITCH ENGAGE, TIMES OF GRACE, THE WEAPON, STOKE THE FIRE PODCAST*

JESSE: We're being divided by hate, and it's actually designed. Call me a nut or whatever, but do your own research. There are people who are sitting there literally trying to figure out how to keep us divided because we're easier to control that way. When people talk about left and right, Republican and Democrat, and all that nonsense, it's just white noise to divide us. If we're divided, we can't rise up and fight back against the few people who are pulling the fucking strings.

As a writer, with the gift that I have and the privilege that I have, the least that I can do is talk to people and say, "Racism is fucking bullshit." The fact that we still harp on about race and the color of somebody's skin is such fucking bullshit. And that's something that really needs to be addressed because there's a lot of ignorance and bickering online. To me, it's like, "How the fuck can people not see that we should all have equal rights?"

VINNIE STIGMA—*AGNOSTIC FRONT*

VINNIE: It doesn't matter to me what race or religion or gender you are. I don't give a fuck! Either you're a good person or a bad person. It doesn't matter who robbed your wallet—that's a bad person.

MATT: I look at life in very much the same way: you're either an asshole or you're not. If you're a good person then you're okay with me, regardless of skin tone, or who you worship, or who you sleep with.

VINNIE: Right. Who cares? Racism is a self-inflicted wound. And jealousy is a self-inflicted wound. It'll only hurt you. So fuck it! Just be a good person. Nothing else matters—at least not in my life.

LINUS OF HOLLYWOOD—*NERF HERDER, SOLO ARTIST, PRODUCER*

LINUS: It's weird being in a position where if you say things, like, "I think everyone should have equal rights," or, "I think it's really bad that children are getting shot at school," that makes you a radical left-wing socialist. I just don't understand what the other side of these arguments are. And I'm a big supporter of free speech. If you want to be a racist, or you decide that you don't like gay people—or whatever your deal is—then you have the right to feel that way. But when you start legislating against people's rights, that's where I draw the line.

MATT: Why do you think the US is seeing such a shift toward right-wing nationalist ideologies?

LINUS: I think a lot of people in Middle America are busy working their jobs and trying to support their family, so they don't have a ton of time to absorb every nook and cranny of politics. And the general culture of those areas is pro-gun, pro-Bible, and a little anti-gay, etc. That's just the way they're brought up. And most of those people probably choose to watch Fox News because that channel falls in line with their general way of thinking. But unfortunately there's so much propaganda now being fed through that channel, which is where most people in Middle America are getting their news.

MATT: And accepting it as fact?

LINUS: Yeah. He [Donald Trump] has a forty percent approval rating right now. He's literally divided the whole country. He lies every single day, and you can find evidence of this, and people still support him. That's the part that's hard for me to reconcile, and that's the part that breaks my heart the most.

MATT: I can't imagine there are that many Trump supporters in LA.

LINUS: If you look at a map of where people vote blue, or Democratic, it's people that live in cities, it's people that live with diversity every day. They live with gay people, they live with Muslims, they live with people of color. And we like it; we like living in a city that's multi-cultural. It's the people that live in these small towns—and I grew up in a small town that was eighty percent white—who don't have a lot of experience with different cultures; they're the ones who are taught to fear or blame these people. But when you live in a city like LA, you look around and you say, "We're all just people."

MATT: The greatest irony is that *everyone* who lives in America, regardless of their race or whatever, *is* an immigrant—unless you're a Native American, of course. But the chances are your ancestors weren't born on this land, they came here from another, and that's the most tragic irony of all.

LINUS: It's also crazy when people go on about how American they are, and then they go to white supremacist Nazi marches. We defeated the Nazis in World War II, and now all of a sudden, it's an American thing to do, to walk around wearing swastikas? I think another problem with America is that we're a wealthy country and people just have too much free time on their hands. Have you been reading about the incels and this whole thing?

MATT: No, but it already sounds stupid.

LINUS: The abbreviation is "involuntarily celibate." It's these men who can't get laid, and they're furious at women because they can't get laid. I don't know if you remember the guy in Toronto who drove a van into a crowd of people?

MATT: That rings a bell.

LINUS: That's why he did it. That was the whole thing that he had in his head. It's complete insanity. There was another kid in Santa Barbara who went on a shooting spree, and he filmed this video right before he did it about how he was upset at women because none of them would sleep with him. That's called welcome to life, my friend. It's just insanity. There's a whole community of these incels— there's Reddit forums of these people who have this weird ideology about how women are evil because they won't sleep with them— and I'm just like, "Who even has time to develop and cultivate this philosophy that gets you so worked up that you're running people over because you can't get laid." Do you know what I mean? Why don't you try waking up with a purpose and doing something that's fulfilling to you instead?

MATT: It's fucking scary times, man. Speaking of waking up with a purpose, what are you working on at the moment?

LINUS: I don't have anything going on right now. I'm just trying to get laid.

KEVIN KERSLAKE—*FILMMAKER*

MATT: I had no idea how bigoted people were toward The Runaways, just because they were girls playing rock music. I had no idea they faced that much animosity and hatred from the American media.

KEVIN: It's nuts. I didn't know that either, to be honest. That was a shocker. Joan [Jett] is such a bad ass, and she can hold her own on stage with any man, so you don't even look at her in gender terms, in the same way that you don't look at people like Jimmy Page in gender terms. It was horrifying to go back and track her journey through finding kindred spirits and forming The Runaways, and how much shit they got. It got violent too, just because girls wanted to play rock 'n' roll.

MATT: She said she had a car battery thrown at her one night.

KEVIN: Yeah. There was violent opposition to girls just playing music. Of course, we're all familiar with how difficult it is for women to make their way in a man's world, whether it's the music industry, or politics, or whatever. And I considered myself pretty dialed in to that stuff. But to learn about all the shit that they got on a daily basis, for decades—

MATT: Not just shit either. Genuine hatred.

KEVIN: It's venomous. Record companies used to actively work against their success, and that's obviously not part of their job description. It's supposed to be the opposite of that. And I think right now, especially in this day and age where we've got a guy who proudly cocks to that sort of behavior in the White House, and a whole movement that's reacting to that—

MATT: Was all of that going on while you were editing the film?

KEVIN: Yeah, the Me Too Movement popped toward the tail end of the edit. Obviously equality is always on the table, but that obviously turbocharged things.

MATT: It must've felt like you were working on something very timely and vital.

KEVIN: It did. And there's a lot of stuff in there outside of her musical career, like being an instrument for change on the planet and a champion for underdogs and people who don't have a voice.

MATT: Yeah, it's not even just a gender thing: it's anyone who's been spat on, trampled on, marginalized, and disrespected.

KEVIN. Yeah. Human rights, animal rights—all that stuff. Joan's been very active in the name of bettering life on the planet.

MATT: We need more people like Joan Jett.

KEVIN: We do. And she's so humble about it. She's not beating on her chest or taking selfies at an issue related event. She just goes in there and does the work. There's an integrity about her activism that I think is really refreshing, and the nobility of it shines through.

JESSE HUGHES—EAGLES OF DEATH METAL, BOOTS ELECTRIC

MATT: Are you close to reconnecting with the joy that rock 'n' roll music gave you before what happened out in Paris?

JESSE: That joy never left me. It never left me. Nothing ever took it from me—truly. There was a moment or two where I had something far more terrible to simultaneously deal with. But I dealt with it simultaneously, by surrounding myself with the finest fucking friends you could ask for—on top of Joshua Homme. I have the luxury and the incredible honor to be in a band with friends who are at the top of their fucking game. And it's a lot easier to get out of bed when you have a reason to—a real reason to, you know what I mean?

I never been someone who's a "why me" kind of dude. Why not me? Whatever that is. Everyone is going to be called upon to defend the neighborhood at some point. Be ready. And don't worry about how terrible it's going to be. Just make sure you're doing the best that you can by your friends, and if they're doing that then it will take care of itself. I don't have it in me to let the bad guys win. I just don't have it in me. I don't.

Even if we're talking about what happened three-and-a-half years ago, there was a terrible joy that I was able to spread. A terrible joy and a terrible happiness. I was able to measure the quality of the people in that moment by how they reacted, and I was able to spread the testimony of what I saw that night, which was the greatest examples of love that I've ever seen in my life.

The nation of France put its cape around us and pulled us into its bosom and protected us. And rockers around the world united in a decent cause. These are all beautiful things that I'm able to spread at a great cost. These are the sorts of things that, if I could choose, I wish I'd never fucking seen them and would never be able to tell you about them. But that isn't going to happen. So the honor has fallen to me. And it's a terrible honor—I'm talking about that moment, three-and-a-half years ago.

MATT: I was at the return show that you guys did at L'Olympia in Paris, and it was one of the most special and overwhelmingly beautiful experiences I've ever been a part of. And I saw firsthand how much the people of France truly had the band's back—and vice versa.

JESSE: They truly had our backs. And I mean this with no disrespect, but nobody's ever really going to fucking be able to understand certain things unless it happens to them. And when are you ever really going to see the morality of a nation? Most people only get to know a country based on their own personal friendships; I got to see the character of a country in a moment, and it blew me away.

What I'm here to say is that my experiences have led me to this conclusion: it's a beautiful world filled with beautiful people and a lot of love. So much love that it's willing to sacrifice itself to protect its friends. I think that's a beautiful message. Some people might think I'm fucking crazy for coming to that solution, but I don't really give a shit. I honestly don't give a rat's ass what an asshole thinks, even if they're a loudmouth asshole. I'm a rock 'n' roller; I came here to shake my dick and have a good time. Occasionally, that pisses some people off. But so be it. I've still got a three-quarter chub right now in a room with six dudes.

MATT: So the Jesse Hughes that we know and love is still very much alive and kicking?

JESSE: Hell yes.

MATT: That makes me very happy, dude. It really does.

JESSE: Good, good, good. Honestly, I've never had nightmares. I haven't had any trouble sleeping—none of that shit. None of it. I just want to make sure I earn everything that I've got. That's it. But nothing is going to stop me from being horny. And it isn't going to stop me from loving rock 'n' roll. If it did, it would let these assholes win. And when it comes to the vile, their names shall never be known, because they are nothing, and they have only ever been nothing—to me.

Really, the testament of what we're seeing is that rock 'n' roll is a thing that happens between the whole gang. There's the monkey with the guitars that shakes his dick on stage, and there's the ones who come to the show. I'm still here, not just because I had a will to persevere, but because the rock 'n' rollers out there were unwilling for me to go anywhere. That was made very clear. And that was probably the first source of any strength that I had: the weird letters that you only see in movies, where they're like, "You can't stop doing this." Shit like that. Those people aren't willing for me to age even one day. So, I guess I'll live forever.

MATT: Let's talk about this new covers album that you just put out. How did you go about choosing the songs for it?

JESSE: The reason I chose all these songs for the covers record is this is the playlist of songs that I used to walk myself out of the bad shit that happened to us. Originally, Joshua wanted me to write a record to get this shit out. But I put forth the idea that maybe the songs had already been written. So maybe I can cover these songs, and maybe that'll be easier on me.

MATT: They also say all the things that you'd want to say so perfectly.

JESSE: That's exactly what I'm saying: it's like they were written for me in a playlist. When I get up in the morning, I rise to music. I prepare for anything that I do to music—it's a known fact to anyone who knows me. And that didn't change when it came to dealing with something terrible. I would use music to get myself to a place where I felt like I could go out and take some punches. This album is that playlist.

MATT: The Cat Stevens cover ["Trouble"] crushes me.

JESSE: It's one of the most beautiful songs I've ever heard in my life. And it really was like he was writing what I was feeling, you know? This album is almost like a statement to the fans, and the spirits, and whatever else. And it worked: I feel better about a lot of things. I really do believe in rock 'n' roll. I *really* fucking believe in rock 'n' roll. If you approach it with the right attitude, it can save your life. And it can help you feel better, just about things in general. There was an intensity and some real voodoo magic that went into this record. I believe in the good Lord, and therefore I believe in the devil, and therefore I believe in voodoo magic. It's real.

MATT: Especially in music—music is magic.

JESSE: I feel like there's a lot of magicians in our world running around performing fabulous tricks. But there's only a few wizards who can really fold fucking time itself. And I've always endeavored to be a wizard; I don't want to do tricks; I want to do magic for real. And rock 'n' roll is the best medium through which that can be achieved.

MATT: You're looking well, dude. You seem really happy. And I'm pleased and inspired to know that the show will go on.

JESSE: Thank you, brother. It ain't ever going to stop. I love you, dude.

JESSE MALIN—*HEART ATTACK, D GENERATION, SOLO ARTIST*

MATT: Didn't the merch seller, who was killed during the Eagles of Death Metal show at the Bataclan, used to work with your band?

JESSE: Nick Alexander, yeah. He did his first tour as a merch person with my band on *The Fine Art of Self Destruction* tour. He was a guy that was around—he was friends with some folks—and he just a cool dude. We wound up doing two or three tours together, and then he went on to work for everybody. The last time I think I saw him before the Bataclan was when we were out here in Camden playing some shows with The Replacements at the Roundhouse. I saw Nick that day while he was working, and he was just the same as he always was—so sweet. I gave him a big hug.

Unfortunately, he was there at the Bataclan with the Eagles. He was protecting another girl, and he laid over her and got shot. It was heartbreaking. When you travel and tour with people, you live with them so intimately, and they become part of your family. I'm also close with Dave Catching, and I don't think he tours with them anymore, but he was the guitarist in Eagles of Death Metal and Queens of the Stone Age for many years, and he runs the Rancho De La Luna.

MATT: I know Dave very well. He's an absolute sweetheart.

JESSE: He really is. And watching those clips, you see him and he hears the shots, and he's looking in complete disbelief, like he couldn't believe it was really happening. I know that room, too. I played the Bataclan years ago with Ryan Adams.

MATT: I got to play there in February, and it was such a huge honor. The occasion was so joyful, and to see people in that room smiling and laughing after what happened in there was truly special. I guess when something like that happens, it really hits home how small this community is.

JESSE: Yeah, it's a really small planet. You learn that very quickly touring and travelling and finding people through music and a need to connect—to feel like we're not alone. And there's always horrible things going on in the world, with violence and terrorist attacks and all kinds of stuff like that. But what happened at the Bataclan was right in our back yard, in the rock 'n' roll community, and it felt extra personal. It will never be forgotten. We just have to keep spreading the positive word and give people more love in this life.

CULTURAL COMMENTARY PLAYLIST

DUSTIN KENSRUE—"CARRY THE FIRE"

TOM MORELLO (FEAT. KNIFE PARTY)—"BATTLE SIRENS"

HYRO THE HERO—"LET THE SNAKE SHOW"

2PAC—"HIT 'EM UP"

THE BRONX—"YOUTH WASTED"

EVERY TIME I DIE—"POST-BOREDOM"

AMEN—"COMA AMERICA"

REFUSED—"ELEKTRA"

JANE'S ADDICTION—"JANE SAYS"

PUBLIC ENEMY—"911 IS A JOKE"

HYRO THE HERO—"CLOSED CASKET"

KILLSWITCH ENGAGE—"HATE BY DESIGN"

AGNOSTIC FRONT—"FOR MY FAMILY"

LINUS OF HOLLYWOOD—"AT ALL"

JOAN JETT—"BAD REPUTATION"

EAGLES OF DEATH METAL—"SAVE A PRAYER"

JESSE MALIN—"THE FINE ART OF SELF-DESTRUCTION"

ODDS & ENDS

"Talk about a weekend of weirdness."

I HAVEN'T EXACTLY SAVED the best for last. But I almost have. I love this chapter. There's no way I could follow the last one while keeping it serious, so all that's left to do is flip the tone and lighten the mood. Outtakes, odds and ends, miscellaneous—whatever you want to call it. This chapter is a collection of anecdotes that wouldn't neatly fit into any of the other chapters in the book, but are nevertheless worthy of inclusion, and of interest, especially if you're a lifelong rock 'n' roll fan like myself. And once again, you've made it this far through a book based solely on stories about music, art, and culture, so I'm guessing we're on the same team.

These segments also highlight the beauty of podcasting. Because podcasts are longform conversations, they allow the narrative to veer off into all kinds of awesome avenues and alleyways, and you uncover stories that you don't get from more generic Q&As—like swimming with sharks, wrestling with midgets, touring with Bon Jovi, fighting with Slayer, partying with Sam Kinison, making music videos with Michael Madsen, and inventing the wall of death. Let's jump into it. Odds and ends. Here we go!

GREG ATTONITO—*THE BOUNCING SOULS*

MATT: I want to ask you about "Lean on Sheena." That's an all-time favorite song of mine; I don't know if it's the lyrics, the melody, or the combination of the two, but there's something about that song that's musical perfection to me.

GREG: That's great to hear. Do you know the history of it?

MATT: No, but I want to.

GREG: Okay. Do you know The Mighty Mighty Bosstones?

MATT: Of course.

GREG: Do you know their bass player, Joe Gittleman?

MATT: Not personally. But I know who he is.

GREG: Well, here's a fun fact for you: Joe had a side project during the early 2000s called Avoid One Thing, and they put out a record that had that song on it. So Joe wrote that song.

MATT: Wow! I had no idea.

GREG: Yeah, and we were recording *The Gold Record*, which was produced by Ted Hutt, who's actually from London. He was friends with Joe and kind of at the last minute dropped it on us, like, "I've got this idea. And he's a friend of yours—guys you like, you know?" He was pretty delicate about it, which was funny. It was literally the day before we started tracking. He was like, "Check this out, guys." He almost slipped it in there. He was like, "We could just track the drums, then, you know, see how it goes." And we thought it was a cool song, so we liked the idea. Joe Sib from SideOneDummy Records was also instrumental in making it happen. We call him the Mayor of Broville because he's always like, "What's up, bro?" He's the mayor of California bro culture. And he was on Ted, too. He was like, "You gotta get The Souls to record 'Lean on Sheena,' bro." And Ted agreed with him. So they hatched this little plan to try and get us to do it.

MATT: I never knew any of this.

GREG: It's a cool story. And I'll just finish it by sharing that Joe's original version had four of the same verses. And I was like, "I get it—the Ramones. It *can* work." But I said to Ted after the third verse, "I can't sing it a fourth time. I just can't do it." And Ted was like, "Let's see if we can get Joe on the phone." So I called Joe Gittleman. He was all excited that we were going to record the song, by the way. He was beside himself. And I was like, "Dude, what's this song about?" He said, "I don't really know, it's sort of an unfinished idea. So I completely get what you're saying about that fourth verse because it's not quite done; I didn't finish it." Then he and I kind of hashed it out and wrote that fourth verse together.

MATT: Over the phone?

GREG: Yeah, because I had to track the vocals in a day or two. So we figured it out. And the rest is history.

JOHN FELDMANN—*GOLDFINGER, PRODUCER, SONGWITER, A&R EXECUTIVE*

JOHN: I'd written "Superman" between the first album [*Goldfinger*] and *Hang-Ups*. The plan was to put out a split seven-inch with us and Reel Big Fish, so I had Aaron [Barrett] sing on "Superman"—he's singing all the harmonies on the song. And it just randomly became what it is because of *Tony Hawk's Pro Skater*. It wasn't like we ever expected it to be a single or anything like that. It was just meant to be an in-between album song.

MATT: I think for me, and everyone my age, that was how we discovered Goldfinger—here in the UK at least. Do you remember playing in the UK for the first time after the game came out? And was it an instant moment of recognition, like, "Shit! This is happening!"

JOHN: For sure. It was 1999, and we were opening for the Bloodhound Gang. "Superman" was halfway through the set, and people just went fucking ballistic. I didn't even put it together at first; I had no idea it was this video game that people were hearing the song from until about three weeks later when someone connected the dots, and said, "That's why the song is so big." It was really cool.

LINUS OF HOLLYWOOD—*NERF HERDER, SOLO ARTIST, PRODUCER*

LINUS: I play in Nerf Herder now, and before I was in the band they did the *Buffy [the Vampire Slayer]* theme. And they were on an episode of the show.

MATT: That's one of my favorite TV shows of all-time.

LINUS: Really?

MATT: Yeah, I think it's fantastic. There's one episode where…have you seen all of them?

LINUS: I have seen *none* of them. And I don't want to ruin my Nerf Herder credibility, but I'm probably the least up on all the pop culture references that those guys allude to—all the *Star Wars* and the *Star Trek* and the *Buffy* stuff.

MATT: I won't even go down the rabbit hole with my story then. Do you get a lot of *Buffy* fans still coming to Nerf Herder shows? Is that a section of the fanbase that you still see to this day?

LINUS: Yeah, for sure. I was a Nerf Herder fan before I was in the band, and I was definitely coming more from the pop-punk, funny lyrics angle, as opposed to the nerd references. But a big part of our current career is playing Comic Con and Dragon Con, and all those other Nerd Cons. And the main reason we're there is because we're the band that did the *Buffy* theme.

DEAN KARR—*DIRECTOR, PHOTOGRAPHER*

MATT: Were Deftones happy to stand on those cages in the middle of the ocean for the "My Own Summer" video?

DEAN: Yeah, we had a blast shooting that one.

MATT: Where was it filmed? It looks like it was a pretty cold day.

DEAN: That's just the way I colored it. It was actually just outside LA at Lake Piru, and we had prosthetic sharks cutting through the water. We set it up so it looked as dangerous as it could when they went under water. Then we went to Australia to film white sharks, but we didn't even see a freakin' white shark. We went on a six-day expedition on an eighty-foot prawn trawler, and we were with the right people, but we didn't see one. So I had to come back and license a bunch of shark footage. I'd waited my whole life to do that, and I kind of came back with my tail between my legs. But now I go to Mexico each year, and I swim with these beauties.

MATT: Mexico's the spot, is it?

DEAN: Yeah. It's so clear. I was in the water plenty in Australia, and it's kind of murky down there, as I know it is in South Africa. But where I go in Mexico, it's eighteen hours straight out to sea, and we live on a 120-foot boat for five days. I take twenty friends, and there'll be a dozen or so white sharks in the water, all twelve-to-eighteen-feet long.

MATT: Better you than me, mate.

ALAN ROBERT—*LIFE OF AGONY, COMIC BOOK CREATOR*

ALAN: In college, I had this idea for a comic book that I never finished. So by 2009, when the band started to slow down a bit, I was so determined to get this idea out of my head and make it real. I went through a bunch of artists that worked for Marvel to help bring the story to life because I wasn't that confident in my own drawings at that time. But I must've waited six months, and I never got one sketch from those guys. I got so frustrated, and I said to myself, "I'm going to draw it myself. I don't care what it looks like." So I did. And through Twitter, I got myself a publishing deal.

MATT: Through Twitter?

ALAN: Yeah.

MATT: How? Did you just tweet some work?

ALAN: No, I was just connecting with some people in the industry, and I noticed this one cat liked heavy metal. He made some posts about Motörhead, so I connected with him, and he was like, "Oh, I bought your record." At the time, I actually just thought he was the writer of a book that I liked, but he turned out to be the editor-in-chief of one of the biggest indie comic book publishers [IDW Publishing]. They did *30 Days of Night*, a lot of horror books, and eventually *G.I. Joe, Transformers,* and *Star Trek*. They're a powerhouse now. And they're the company that gave me my first shot.

My first book was *Wire Hangers*, which started as a monthly comic book and then got collected into a graphic novel. So while I still had their ear, I pitched them another story for this book called *Crawl to Me*. Then after that I did *Killogy*, which I incorporated Marky Ramone, Doyle from the Misfits, and Frank Vincent into.

MATT: What gave you the idea to pair the guy from *Goodfellas* with a Misfit and a Ramone? Did you just think, these are some interesting people that I've grown up with as pop culture icons, and I'd like to see them play off each other in this fictional world?

ALAN: The original idea was to make three *Twilight Zone*–type stories that intersected. When I started drawing the characters, they just kept looking like these heroes from my childhood, and I was like, "Maybe I just pitch these guys the idea of starring in my comic book?" I don't think that had ever been done before—to cast a comic book without coming off a TV show or something like that. And I was able to convince all of them before they saw any pages or anything; I just drew up the covers of them in action and each one said, "Yes."

So all of a sudden I had my own comic book with all my heroes in it. After that, we were able to adapt it into an animation using their voices. There's a six-minute proof of concept video that you can see online at killogyanimated.com. We worked with this Canadian 3D animation studio, which was fantastic. They took my artwork and were able to make 3D characters out of it. They made all these 3D environments, too. And the audio was very DIY: I went over to Frank Vincent's house, we went into the kitchen with my laptop, and he just did the voiceover right there in front of me. Then I went to Marky Ramone's studio to get a couple of lines from him.

MATT: I've never heard Doyle from the Misfits talk, but those other two have such distinct New York accents. Is Doyle's voice like that as well?

ALAN: Doyle is a real character. He's a very funny guy, and he's very New York. He's a sweetheart. It was so much fun. And it was very exciting to work with those guys and get to know them on a personal level—as friends. Even after we did all the comics and the animation, before Frank Vincent died, he would come and check up on me every couple of weeks. We did some conventions together and stuff like that, and we became very friendly.

MATT: What was he like? I loved him in *The Sopranos*. And he's great in all the Martin Scorsese movies: *Raging Bull*, *Goodfellas*, *Casino*. He was a great actor.

ALAN: He was very cool, just a very sweet man. He was a musician as well: he was a drummer when he was younger, so we'd trade a lot of musician stories. He had a band with Joe Pesci back in the day.

MATT: Really?

ALAN: Yeah, they were a local New Jersey band, and they'd wear all the suits and stuff like that. It was a five-piece band. Joe Pesci played guitar and sang, Frank Vincent was behind the drums, and in between the songs those two would have this banter back and forth. They used to make a lot of people laugh, so eventually they became a comedy double act.

MATT: No way! And that's how Scorsese became aware of them?

ALAN: Yeah, and they had this kind of rhythm together, so when Pesci got *Raging Bull*, he said, "I've got someone to play Salvy." They just had this chemistry that was undeniable.

MATT: The chemistry between Joe Pesci and Robert De Niro is undeniable, too. As you say, it's this rhythmical thing.

ALAN: Absolutely. It's all about timing. Frank and I talked about timing a lot. I actually interviewed him for an interview in the back of the *Killogy* graphic novel. I have that whole recording somewhere.

I should really edit it for the public at some point. It's so good. He's got great stories.

MATT: Would you ever consider doing a podcast?

ALAN: Yeah. You know what it is, though; I spend so much time drawing, writing, and playing music. It's really hard to find the time to do anything else. Plus, we're developing each of these comics into films and TV shows. I've been at it for years, and I'm just starting to see one of them gain momentum. But you need so many things to align to make it happen, besides the obvious things like the money, the script, the right producers, a distributor, and the acting talent. You need all that stuff to align and for everyone to be on the same page with the same vision to work within a schedule to execute it. And I've learned that just because you have three out of the five pieces, that doesn't necessarily mean that it's happening.

MATT: It's not a DIY project like the Killogy novels, where you can just go out there and make it happen.

ALAN: Not at all. I wish it was.

CHARLIE PAULSON—*GOLDFINGER, BLACK PRESIDENT*

MATT: Weren't you in a movie directed by Tobe Hooper?

CHARLIE: Yes. Rest in peace.

MATT: What was that like?

CHARLIE: It was fucking awesome.

MATT: For anyone who doesn't know the name, he obviously directed *Texas Chainsaw Massacre* and *Poltergeist*. He's a horror legend.

CHARLIE: Yeah, a horror legend, for sure. My part was originally supposed to be for Glenn Danzig, but apparently he just couldn't act. From what I'm told, he was so bad that it wasn't even like, "It doesn't matter because it's Glenn Danzig." He couldn't remember his lines or anything. So they held auditions for the part, and I got it. This was a long time ago—about thirteen years ago—so I wasn't very experienced, and I had this one scene with a lot of dialogue. We shot a couple of takes, then Tobe pulled me aside and essentially said, "Forget about acting. Have the conversation with this woman as yourself."

He also did this thing that made me feel more comfortable, where he came up to me and said, "Some of these actors are having a hard time, and you're such a natural." He could have been full of shit when he said that, by the way. But it was calculated. He said, "You're such a natural, I would love it if you could practice their scenes with them, just so they can relax a little bit and maybe get some of what you have." I didn't have anything. But he was doing that to make me feel good and to make me feel comfortable in front of the camera.

The thing about acting is listening. When you're on camera and you've got a head full of all these lines that you've memorized, a lot of the time you're just in your own head, and you're waiting to say the next thing that you memorized; you're not actually having a moment or listening to the other actor. But if I'm in that scene thinking, "I'm here to be of service and to help them," then I actually have to fucking listen to them. So Tobe was amazing. He really understood actors, and he really helped me out a lot.

MATT: Do you go to acting classes?

CHARLIE: I did go to one class for a little bit, which was ironically held in the building that used to be the storage space where Guns N' Roses lived and rehearsed—on Sunset [Blvd.] & [N] Gardner [St.], right next to the Guitar Center. Now there's a restaurant, an acting studio, and a little theater there. But it used to be a huge storage space, and Guns N' Roses all lived in there with their gear, and they rehearsed and did whatever else that they got up to in there. And that was the same fucking room where my acting class took place. So everything is full circle.

KEITH BUCKLEY—*EVERY TIME I DIE, THE DAMNED THINGS, AUTHOR*

MATT: As a Buffalo native, how do you feel about Vincent Gallo and *Buffalo '66*?

KEITH: I think he's great. But I think there's an overall feeling in Buffalo that he's the one that got out. Everyone that I know who knew him had been proud of him until he actively disavowed the city. And obviously there's no reason to be proud of where you were accidentally born. You didn't have anything to do with it, you just happened to pop up in the place where your parents fucked, so you shouldn't feel like it's your place, because it's really not. But when Vincent Gallo did get out, I suppose he could've tipped his hat to the place that raised him. Instead, he just said, "Fuck that place. Everyone there is a loser. Fuck all these idiots." And really, where's the lie? But he didn't have to say it. He didn't have to rub it in. And I think the reason I'm bitter is because with *Buffalo '66*, he said all the things that I wanted to say, but he did it first, and he did it best. I really wanted to do that, and I felt like it was my calling, but he already did it. I actually went to the casting call for that movie.

MATT: Really? I didn't know that.

KEITH: Yeah, I was about fifteen or sixteen years old, and they had an open casting call for *Buffalo '66*. There wasn't any readings or anything like that. Everyone was in a line, and he just kind of came down and picked out the people who he thought looked the most Buffalonian. The guy next to me was very vocal about his acting past, and he was talking about all the plays that he'd done to anyone who would listen. He was so obnoxious; I was just like, "Somebody shut this guy up." But he got picked, and when he got picked, he was ecstatic, and he felt like that was his big break. If you've seen the movie, it's the guy in the bathroom—

MATT: Who looks at Vincent Gallo's dick?

KEITH: That's the guy. And he thought that was going to be his big break. But instead he gets called a derogatory term, and he has his face mashed into a wall.

MATT: It could've been you, Keith.

KEITH: It could've been me, man.

MATT: Vincent Gallo is also in one of the Glassjaw videos. How did that come about?

KEITH: So, Vincent Gallo has a website [www.vincentgallo.com] where he sells anything. He's a shameless self-promoter.

MATT: He even sells his own semen.

KEITH: Yep, he sells his semen online—you can still buy it. He's a sicko. But on that website, he sells an afternoon with him, and you can pay like $10,000 to hang out with him. Glassjaw found out about that, and they hired him for $10,000, which was their video budget, and they put him to work. I guess that's a pretty cool thing to do, as I'm sure Vincent Gallo thought someone would hire him just to hang out and superfan on him and feed his ego. But instead it's this band who are putting him to work, and they don't really give a shit about him, so the joke's on him.

MATT: How did you wind up with Michael Madsen in the music video to "Kill the Music"?

KEITH: The director [Darren Doane] was somehow owed a favor by a friend that knew Michael Madsen. It was a long, weird story. And somehow Michael Madsen agreed to do it, but only if we let him bring his son to the set so he could do some graffiti. We were just, like, "All right. Is this some weird rich person thing?" Who the fuck knows what demands these people have. So they had to set up this area with all this plaster and cardboard where his son could do graffiti all day, while Michael Madsen was in the video. He was very intimidating at first. And he brought a suit from *Reservoir Dogs*, which was crazy.

MATT: I love it. My friend Thomas Nicholas made a film with him a while back, and apparently he still has the car from *Reservoir Dogs* on his driveway.

KEITH: And here was me thinking you had to give all that shit back. He was a little standoffish at first, but then as the day went on he got more and more involved. He was also drinking very heavily. And I had a drink with him in the hope that it would open things up between us. He leaned into me at one point and said, "I'm going to tell you a joke that Al told me." And I was like, "Who's Al?" He goes, "Al Pacino—on the set of *Donnie Brasco*." I was like, "Are you fucking kidding me? This guy just referred to Al Pacino as *Al*," just assuming that I'd know who he was talking about. I ran off right away to brag about it, and I never heard the story or anything, and by the time I got back he was gone. So I'll never know the joke that Al told Michael Madsen.

JESSE LEACH—*KILLSWITCH ENGAGE, TIMES OF GRACE, THE WEAPON, STOKE THE FIRE PODCAST*

MATT: I wonder if we can talk about what happened to your throat, the recovery steps that you took to get your voice back, and what you learned in the process?

JESSE: I've been doing this for twenty-four years now. I started out as a punk—I'm still a punk, but I sing in a metal band now—where all I did was yell. And at some point, I was like, "I want to try this singing thing out." To be quite honest, I've never been very good at it, because I never had proper training. So I've been doing it improperly for twenty-something years. In the studio it's one thing: you're calm and relaxed. But when you put somebody in a live situation, your adrenaline is going and you get cottonmouth, and all these things come into play.

I didn't have the training or that muscle memory that good vocalists have prior to touring a bunch. I rejoined Killswitch attempting to do my best with songs that I didn't write or sing. And Howard Jones has this bellowing, beautiful voice. I was having a really hard time singing his songs, to the point where I'd come off stage and I'd be spitting blood into the bathroom sink, thinking to myself, "Am I going to fucking die? Do I have cancer? What is wrong with me?"

I was doing vocals for this recent record [*Incarnate*], and I went to sing a note that I can hit easily, and Adam [Dutkiewicz] was like, "You're not hitting that note at all. You're not even close. You sound off." So I got home, and I went to see my doctor. He looked me dead in the eye and said, "Stop talking. I'm going to put you on a high dose of prednisone," which is steroids for the muscles, and he told me that I couldn't speak for a week. When I went back for the follow-up appointment, my doctor's face was as white as a ghost. He just looked at me and said, "This isn't good, they haven't moved, your nodules are still there." Normally in the past I've gotten nodules, then I take the steroids, and they go away. But these weren't going away, and they were calloused, which means they'd been there for years.

After that my doctor sent me to another guy, and he did the same thing: he looked at me and said, "This is not good." And this was the guy who did Adele's vocal surgery, so he's one of the top three in the nation for what he does. I was just looking for an ounce of hope, as the next tour coming up was with Iron Maiden, and that doctor looked me in the eye and said, "I can't promise you anything, but I think we're going to get you to Iron Maiden. I think it's going to be okay."

Fast-forward a few weeks, and I'm opening up for Iron Maiden in front of eleven thousand people in Tallinn, Estonia. I was doing vibrato and things that my voice had never even done before. Adam looked at me and said, "Sounding good." And I cried. I drank a lot that night, which I probably shouldn't have done, but I wanted to celebrate. And I completed six weeks on tour with Iron Maiden. There was no blood, I sang better than ever before, and I can actually hit notes now. It's great. It's fucking awesome. So thank you modern science, and thank you Melissa Cross [legendary vocal instructor] for saving my career.

MATT: And what was it like touring with Iron Maiden?

JESSE: Even if you don't know who Iron Maiden is, to see their live show is insane. It's like a mixture of a Broadway musical and one of the most entertaining metal shows that you'll see. You even said this last night, which I love: there's a little bit of Monty Python thrown in there. It can get a little camp. But they're the originators of camp, and you have to tip your hat to them. They always keep everybody entertained. But life on the road with Maiden is exactly what you'd expect—it's nuts. If you would've told me as an eleven-year-old boy that I'd be shaking hands and hanging out with members of Iron Maiden one day, I would've told you, "Fuck right off. That will never happen in a million years."

Day one of tour, Bruce [Dickinson] walked into our dressing room and gave us two bottles of champagne and a case of Trooper beer. He said, "Welcome to the tour," and shook each of our hands. We were all like, "Holy shit! That just fucking happened." After our set, Bruce then shows up dressed as a fucking pirate or something with a cape and a sword, and he asked us, "How was it lads?" We were like, "Good, good, good." And Adam [Dutkiewicz] was like, "You look fucking sexy," to which Bruce replied, "I didn't know you cared, mate." That was the first show, and after it was done we popped the bottles of champagne and poured them all over each other. We were like, "We're on tour with Iron fucking Maiden."

For those who don't know, and many people don't know, my dad was a Christian minister when I was growing up. He was the kind of guy that thought heavy metal music was satanic back in the 1980s. I wasn't able to listen to it until my brother and I started smuggling in cassette tapes from private school. And the first tape that got smuggled through was *The Number of the Beast*. Of course everyone knows the cover with the devil, which looks very satanic, but we also know that Maiden are a bunch of history dorks, and they're not satanic in the least bit. But my father found the tape, and I have never seen that man get so angry. He literally smashed it to pieces in front of my brother and me. He said, "No devil's music in my house!"

When I first found out I was going on tour with Iron Maiden, I was out for dinner with my parents, and I leaned over to my pop and said, "Guess who I'm going on tour with?" It was a great moment of redemption. And thankfully my dad's loosened the fuck up these days. He wears Killswitch hoodies, drinks whiskey, and swears like a sailor with me behind closed doors. So he's lightened up a lot.

CHRIS DEMAKES—*LESS THAN JAKE, CHRIS DEMAKES A PODCAST*

MATT: When did you first start wearing costumes on stage?

CHRIS: The costumes were bred out of boredom. It was before smart phones and all these things that now occupy our hands and minds, and I always liked to dress up, but it wasn't all the time. Then we were out on the road with Skankin' Pickle, who we love, and their trombone player Gerry [Lundquist] used to do this bit where he'd pretend that he was Hulk Hogan, and he'd rip his shirt off. He'd go out to thrift stores and buy a different shirt every day to rip off his back, and I'd follow him around town to these thrift stores, and be like, "That's a funny wig. That's a funny pair of glasses. That's a gaudy gold necklace or watch. That's a horrible pair of pants." And I just started amassing these costumes.

MATT: And you actually invented characters, too. The people who I dress up as when I'm DJing are pop culture figures that people know, but you'd invent your own characters with names and backstories and all that stuff. You'd go full method!

CHRIS: Yeah, it was ridiculous. And I really paid attention to detail; I never half-assed it; I was never going to have the right pants and shirt and wig for a specific time period, but then you looked down and I had shoes that were current.

MATT: Then the myth is unraveled, and the character is broken.

CHRIS: Right. So unlike yourself, these were unknown characters that I invented. And a lot of them were inspired by living in Florida; I would see these guys at my Little League games. I basically started doing it just to get a laugh from the band.

MATT: Tell me about what happened at the Warped Tour in Spain. Less Than Jake were an hour late going on stage because of some technical difficulties, so you filled the time creatively, right?

CHRIS: Yeah, it was the European Warped Tour and Ignite and Pennywise were there. Ignite had just finished their set, and we were scheduled to go on next, but our set kept getting pushed back, so I donned what I used to call my "Richard Simmons Fitness Guru" outfit. I had on tight nut-hugging pink shorts, socks pulled up to the knees, really bad shoes, and a terrible gold necklace. And I went out into this bull ring to entertain the crowd. At first, they loved it: they were cheering for me and everything. The PA came back on, and I did an acapella version of "You Shook Me All Night Long" by AC/DC. But I went on a little too long and cups of piss started flying up at me, so I got off the stage. Then we got told that the problems had been fixed, and it was time to play. So I got into an empty road case and our roadie at the time, Mr. Skull, pushed me out on stage. I popped out of this road case with my guitar and everyone was just like, "Oh, that's who that was."

MATT: The big reveal.

CHRIS: Yeah, the big reveal wasn't the greatest reveal. But that was the first time that Fletcher [Dragge] from Pennywise ever laughed at us, so that was a big moment for me.

MATT: You got the Fletcher seal of approval.

CHRIS: Yeah, he finally gave in.

MATT: Who were the biggest hell-raisers that you toured with back in the nineties? Aside from Fletcher, obviously.

CHRIS: Guttermouth.

MATT: They're still crazy. They did Slam Dunk Festival last year, and Mark [Adkins] came out at midday, necked an entire bottle of red wine, then proceeded to get butt-naked on stage. Nobody does that shit anymore—with smart phones it's not a smart move.

CHRIS: No, but Mark does.

MATT: He doesn't give a fuck, does he?

CHRIS: No, especially not back in the nineties. Those guys were out of control—every single one of them. I won't mention which guy in the band, but we were backstage this one time, and he pulled out a container with about a thousand pills in there—of all different variants, shapes, and sizes. We were like, "Wow! These guys are not messing around." The Pietasters were nuts, too. And Frenzal Rhomb was another one. Those three bands had a different resolution about them than most people: they'd go all night, survive on minimal sleep, and when you turned up at the club the next day, they'd already be drinking again.

MATT: Tell me about the Bon Jovi tour. How did that one come about?

CHRIS: Oh, man. In the summer of 2000, we got this phone call from our agent, who also represented Bon Jovi at that time, and they were putting together this tour, so they threw our name in the hat. It was thrown in with bands like Sugar Ray, Eve 6, Smash Mouth, Dishwalla, Marcy Playground, and all these radio-friendly-pop-rock bands that were happening at that time. And all those other bands turned down the tour because Bon Jovi was kind of looked on as passé by 2000. And people didn't yet realize the value of what we now call soccer moms and the money that these people have. So we got the tour. And in-between us saying yes in July and the start of the tour in November, *VH1* in America—by that point the new *MTV* for people who were in their thirties—picked up the Bon Jovi song, "It's My Life," and it went through the roof.

MATT: Is that around the time that song was released? I didn't realize that—I just thought it was another one of their hits from the eighties.

CHRIS: No, it came out in 2000. And in the lead-up to that tour the song and the album [*Crush*] blew up. Every single show of the tour sold out, 15–20,000 tickets per night. And it was just us supporting them.

MATT: How were the shows?

CHRIS: Hilarious. The doors were only open for half an hour before we came out, and there'd be guys down the front with ties on reading the *Wall Street Journal*. I'm not even kidding you; there'd be guys in the front row reading the paper while we were on. So we teared the crowd apart every night. We'd be like, "Holy shit! Lita Ford is here." And it would just be some old blonde woman in the crowd.

MATT: How did that go over?

CHRIS: They received it well. And on the second date of the tour, Tico Torres—who's the drummer in Bon Jovi—came up to me and said, "Hey! You killed me the other night when you said, 'Hi, we're Winger from Florida.' Winger! HA!" He thought it was hilarious. He got that we weren't making fun of them; we were making fun of the whole scene. And Jon Bon Jovi didn't want to be attached to that whole thing at all.

MATT: Did the band treat you well?

CHRIS: Kind of. Heather Locklear was married to Richie Sambora at the time, and she had her own dressing room while we were put in a broom closet. But what were they going to do? Give the support band a dressing room and put her in the broom closet? No way! That's his wife.

BEN OSMUNDSON—*ZEBRAHEAD*

MATT: Have you got any funny tour stories?

BEN: We were at a festival in Germany once, and there was this weird altercation that went down, where one of the crew guys from Slayer ended up getting into a fight with our manager, who also managed Motörhead. And somehow we ended up in the middle of it. It ended up us versus Slayer in this huge fight. It was the craziest thing ever. And I grew up following Slayer from show to show. They're my favorite band ever. So when all of this was going down, I was like, "No! I love Slayer!" But it was all just a weird misunderstanding, and later that night, we ended up in their dressing room, as it was Tom Araya's birthday. We were eating Tom Araya's birthday cake and singing happy birthday to him, and I was drinking tequila shots with Kerry King. I'll never forget that. It was the most awesome thing ever.

MATT: Everyone loves a happy ending.

BEN: That story actually progressed—I have to tell you part two. The tour manager of Slayer didn't know that the beef was squashed, so the next day we're playing this festival in Austria, and we had some friends there who work with Green Day. They came up to us and said, "Hey, man. We were told there's this big conflict between Slayer and Zebrahead, and that if something goes down, we need to stay out of it. We just want you guys to know about it." We were like, *"What? We had birthday cake and shots with them last night. And now all of a sudden Green Day knows that there was a feud between Slayer and Zebrahead?"* Slayer would fucking kill us by the way because we don't know how to fight. We were like, "There is no beef! There is no anything! It was all just a big misunderstanding." Talk about a weekend of weirdness.

JESSE MALIN—*HEART ATTACK, D GENERATION, SOLO ARTIST*

MATT: What's been some of your all-time favorite live shows as a punter?

JESSE: Seeing Neil Young on the *Ragged Glory* tour with Social Distortion opening. It was around Desert Storm time, and it was unbelievable. Crazy Horse and Neil Young just have this magical telepathic connection. And seeing the Bad Brains at CBGB when they were just coming up, and seeing them open up for the Dead Kennedys at Bond's [Bond International Casino] in 1981. They were probably some of the best live shows I've ever seen. Iggy Pop at The Ritz in New York in 1986 was also a great show, as was the Dead Kennedys at Irving Plaza in 1981, and The Clash on the *London Calling* tour, with Lee Dorsey and The B Girls.

I also saw The Rolling Stones recently, and they were so good. I don't know if it's because they have something to prove or what, but I saw them a bunch of times in the 1990s and 2000s, and it was always good but not great. This was *great*. Mick Jagger would've been good if he was twenty, forget that he had a heart operation and he's seventy-six. And I think there is something to the fact that people tape shows and record them on their phones now. Everything you do is like growing up in public, and it's forced people to up their game. Seeing Tom Waits in New York on the *Mule Variations* tour was also very special.

MATT: I've never seen Tom Waits live. He's at the very top of my list of people that I'd love to see.

JESSE: I also saw Robert De Niro in a play on Broadway called *Cuba & His Teddy Bear* with Ralph Macchio. It was about a drug dealer on the Lower East Side. That was pretty amazing. I saw Al Pacino in a play called *Chinese Coffee* as well. And I recently saw Sam Rockwell in *Fool for Love*—the Sam Shepard play—and that was insane. Sometimes the best performances are without guitars. But I have to tell you, that Bad Brains period from the early eighties was like seeing something from another planet.

LOU KOLLER—*SICK OF IT ALL*

MATT: Did Sick of It All invent the Wall of Death? Is that safe to say?

LOU: It's something that we did as kids. I remember my first one ever was in the late eighties. Dead Kennedys were playing in New York City, and they used to stack the bill. It was Dead Kennedys, DOA, and Reagan Youth. We were in the pit running around like idiots, and that was just natural to do. Nowadays, you have to tell people, "Do a circle pit!" I fucking hate it. I don't want to do it. But if I don't, nobody does it. They're not feeling it anymore. I don't know what it is.

MATT: They're filming it, that's what it is.

LOU: Exactly. So fast-forward to 1997, and the first one that I remember doing was at a festival in Holland with The Offspring, Joe Strummer, Silverchair, and Sick of It All. We were playing, everybody was on stage watching us, and we were having a really good show. We were getting ready to do *Scratch the Surface*, and I was like, "Everybody separate." And the whole place just separated—I'm talking a good three thousand people. When we started the song, they all crashed into each other, and it looked like the crowd had been hit by a bomb—everybody fell on top of each other and people were twisted in knots. I was like, "Holy shit. I shouldn't have done that." But the look on everybody's face—in the crowd, on the stage, even the security—was like, "These guys are the greatest band in the world."

I can pinpoint the show where every band stole that move from us, too. We did a festival once, and it was this huge tent that held about five thousand people. On one end, it was Slipknot, Sepultura, Papa Roach, and Mudvayne. And on the other side it was Sick of It All, Pennywise, L7, and a bunch of other punk and hardcore bands. When we did the Wall of Death, everybody from both sides was watching. Then two nights later, we got a message from a friend of ours, and she was like, "I was just in London, and Papa Roach did your Braveheart thing," because we used to call it The Braveheart. I was like, "Motherfuckers!" And that was it, the next thing we knew it was everywhere.

MATT: That's a beautiful thing, though—to invent something brand new.

LOU: Yeah, if only we could get royalties.

TOMMY LEE—*MÖTLEY CRÜE, METHODS OF MAYHEM, SOLO ARTIST*

MATT: Let's talk about Fred Durst. I keep meaning to try and track down his film with John Travolta: *The Fanatic.* Have you seen it?

TOMMY: It's fucking wicked.

MATT: I need to check it out. I enjoyed the basketball comedy that he did with Ice Cube [*The Longshots*], and I liked the one with Jesse Eisenberg from *Zombieland* and *The Social Network* [*The Education of Charlie Banks*]. But all I keep hearing is that John Travolta is off-the-chain in that film as this crazy psychotic character. Did you do both the music videos from your solo album [*Andro*] with Fred Durst?

TOMMY: Yes.

MATT: How long have you two known each other? And what was it like working with him on the videos for "Knock Me Down" and "Tops"?

TOMMY: I think I knew Fred slightly before 2000, but in 2000, we worked together on the music and video for "Get Naked" with Methods of Mayhem. That's when Fred and I became really close, and we've been friends together for a long time. He's awesome, man. When it came time to do some videos for my new record, Fred was my first fucking choice. If ever there was a guy who was going to get it, it would be Fred. He loves the fucking heavy screamo shit that makes you want to break stuff, and he also loves dance music and hip-hop. He was going to get those first two tracks that I dropped better than anybody else. So it was a no-brainer; I didn't even want to talk to anybody else.

MATT: Do you know John Travolta? I saw a picture on your Instagram a while back of you and your son hanging out with him. Are you guys friends?

TOMMY: Yeah, he was just over here on Saturday with his family. He just got a place literally four minutes away from mine.

MATT: What an icon. From *Saturday Night Fever* to *Pulp Fiction*, they were two of the most important films and cultural moments of their respective eras. And John Travolta is right there, smack bang in the center of both of them. Is he a cool guy?

TOMMY: I'm sure anybody who knows him will tell you this: he's probably the sweetest man I've ever met. Hands down, he's just the sweetest man. Nothing but love flies around that guy. He's wonderful, man. And I'm proud to call him a friend. He's a really good dude. You'd love him.

MATT: You've obviously hung out and spent time with the best of them over the years. Did you ever cut loose with Sam Kinison back in the day?

TOMMY: Dude, we used to get fucking bananas. God bless him. I miss that guy. That was during a crazy time, and Sam was like the Mötley Crüe of comedy. He literally ran it until the fucking wheels fell off. He was going at it—non-stop partying, just being that guy. He was funny as fuck. I had so many good times with him. Every time we hung out, my face would hurt from laughing so much. My jaw would be so fucking sore.

MATT: I can't get enough of his stand-up. You wouldn't get away with a lot of stuff that he said back then today, but he was just on a higher plane, wasn't he? Like Richard Pryor or George Carlin.

TOMMY: Absolutely. He was definitely on his own program.

DAVE FORTMAN—*UGLY KID JOE, PRODUCER*

MATT: What are your memories of Lynn Strait? Was he a special guy?

DAVE: Lynn? I loved him to death. He was a great guy; we were really close. He came over and gave me a cigar when I had a kid—all that shit. But he was a reckless guy, man. He was a fantastic human, but he had his problems with heroin and whatnot. I moved back to Louisiana just before he died, and his girlfriend Karen was all distraught, so she flew down here, and we took her to my grandma's house, and we had the old school southern vibe going on. It was real laid back, and you could sit out on the porch, so that gave her some time to chill out.

One of Lynn's school friends was recording down in Louisiana right after he died. This guy was sitting in the control room with me the day they were having the wake for Lynn. This is a guy that went to school with him in Montecito, and they used to run around and steal church PA's together. He said the funniest fucking thing to me. I said, "It's a bummer we can't be out there." And he said, "Yeah, because then everybody could talk about what Lynn stole from all of us, and we could find out where all of our shit went." I was like, "That's the fucking funniest shit." He said, "Yeah, dude. Lynn ripped everybody off. In the eighties, we ripped of the Montecito church PA to use at our practice room." It was hilarious. I certainly had some good moments with Lynn. And it was great to see him get a record deal and influence the world. That was fantastic. He was quite the boy.

VINNIE STIGMA—*AGNOSTIC FRONT*

VINNIE: I love making prank calls. One night, I was partying with a couple of wrestlers—Corey Graves and a couple of other guys. I was having a great time in Florida after we played this big show. And Mike Gallo comes up to me, and he says, "Vinnie, there's a guy downstairs who wants to see you." I was like, "Yeah, yeah. I'm talking to my rock star friends." And he said, "Vinnie, you've gotta come down and talk to this guy." So I went down there, and I saw this big fucking guy. He said, "Stigma! You prank called me." I said, "*I did?*" And he said, "You don't know what that meant to me, Vinnie. I was in Afghanistan when you called. And we listened to your message over and over again." Because I left him a message saying, "You cock sucker! You didn't come to my fucking show!"

MATT: And that helped keep him sane and provide him with some joy in a dark situation?

VINNIE: Yeah. Then he started crying. And his wife was crying. I started crying, too. And Gallo ran away. So a little stupid thing like that can mean a lot. I was in Houston, Texas, one other night, and some guy brought his son to the show. His son was challenged, you know what I mean? And I brought him up on stage for the whole show. On the load out the guy came up to me, and he said, "Vinnie, you made my son's day. You made him feel so special. Thank you." Stuff like that costs you nothing. So all you rock star motherfuckers out there better fucking get with it because those are the real people out there, and they make you who the fuck you are. I appreciate everybody who comes to my show.

WALTER SCHREIFELS—*GORLLIA BISCUITS, YOUTH OF TODAY, QUICKSAND, RIVAL SCHOOLS*

MATT: Your birthday is March 10, right?

WALTER: That's right.

MATT: One day before me.

WALTER: No shit!

MATT: I'm March 11.

WALTER: Pisces.

MATT: Do you take interest in star signs and astrology and all that stuff?

WALTER: I guess I wouldn't plan my life by it, but I certainly don't discount it. There were so many years where human beings were alive and the stars were the main way of indicating what life was about, and why we were here—these deep-seated philosophical questions. As soon as our brains could start asking those kinds of questions, pre-religion, we were looking at the stars. And we had the time back then, because there wasn't any distractions, to correlate the movement of the stars with what was going on in our lives. And somehow there's enough correlations that it's still relevant today. So I wouldn't say that I'm really into it, or that I know a lot about it, but it is kind of nice when you read your horoscope and it's something cool.

MATT: You're right.

WALTER: Or you're like, "Shit! That's happening to me right now. Damn."

MATT: I was just reading up today about the strengths, weaknesses, characteristics, and qualities that make up a typical Pisces, and I was going through the list, like, "This is almost me to a tee."

WALTER: Same.

MATT: Intuitive, emotional, sensitive, compassionate, prone to sadness, overly trusting. I was like, "Tick. Tick. Tick. That's all me."

WALTER: Yep. And I think it's cool. I like being a Pisces. I'm happy with that sign.

ODDS & ENDS PLAYLIST

THE BOUNCING SOULS—"LEAN ON SHEENA"

GOLDFINGER—"SUPERMAN"

NERF HERDER—"BUFFY THE VAMPIRE SLAYER THEME"

DEFTONES—"MY OWN SUMMER (SHOVE IT)"

MISFITS—"SKULLS"

GLASSJAW—"COSMOPOLITAN BLOOD LOSS"

EVERY TIME I DIE—"KILL THE MUSIC"

KILLSWITCH ENGAGE—"STRENGTH OF THE MIND"

IRON MAIDEN—"THE TROOPER"

LESS THAN JAKE—"DOPEMAN"

BON JOVI—"IT'S MY LIFE"

ZEBRAHEAD—"CALL YOUR FRIENDS"

SLAYER—"RAINING BLOOD"

BAD BRAINS—"I AGAINST I"

SICK OF IT ALL—"SCRATCH THE SURFACE"

METHODS OF MAYHEM—"GET NAKED"

SAM KINISON—"WILD THING"

SNOT—"SNOT"

AGNOSTIC FRONT—"THE ELIMINATOR"

RIVAL SCHOOLS—"WRING IT OUT"

AFTERWORD

"You have to stick by what you believe in."

WHILE COMPILING THE STORIES for this second installment of
what will hopefully become a trilogy of collected interviews,
Joey Jordison from Slipknot passed away. In the wake of his death,
I was reminded of an unpublished podcast from four years prior,
which I'd recorded but ultimately decided not to use because it was
too short (around twenty minutes) to sit alongside the rest of my *Life
In The Stocks* podcasts, which usually run for an hour or more.

Unfortunately, I was too far along with the writing of the book to
include Joey in any of the chapters in a way that made sense, but I've
decided to end it with this unpublished interview. And it's particularly
poignant now that he's gone. The conversation took place backstage at
the 100 Club in London on Wednesday February 15, 2017, before Joey
played a one-off gig with his band, Vimic. It was our last interaction
before he died.

I'd interviewed Joey a few times over the years for the various
projects he was in (Slipknot, Murderdolls, Sinsaenum), but we bonded
the most during a 2016 interview for *Metal Hammer* on his top ten
favorite drummers. We spent fifteen minutes talking about drummers
for the feature and about an hour afterward discussing how we'd both
suffered from serious spinal injuries and narrowly avoided death. And
that's the thing with unique trauma: it connects you to other people
who've been through the same thing in an almost telepathic way.

Joey and I had both also lost our dream jobs and been given
the boot without notice by our former employers—Joey by Slipknot,

me by Kerrang! Radio. And we both found ourselves at a very similar crossroads in life, with a newfound appreciation of the mere experience of living after finding ourselves so close to death. And this is something that I'd like to share with you here: *your job does not define you.* Even if you have the best job in the world, you are so much more than what you do for a living. And as long as you are *living*, there will always something to *live* for. Try to remember that when things get tough.

I don't claim to have known the late drum legend well, but the last two conversations that we shared left an indelible mark on me, and I was deeply saddened to hear of his passing. I know that his music affected a lot of people, too. And I thought it would be nice to end the book with a tribute to Joey.

Personally, I have no idea what went down between him and the rest of the guys in Slipknot. Only the people in the inner circle of that sanctum will ever really know the truth. But one thing I do know is this: Joey was in a really resilient and positive place on the afternoon that I last spoke to him. And that's the Joey Jordison that I'd like to remember.

Rest in peace, JJ. You will always be #1.

JOEY JORDISON—*SLIPKNOT, MURDERDOLLS, SINSAENUM, VIMIC*

MATT: The last time we spoke, I was telling you about the spinal injury that I endured. And we bonded over our mutual experiences with rehabilitation and recovery. Can you remind me again how you pronounce the disease that you suffer from?

JOEY: It's acute transverse myelitis.

MATT: And correct me if I'm wrong, but that's essentially when the spinal cord inflames.

JOEY: Yep.

MATT: Then that cuts off the electrical current to your body.

JOEY: Correct.

MATT: And your limbs stop functioning properly.

JOEY: Yeah.

MATT: Is it just your legs? Or is it your arms as well?

JOEY: No, it was just my legs.

MATT: Did they completely shut down?

JOEY: Yeah, they got totally wiped out.

MATT: Mentally, how do you process something like that?

JOEY: You don't. The only thing you can do is accept it—that's how I got through it. It was the most devastating thing I've ever gone through. I couldn't believe it was happening to me. And the thing is, I could've sat and cried and bitched and whined about it. But what I did—and honestly this was the toughest thing for me—was accept it. I told myself, "No matter what, I will not let this beat me. And I will walk again, no matter what. I don't care what the doctors say." It took a lot of courage for me to be able to convince myself that I was going to be able to do this. But as you can see…no problem!

MATT: You're kicking ass.

JOEY: Yep. And you have to realize, man, when that happened, I couldn't move my legs whatsoever. They were completely gone. And it took a lot of determination and hard work just to be able to move my legs again, let alone walk. But you just have to believe in yourself and have a goal and never give up. Never accept the fact that what they're telling you is for real or the final word. I just sought out the best trainers that I could find and I stuck with it. And I couldn't have done it without my lady. Without her support, I don't know what I would've done. She found the trainers for me, and they became like my best friends. I started at this place called Absolute Performance Therapy in Waukee, Iowa, which is not too far from where I live. And now I'm at Life Time gym in Des Moines with my trainer Caleb.

MATT: It's kind of a cliched phrase, but from my experience, and undoubtedly from yours, at rock bottom is truly where you find yourself.

JOEY: It is.

MATT: Right? Your character, your strength—

JOEY: Yep.

MATT: And also those who matter.

JOEY: Absolutely.

MATT: For me, that was my friends and family, as I was single at the time of my accident. And my family and I have always been kind of close in our own unique way, but the experience that I went through after breaking my back really solidified our relationship and connection with each other.

JOEY: Yeah, you really realize what's important in life. And no disrespect as to why I'm here in London talking to you today, but sometimes it's not all about music and touring and making records. I honestly think it happened to me for a reason: to make me wake the fuck up and stop taking life for granted. I don't want to get into certain things, but it really made me wake up and look at life in a completely different way. And the fact that I came out of it made me one of the lucky ones because some people don't make it back, so don't fucking take it for granted.

MATT: Amen.

JOEY: A lot of people don't necessarily have these gifts that I've been blessed with, and when this thing happened to me it was one of the best things that ever did happen to me because it made me absolutely appreciate everything that I have in life, which I might've been taking for granted and didn't realize I was doing so. So it kicked my ass, man— physically and emotionally. It made me wake up in a lot of ways. And honestly as much as it sucked, it's probably one of the best things that ever happened to me.

MATT: I feel the same way, man. As you say, some people have gifts, and you should never take them for granted. But also, don't take for granted the fact that you can go to the toilet and take a shit.

JOEY: Oh, I know.

MATT: Do you know what I mean?

JOEY: Yeah.

MATT: Or the fact that you can breathe air into your lungs.

JOEY: Yeah. When I couldn't walk, I used to have to get my girlfriend to fucking lift me onto the toilet. I was like, "What the fuck happened to me?" I couldn't fucking play drums—that was enough to crush me right there. But I also couldn't drive a car or go to the store, and I couldn't even go to the bathroom on my own. I was fucking paralyzed, man. And the fact that I made it back is a fucking miracle. It's hard for me to talk about this because it gets me a little emotional and shit. But I truly believe that I came back for a reason. So I really have to pay attention and just keep doing the best that I can, one day at a time. I'm just very grateful and thankful that I was able to come out of this.

MATT: With what we've both been through as well, all ego goes right out the window.

JOEY: Oh, yeah. It's gone—completely. I've been there, and I know exactly how you feel. There's a reason that we came out of it, and you have to pay attention to that gift. I know people who have the disease that I have, that I've been able to meet, and they haven't been able to come out the other side. That really fucks with you.

MATT: There's almost a weird sense of guilt that comes with that, like, "Why me and not this guy?"

JOEY: Exactly. But I have to believe that I came back for a reason, and obviously I'm still here to make music. And I'm still here to talk to you. I try not to think about it too much because I start getting inside my head too much. But there's not a word in the English language—or indeed any language—that can express the thanks and gratitude that I have. There's something else out there looking out for me.

MATT: I believe that, too—whatever it is.

JOEY: Yep. There's definitely something on my side.

MATT: Can we talk about Slipknot?

JOEY: Yeah, absolutely. It depends on what the question is, though.

MATT: Why did you leave the band? Was it purely down to your inability to go on performing at the level that Slipknot required?

JOEY: During the last couple of shows that I did for Slipknot, this disease was hitting me hard. But I didn't know what it was; I had no fucking clue. Before one of the very last shows that I did with the band, I was packing my bags, and I was so fucking unbalanced. If you're hungover, or you're got asthma or a cold or whatever, you're a little shaky, but you can still fucking walk. But I was packing my bags, and I was shaking like a leaf; my legs were quivering and my back was on fire. It was unlike anything I'd ever experienced before. I finally made it to my front door, and I came outside, then I took my first step off my porch, and I collapsed onto the cement. At this point, I was in absolute fucking panic; I had a show to do, and I was like, "How am I going to explain this to the band? They're just going to think that I'm fucked up." And that's probably what anyone would think—even I didn't know what the hell was happening to me. But somehow I made it through the show, and I came home, and I went straight to see the doctor. They admitted me right away, and they kept me there for three months.

MATT: That's exactly how long I spent in hospital with my broken back. So at this point, are you involved in the discussions with the rest of the band?

JOEY: What do you mean?

MATT: Did they discuss your exit from the band with you?

JOEY: No, I had no warning or anything. I got a letter in the mail. A *letter!* After all we've fucking been through—no meeting, no phone call, no warning, no nothing. I got a fucking note in the mail.

MATT: Brutal.

JOEY: A fucking note in the fucking mail. That's how it went down. And I've been in contact with a few members since then. But I've moved on with Vimic and Sinsaenum, and just my life in general. That stuff is in the past now.

MATT: It's very much in the past for you?

JOEY: Yeah, it's gone. I don't even think about it anymore. Everything that I've been through with Slipknot and the acute transverse myelitis has led me to a point in my life where I look at things very differently. I'm here talking to you now for a reason. We [Vimic] just signed with Universal. I'm back with Danny Nozell, who I grew up with and who was our very first tour manager in Slipknot. And I'm back with Steve Ross, who was our first manager in Slipknot. So it's all come full circle, and it's actually really cool. It's just been a bit of a tough road getting here. But I've been working really hard and keeping positive. And that's all I can really do.

MATT: Before I let you go, can we talk about the night that you played with Metallica at Download Festival in 2004?

JOEY: Sure. Slipknot was opening for Metallica on like a two-month run through Europe around that time, and I was sitting backstage at Download right after we got done playing. I was still in my coveralls, and I had makeup all over my face, and my mask was still on top of my head. I'd barely got off the stage when my manager came into my dressing room, and said, "James needs to talk to you." Right then I was like, "Oh, my God! What the fuck did I do?" I thought I was in some deep shit for something. So I went over there, and they explained that Lars [Ulrich] wasn't going to be able to make the show. So would I be able to fill in? I was like, "Is this a joke or what?" I thought they were literally pulling a prank on me. But they were so matter-of-fact about it. They were like, "Yeah, Lars can't make it to this one, so we were wondering if you could help us out? We have a rehearsal room over here. What songs do you know?" That's when I knew it was for real. We actually jammed a lot of songs together that we didn't get to play live because we went on so late, and they had a curfew and all that shit. And playing the show was amazing, but honestly what was even cooler was when I went into their little warm-up room and I sat down, it was just the four of us, and they instantly made me feel right at home. We just started playing and that was it—the rest is history.

MATT: What a class act.

JOEY: They are. They made me feel really comfortable and really at home.

MATT: What about Rob Zombie? I saw you play with him in, I want to say, 2010?

JOEY: Yeah, it was 2010.

MATT: I interviewed him before the show in Birmingham. And I said to him, "Please play 'What?' tonight, Rob. I love that song so much." And he said, "We haven't been playing that one. But I'll ask Joey, and we'll throw it in." Sure enough that night you played "What?" And Rob dedicated the song to me and my Kerrang! Radio colleague, Johnny Doom. It was killer.

JOEY: I absolutely remember that. You never know what Rob's going to do, man. But I loved playing "What?" That song fucking rocks.

MATT: It's proper garage punk, isn't it?

JOEY: Yeah, it's sleazy. I had such a great time playing with Rob and John [5] and Piggy [D.]. They were great guys, and I had a great time on that tour.

MATT: Final question. You're obviously known as one of the best drummers in the world, so there must have been offers to join other big established bands after you left Slipknot. Was that ever an option for you? Or because you're a songwriter as well, and because you're on this personal journey through your recovery, did you want to start your own band as opposed to just being a gun for hire?

JOEY: I'm not going to mention the names of the bands because I don't want to start any shit, but I have had a few offers from bands who are much bigger than Vimic. But at the same time, all the guys in Vimic have put in so much work into this band, and to abandon that just to go and play in a bigger band, there's no integrity in that. I have to stick by my brothers and what we created; if I don't see it through properly then that's not being an artist. You don't go someplace just for fame and money. That's not being an artist. I have to stick by my friends and my songwriting partners and my management because this project has taken a long time to even get moving. If I abandoned it now, it would all be for nothing and a complete waste of time. I believe in this band one hundred percent, that's why we're out on this tour. So I'm just going to stay on this track and see where it lands.

MATT: I feel you, brother. The reward is far greater when you've built it yourself.

JOEY: Exactly. I can go and join another band any time, but it's not my band, I'm just playing their songs. Vimic is completely my creation from just a small inkling of a thought about a band, and we just played South America with Megadeth and now we're in London. And we just signed with Universal. So what I'd like to say is this: hard work and patience pays off. And just because something seems like it's better at the time, it doesn't mean it is. You have to stick by what you believe in. That's why I'm out here doing this. I can't abandon my guys, I just can't do it.

MATT: It's great to see you looking so happy and healthy.

JOEY: Thanks, dude. I really appreciate it.

MATT: And good luck with the ongoing rehabilitation.

JOEY: Thanks a lot—you too!

GUEST LIST

(In Alphabetical Order)

ALAN ROBERT

Alan Robert is a musician, songwriter, visual artist, and comic book creator. He's the bassist and founding member of Life Of Agony, a legendary alternative metal band from Brooklyn, New York. He's also known for his graphic novels, *Wire Hangers*, *Crawl to Me*, and *Killogy*, and his best-selling horror-themed coloring book series, *The Beauty of Horror*. (Episode 070—09/11/2018)

BEN OSMUNDSON

Ben Osmundson is the bass player in Zebrahead, a rap-rock-pop-punk-party band from Orange County, California. They formed in 1996 and have released thirteen studio albums to date. They've also played Slam Dunk festival in the UK more times than any other band. And they're the most fun live band you will ever see—*ever*! (Episode 062—07/12/2018)

CASEY CHAOS

Casey Chaos is a super unique individual. He's unlike anyone I've ever met. As well as fronting Amen and writing all the music for everything that band has ever released, he's also been a professional skateboarder, sung with The Damned, played bass in Christian Death, cowrote one of System of a Down's best songs ("B.Y.O.B."), and collaborated with everyone from Iggy Pop and Josh Homme to Ross Robinson and Dave

LIFE IN THE STOCKS VOL. 2

Lombardo. He also has the best stories, some of which are captured in this book. (Episode 069—08/29/2018)

CHARLIE PAULSON

As well as being lead guitarist and an original member of famed LA ska punk band Goldfinger, Charlie Paulson was also in the short-lived rock 'n' roll band Black President with Greg Hetson of the Circle Jerks and Bad Religion, who also happens to be in this book. Another thing I'll say about Charlie is this: the man is an encyclopedia of LA punk history. I hope to write a book with him some day about just that. (Episode 135—11/18/2019)

CHRIS DEMAKES

Chris DeMakes is the lead guitarist and vocalist in Less Than Jake, a ska punk band from Gainesville, Florida. I've done three full UK tours with Less Than Jake, plus a couple of festival appearances, which means I've seen them live more than any other band. And they were one of my favorite groups growing up, so to now call them friends is an absolute trip. Chris also hosts his own amazing podcast, *Chris DeMakes A Podcast*. Check it out! (Episode 162—05/12/2020)

CHUCK D

Chuck D is a stone cold legend. I'd be very surprised if you didn't already know that. So what else is there for me to add? Listen to Public Enemy—*Fear of a Black Planet* and *It Takes a Nation of Millions to Hold Us Back* are essential records. Read his book, *Fight the Power: Rap, Race, and Reality*. Check out his radio station: rapstation.com. And be sure to take notes as the great Mr. Chuck drops science on you. Nobody does it better. (Episode 170—07/10/2020)

DAVE FORTMAN

Dave Fortman is a celebrated songwriter, musician, and record producer. He's worked with everyone from Godsmack and Simple Plan to Slipknot and Evanescence, and the bands he's produced have sold over thirty million albums worldwide. When he's not producing multi-platinum selling records, he also plays guitar in Ugly Kid Joe, who are the only act in the world with a platinum selling EP to their name. (Episode 054—04/23/2018)

DEAN KARR

Dean Karr is a renowned filmmaker and photographer. Think of any iconic music video or album cover from the nineties alternative rock and metal era, and chances are he shot it. You could spend hours going down the YouTube rabbit hole with this guy's filmography. You probably should. Tool, Pantera, Slipknot, Deftones, Korn, Alice Cooper, Ozzy Osbourne—he's worked with all of them. And it's a huge honor to feature some of his work in this book. Cheers Dean! (Episode 072—09/17/2018)

DENNIS LYXZÉN

Dennis Lyxzén is the lead singer in Refused, INVSN, and Fake Names. He also fronted AC4, The (International) Noise Conspiracy, and countless other incendiary, rebel rousing bands. He's a modern-day punk legend, and the snappiest dresser in rock 'n' roll. The revolution never looked or sounded so good as when this man is leading the charge. (Episode 151—02/10/2020)

DUSTIN KENSRUE

Dustin Kensrue is a singer, songwriter, and former worship leader. He's the lead vocalist and rhythm guitarist in Irvine post-hardcore quartet Thrice, as well as being a successful solo artist in his own right. And he hosts his own podcast, *Carry the Fire*. You'd be hard-pressed to find a rock front man with more knowledge, understanding, and appreciation of the intricacies and complexities of religion, and I thoroughly enjoyed picking Dustin's brain on all that stuff for my podcast. (Episode 152—02/24/2020)

GENE SIMMONS

Gene Simmons, ladies and gentlemen. The illustrious Gene Simmons. Probably the most misunderstood man in rock 'n' roll. He's as maligned as he is adored—perhaps even more so. But I won't hear a bad word said about him. We've done countless interviews together over the years, and I've had the pleasure of spending several hours in his company, and he's always been nothing but courteous and cool to me. He's a great guy. And Kiss are one of the all-time iconic American bands. So there you go. Make Gene Simmons great again! (Episode 049—03/21/2018)

GREG ATTONITO

Greg Attonito is an artist and musician, and the lead singer in New Jersey punk band, The Bouncing Souls. He's also a bona fide sweetheart and one of the nicest people I've ever met. Love and respect, Greg. I look forward to seeing you in person when all this madness is over. Bouncing Souls forever! (Episode 148—01/20/2020)

GREG HETSON

Greg Hetson is a punk rock legend. He's played guitar in Redd Kross, Circle Jerks, and Bad Religion, and his place in the pantheon of hardcore punk is cemented for all-time. These days he can be found jamming with punk rock supergroup Punk Rock Karaoke and the newly reformed Circle Jerks. I can't wait to see that band live when they finally make it over to the UK. (Episode 147—01/13/2020)

HYRO THE HERO

Hyro The Hero is a rapper from Houston, Texas. His debut album, *Birth, School, Work, Death*, was produced by the one and only Ross Robinson, and it came out when I was just starting out in this game, so Hyro and I go way back to the start of both of our careers. I'll never forget the night we presented Jared Leto with a Kerrang! award in 2011. It's hard to believe that was a decade ago. It's been a crazy ride, brother. And in many ways it's just getting started. (Episode 064—07/22/2018)

JESSE HUGHES

Jesse Hughes is truly one of God's own prototypes: too weird to live, too rare to die. He's the last of a dying breed of larger-than-life rock stars who march to the beat of their own drum. And after everything he's been through, it's a miracle he's still alive. But he assures me the show will go on no matter what life throws at him, which is incredible to hear. The world is a more colorful place with old Boots Electric in it. (Episode 115—07/29/2019)

JESSE LEACH

What can I say about Jesse Leach? As well as fronting Killswitch Engage, Times of Grace, and The Weapon, Jesse is also my cohost on *Stoke The Fire*, which is the best thing I've ever been involved in, and Jesse is a huge reason why. I love you like a brother, brother. And I couldn't be more excited for the future. Fires stoked my friend! Thank you for everything. (Episode 074—10/10/2018)

JESSE MALIN

What is it about Jesses? They're just the best. Jesse Malin wrote the foreword to *Life In The Stocks Volume One*, and he moved me to tears with the kind words that he wrote. I'm honored to call this man a friend. He's one of the most respected musicians in the game, and he's a New York institution. Listen to Heart Attack. Listen to D Generation. And buy all of Jesse's solo albums because this guy is an absolute lifer. (Episode 143—12/18/2019)

JIM ADKINS

Jim Adkins is the lead singer and guitar player in emo pop quintet, Jimmy Eat World. The band formed in Mesa, Arizona, in 1993 and have released ten studio albums to date, selling over one and a half million records worldwide. And their music continues to be enjoyed by legions of new fans with over six million monthly streams on Spotify. Not bad for a group of young punks who started out booking their own gigs, which just goes to show if you follow your heart, then dreams really can come true. And if streaming services start paying artists properly, they might start making money, too. (Episode 133—11/04/2019)

JOBY FORD

Joby Ford is a man of many talents. You'll know him best as the founding member, lead guitarist, and primary songwriter in The Bronx, a punk rock band from Los Angeles, California. But outside of his day job, Joby has designed album sleeves for everyone from The Killers and Paul Westerberg to Alkaline Trio and Every Time I Die. He's also produced records by Face to Face, Trash Talk, Gallows, and Carl Barat from The Libertines, plus The Bronx's charro wearing side-project, Mariachi El Bronx. And he's a great friend. Big up Joby Ford! (Episode 090—02/19/2019)

JOEY CASTILLO

From one Bronx band member to another, Joby Ford is responsible for setting up my interview with Joey Castillo on the Flogging Molly Cruise in 2019. Fun times! But Joey C doesn't just play drums with The Bronx. Oh, no! Over the years, he's also kept the beat in Queens of the Stone Age, Eagles of Death Metal, Danzig, Scott Weiland's band, and The Hives. Joey and I toured together with Zakk Sabbath in 2020, too—another band he plays drums in. And he recently joined the newly reformed Circle Jerks. He's an absolute beast behind the kit, and someone I'm stoked to call a friend. (Episode 146—01/06/2020)

JOEY JORDISON

By all accounts, Joey Jordison was one the greatest drummers to ever sit behind the kit. He was also one of the founding members and principal songwriters in Slipknot—arguably the biggest heavy metal band of the twenty-first century—until exiting the group in 2016. After Slipknot, he soldiered on with Scar the Martyr, Vimic, and Sinsaenum. He also enjoyed stints drumming for Rob Zombie, Korn, Ministry, and Metallica. And he played guitar in the Murderdolls. His death on July 26, 2021, was a huge loss to the metal community, and I've chosen to include this archive interview in the book to honor his memory. RIP Joey Jordison. (Unpublished episode from 2017)

JOHN FELDMANN

It's hard to know what John Feldmann is best known for: his role as lead singer and rhythm guitarist in Goldfinger, or his work as a songwriter, record producer, and music industry mogul, and the man behind huge selling records by Good Charlotte, All Time Low, Panic! at the Disco, The Used, Papa Roach, Blink-182, and countless others. I guess it all depends on the age of the person you're talking to. Some people might even be old enough to remember his short-lived funk rock band, The Electric Love Hogs. But whichever way you've heard of him, chances are you have, because his stamp on modern music is undeniable. On top of all that, I've known Feldy for ten years now, and he's always been a huge champion of my work. I'm forever grateful for that. (Episode 136—10/21/2019)

KEITH BUCKLEY

Keith Buckley is the enigmatic lead singer and chief lyricist in Every Time I Die, who for the uninitiated are an undefinable, raucous rock 'n' roll band from Buffalo, New York. He also fronts one of the world's most unlikely supergroups: The Damned Things. And he's a two-time published author. In short, he's an utterly unique, completely brilliant artist, creative, and human being. He's also solely responsible for me landing a book deal with Rare Bird. So I owe him a great debt. And I consider him a dear friend. (Episode 145—12/30/2019)

KEVIN KERSLAKE

Out of everyone in this book—probably both books, to be honest—Kevin Kerslake's body of work is by far the most impressive. Before reading this book, you might never have heard of him. But you'll definitely know his work. You most likely grew up with it imprinted on your brain, because Kevin directed many of the most iconic, influential, incredible music videos ever committed to film—before the digital revolution took place. His credentials are far too long to list here, but one Google of him will tell you all that you need to know. He shot videos for Nirvana, Soundgarden, Smashing Pumpkins, Red Hot

Chili Peppers, Faith No More, Stone Temple Pilots, Velvet Revolver, and many, many more. His entire back catalogue belongs in the Rock 'n' roll Hall of Fame. He's the GOAT. And a total gent to boot. (Episode 073—10/01/2018)

LINUS OF HOLLYWOOD

My good friend Jaret Reddick (Bowling For Soup) introduced me to Linus Dotson in 2013, and I'm so happy that he did. He's a great guy, not to mention an uber-talented songwriter and producer. He cowrote and produced a bunch of your favorite Bowling For Soup songs. But that's just the tip of the iceberg. Linus has worked with everyone from Cheap Trick to Puff Daddy, and he's in Nerf Nerder, the band most famous for writing the theme tune to *Buffy the Vampire Slayer*. He's also a prolific solo artist. And he has size fourteen feet. And you know what they say about people with big feet! (Episode 063—07/17/2018)

LOU KOLLER

Lou Koller is the lead singer in legendary New York hardcore outfit, Sick of It All. The band formed in Queens in 1986—the same year I was born—and they've played more live shows than you've had hot dinners. The New York and indeed worldwide hardcore scene would not look the way that it does today without the contributions of this man and his fabled band of brothers. And Toby Morse would likely not have a career. Hardcore lives! (Episode 089—02/13/2019)

NADJA PEULEN

Nadja Peulen is best known as the bassist in Coal Chamber, a nu metal band formed by Dez Fafara and Meegs Rascón in Los Angeles, California in 1993. But beyond that, she's one of my favorite people. Each time I'm in LA, we have a great time hanging out and setting the world to rights. I look forward to our next stateside adventure. Don't let that bass get too dusty now, Nadja. Rock 'n' roll needs more fiery females like you, and no one rocks the stage quite like you do. Love and respect. (Episode 094—03/21/2019)

GuestList

PERRY FARRELL

For my money, Perry Farrell is the biggest legend in this book—in both books, for that matter. I even named a chapter in *Life In The Stocks Volume One* after him: "The Hero's Heroes." He's an all-time icon. The godfather of alternative music. The voice of Jane's Addiction. The brains behind Lollapalooza. The shaman. The guru. The rock God. And without Jane's Addiction, the entire alternative rock boom might never have happen—at least not in the way that it did. If you don't know, now you know. (Episode 130—10/21/2019)

RICHARD KRUSPE

Richard Kruspe is the lead guitarist in German Neue Deutsche Härte band, Rammstein. He's been with the industrial metallers since their inception in 1994—the lineup has remained unchanged during that time—and he also sings in the US-based Emigrate. He kindly crashed me a couple of cigarettes during our interview together, and his laid-back demeanor and dry sense of humor left a long-lasting impression. The smokes are on me next time, Richard. Provided we haven't quit by then. (Episode 038—12/05/2017)

SCOTT SHIFLETT

Scott Shiflett is one of the most gifted guitarists in punk rock. Seriously, I know little to nothing about the instrument, but watching him play bass on stage is a masterclass in musicianship. You can catch him doing so in Face to Face. And you can see him play lead guitar in Me First and the Gimme Gimmes. I could happily watch him play all day. He's an amazing conversationalist, too. If you ever get the chance to interview Scott, make sure you take it. He'll do all the talking, and you'll get an incredible interview out of it. (Episode 091—02/26/2019)

TOM MORELLO

Talking of virtuoso musicians, next on our list is the mighty Tom Morello. Like Slash or Jimi Hendrix, Tom Morello is instantly recognizable, not just by his playing, but also by his look. You could even pick his guitar out from a lineup of discarded instruments, which you can't say about many musicians. (Top tip: look out for the one that says, "Arm the Homeless.") In short, Tom Morello is a guitar God. And Rage Against the Machine are simply one of the finest rock 'n' roll bands to ever grace the globe. Audioslave aren't half bad, either. And how many former male strippers do you know with a degree in social studies? From Harvard no less. Then there's the activism. And Axis of Justice. And The Nightwatchman. And his cameo in *Star Trek*. Is there nothing this man can't do? (Episode 082—11/21/2018)

TOMMY LEE

If I had a dollar for every time Tommy Lee said "Fuck!" during our podcast together, I'd be able to retire. That being said, the childlike energy and enthusiasm that he gives off is so infectious. And despite everything that he's been through—the rollercoaster ride of sex, drugs, death, divorce, jail time, and just about anything else you can imagine—he remains just a big kid at heart. And I love him for that. He also played drums in one of the biggest bands *ever*, and he's probably the most famous member of that group. That's partly down to his proficient playing. But it's also (mainly) down to his larger-than-life personality. Tommy Lee is a rock star in every sense of the word. (Episode 180—09/21/2020)

VINNIE STIGMA

Vincent Cappucio, aka Vinnie Stigma, is the lead guitarist and founding member of Agnostic Front, one of the earliest and most important and influential New York hardcore bands. They first formed in 1980 and have had several incarnations and lineup changes over the years. Stigma remains the only constant and original member. He also released a solo album in 2008 called *New York Blood*. And he runs his own tattoo parlor, New York Hardcore Tattoo. As you can probably guess, he's old school New York through and through. (Episode 164—05/25/2020)

WALTER SCHREIFELS

Walter Schreifels is a musician, songwriter, and record producer from New York City. It would be impossible to mention all of his projects—there simply isn't enough space. But let's namecheck the main ones: legendary NYC hardcore bands, Youth of Today and Gorilla Biscuits, post-hardcore outfit Quicksand, melodic punk rock band CIV, and seminal indie rock act, Rival Schools. He's a key figure in the New York music community, and beyond his vast range of creative endeavors, he's just a lovely human being. Sometimes nice guys do finish last. But only on alphabetical guest lists. (Episode 150—02/03/2020)

ACKNOWLEDGMENTS

I USED THE "ACKNOWLEDGMENTS" section of my first book to thank everyone who's had a profound influence on my personal life over the last thirty-five years. Here, I plan to thank all those who've had a positive impact on my professional career since starting out in the music industry in 2010. In no particular order, I'd like to say a heartfelt thank you to the following people for assisting, supporting, encouraging, and facilitating my life in this crazy business of show...

Henry Evans, James Walshe, Johnny Doom, Loz Guest, Alex Baker, Kate Lawler, Danielle Perry, Jon Mahon, Danielle Sammeroff, Sami Westwood, Hayley Codd, Emma Van Duyts, Oli Walkers, Austin Collins, Claire Collins, Tony Cooke, Scott Bartlett, Sam Corbett, Steph Van Spronsen, Nelly Liger, Adam Sagir, Michelle Kerr, Kirsten Sprinks, Alexander Milas, Philip Wilding, Paul Brannigan, Ian Winwood, Ruth Knowles, Konstanze Louden, Tanya Juhasz, Lorre Crimi, Justin Michael, Kerri Kasem, Nikki Sixx, Matt Reynolds, Jon Jones, Chris Dean, Duff Battye, Ben Gazey, Valeria Laghezza, Simon Hargreaves, Hayley Connelly, Matt Hughes, Dante Bonutto, Lailah O'Donnell, Cayleigh Shepherd, James Windle, Chris Goodman, David Cox, Kav Sandhu, Anita Heryet, Alan McGee, Ian Johnsen, Kevin O'Donnell, Vanessa Burt, Lou Mahon, Charlie Caplowe, Dani Cotter, Livy Jenkins, Clare Maxwell, Claire Harris, William Luff, Steve Ager, Judith Fisher, Julie Weir, Anna Maslowicz, James Sherry, Gavin Harry, Stuart Vallans, Lauren Barley, Amanda Emery, Jonathan Green, Lee Dainton, Matthew Pritchard, Dom Joly,

Shaun Ryder, Ralph Steadman, Sadie Williams, Dan Hodge, Jake Szufnarowski, Sean Goulding, Ross Warnock, Christina Austin, Jon McIldowie, Andy Copping, Alan Day, Ian Richards, Reuben Nimmo, James Pattison, James Sharples, Jonathan Owen, Grace O'Grady, Emma Milzani, Lia Kent Mackillop, Sophie Eggleton, Zoe Louise Rockett, Monique Powell, John Feldmann, Jaret Reddick, Laura Jane Grace, Jesse Malin, Danko Jones, Frank Iero, Johnny Fox, Benji Webbe, Arya Goggin, Frank Turner, Nick Horne, Laila Khan, Paul Barnes, Ian Rendall, Chris Shields, Blasko, Zakk Wylde, Talena Rose, Lzzy Hale, John Fred Young, Joel O'Keeffe, Ryan O'Keeffe, Matt Caughthran, Joby Ford, Joey Castillo, Ken Horne, Ginger Wildheart, Chad Ginsburg, Jess Margera, Thomas Ian Nicholas, Sean Smith, Alex Heron, Ollie Route, Simon Young, Eugene Butcher, Tyson Cornell, Ben Ray, Todd Malloy, Jasmine Leah Hussain, Ryan Cornall, Adrian Storry, Olivia Sime, Dawn Mulroy, Tom Dark, Christina White, Matthew Harris, Michelle Sadova Harris, Stephen Hill, Matt Yonker, Chris DeMakes, Roger Lima, Tom Ames, Aaron Barrett, Ralph Saenz, Joe Lester, Ben Osmundson, Dan Palmer, Marc Kantor, Nathen Maxwell, Erik Schrody, Keith Buckley, David Catching, Whitfield Crane, Dane Campbell, Boz Boorer, Steve Diggle, Laura Flanagan, Samantha French Blackwell, Gail Porter, Andy Ellis, Nick Helm, Stuart Whiffen, Christopher Glasson, Rich Wilson, Gerard Edwards, Gene Baxter, Jak Hutchcraft, Dan Cates, Dan Joyce, Mike Locke, David Rudolf, John Bradley, Richard Brake, Thomas Turgoose, Stephen Graham, Hannah Graham, Alice Lowe, Zoe Flower, Paddy Considine, Kevin Kerslake, Dean Karr, Casey Chaos, Nadja Peulen, Hyro Fenton, Benjie Gold, Adam Bantz, Steven Battelle, Alan Williamson, Mark Gibson, Harriet Bevan, Liam Cromby, Alfie Scully, Dan Brown, Craig Jennings, Rou Reynolds, Keith Reynolds, Matt Bigland, Aidan Sinclair, Al Kershaw, Joshua Waters Rudge, Marcia Richards, Jamie Kryiakides, Jonathan Doyle, Dean Ashton, Adrian Preston, Gobinder Jhitta, Jodi Cunningham, Sandra Sorensen, Juliette Carton, Joe Brady, Michael Barrett-Bourmier, Chris Howell,

Dave Pollack, Kent Jamieson, Fat Mike, Jesse Leach, and each and every guest who's appeared on both *Life In The Stocks* and *Stoke The Fire*.

The last person I would like to thank is *you* for buying and reading this book. Look out for the third and final instalment in the not-too-distant future. Listen to all the podcasts in the meantime. And please keep supporting independent creatives. Ciao for now.